Colorado's
Best Fly Fishing

Colorado's Best Fly Fishing

FLIES, ACCESS, AND GUIDES' ADVICE
FOR THE STATE'S PREMIER RIVERS

Landon Mayer

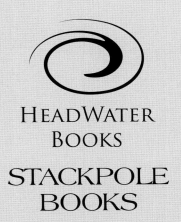

HEADWATER BOOKS

STACKPOLE BOOKS

Published by
STACKPOLE BOOKS
5067 Ritter Road
Mechanicsburg, PA 17055
www.stackpolebooks.com

Printed in the United States

First edition

Main front cover image, Jay Nichols; insets Landon Mayer, Will Blanchard, and Angus Drummond; cover design by Wendy A. Reynolds

Maps by Kumiko Yamazaki

10 9 8 7 6 5 4 3 2

Library of Congress Cataloging-in-Publication Data

Mayer, Landon R.
    Colorado's best fly fishing / Landon Mayer. — 1st ed.
      p.   cm.
    Includes index.
    ISBN-13: 978-0-8117-0731-2 (pbk.)
    ISBN-10: 0-8117-0731-8 (pbk.)
    1. Fly fishing—Colorado—Guidebooks. 2. Colorado—Guidebooks. I. Title.
SH475.M357   2011
799.12'409788—dc22

                                       2010052888

CONTENTS

ACKNOWLEDGMENTS

Thank you, Michelle. Watching someone have the same drive and passion for this sport is a blessing on its own. More powerful than that is your love and support. To our children Lauren, Zachary, Madelyn, and River, family fun on the water makes some of the best days. Thanks to my mother Robbie Mayer Skar and siblings Lauren and Sean.

This book would not be possible without the above-and-beyond hard work of the individuals below. I am proud and grateful to feature their words and experience in this book.

To Jay Nichols, a friend and great individual to work with. Not only do you have an unreal work ethic, but you are one of the best photographers in the industry and have upped the bar for fly-fishing publications. Thank you, Jay, for the opportunity to publish such a memorable project with you.

To Judith Schnell, Amy Lerner, Trish Manney, and everyone at Stackpole Books, thank you for making each book feel like a family affair. It's an honor to publish with such a great company.

To John Barr, for all the knowledge you shared in this book and for being a great friend. You are the prime example of what everyone should strive for in giving back to this industry and the great individuals in it. You play a big part in every project I complete and I am forever grateful.

To Pat Dorsey, it is an honor to guide the same waters with you full-time and involve you in such a vast project. You went above and beyond to help this book be a great wealth of angling information. I am thankful you are a friend.

To Ross Purnell at *Fly Fisherman*, thank you for all your support. I am honored to write for your magazine and have your contributions to this book.

To Frank Martin at *High Country Angler*, thank you for your friendship and guidance in life. The knowledge you share helps others become better people no matter what they do. I thank you and Jack Tallon for making dreams come true through hard work and commitment.

To Angus "Gus" Drummond, thank you for all the support on and off the water. I look forward to all our future projects together.

To Will Sands, thank you for all your efforts in this book and beyond. You are the example of what sharing is all about. Whether it's on the water, in the shop, or at home, you never steer anyone wrong. I look forward to hitting the water again soon.

Passing on the tradition of exploring waters to the next generation is beyond rewarding. Watching the thrill on kids' faces during a hard battle with a brown trout makes every catch more exciting. Lauren, Madelyn, and Zachary made this fish seem larger than life.
MICHELLE MAYER

To Steve Henderson, thank you for the professionalism you have shown on the water and in the shop. Even when passes close down with winter storms you still cranked up the snowmobile and were game to hit the river.

Many other great anglers contributed vital information to this book, like Bob Dye, who took a day off guiding to get on the oars and get work done on this book project, and Devon Ence, who went above and beyond with his contribution to the Conjeos River chapter. Others include John Gierach, Ed Engle, Jackson Streit, Charlie Craven, Greg Garcia, John Flick, Bill Edrington, Taylor Edrington, Larry Kingery, Greg Felt, Brad Befus, Tyler Befus, Steve Gossage, Scottie Miller, Eric Pettine, Barry Reynolds, John Keefover, Jonathan Keisling, Rick Takahashi, Todd Hosman, Jeremiah Johnson, Tim Heng, Dick Rock, Stan Benton, Ben Olson, Grant Houx, Joe Eichelberger, Mike Kruise, Kirk Bien, Brad Tomlinson, Sherry Tomlinson, Jim Cannon, Danny Brennan, Tad Howard, Will Blanchard, Jason Booth, Art Rowell, Jeff Lyons, Kerry Caraghar, Kyle Holt,

Brandon Kramer, Kirk Deeter, Scottie Miller, and Eric Mondragon. I want all of you to know this book is the reflection of the team effort you all participated in, and I am forever grateful.

I also thank the great fly tiers who contributed to this book, including Charlie Craven, Larry Kingery, Brad and Tyler Befus, John Barr, Tim Heng, Will Sands, Rick Takahashi, Greg Garcia, Shane Stalcup, and Ed Engle. I would like to thank Angus Drummond, Will Blanchard, Pat Dorsey, Jay Nichols, Ross Purnell, Joe Eichelberger, and Nick Williams for the breathtaking images. Thanks also to Ross Reels/Ross World Wide, Scientific Angler, Simms, Fishpond, Smith Optics, and Outcast Boats for supporting me.

Our sport will be left with a void without Jonathan Keisling, whose life was cut short in 2010, but his legacy and professionalism carry on. I am truly honored to include him in this book.

I am happy to be a part of such a great community of anglers.

Tight lines,
Landon Mayer

Being in the right place at the right time is the key to success.

B orn and raised in Colorado Springs, I had the good fortune of being able to fish some of the best water in the West only a few hours from home. More important, many great anglers took the time to teach me what they knew. This book is my attempt to pass on the knowledge that so many anglers gave to me and to set the record straight about what are truly the best waters to fish—with information from some of the best anglers and guides in Colorado, as well as my own experience from a lifetime fishing this state (14 years as a full-time guide on the South Platte River).

One constant theme that runs through this book is the importance of timing—timing hatches and migrating runs of trophy trout, or timing your own arrival and departure to make the most of your time, which for many is precious. Timing, I believe, is the key to unlocking the potential of a fishery. There is never just one river that is productive every day of the year. Whether you are fishing a tailwater, freestone river, or spring creek, many variables dictate the quality of the fishing. I am confident this book will help you better understand how to time your next trip.

This book includes what I think are the best fly-fishing experiences in the state. What do I mean by "best," though? Well, it is relative, but for me sometimes size and numbers of trout are important; other times solitude. But in choosing the rivers for this book, I asked myself: "If I could spend a year fishing the state's rivers, where would I go? What hatches would I hit? Where and when would I go to catch fish of a lifetime?" I also thought of things that my friends and I reflect on at the end of the day, everything from that 25-inch brown that attacked a streamer to the way a 6-inch greenback climbed on top of my dry fly. Sometimes, it is the challenge of the fish that we didn't catch that keeps us coming back and striving to learn as much as possible about a particular piece of water.

I wanted to cover only the best fishing in the state, in as much detail as possible, rather than painting with too broad a brush and trying to cover all the state's waters, which are not created equal (at least for trout and the anglers who pursue them). Some rivers in the book, such as the White River, Clear Creek, and the North Platte, have limited public access or short sections of productive water. I wanted to include them but could not justify an entire chapter, so I mention them in other chapters.

In this book, my goal was to capture Colorado's best fly fishing, from where and when to catch trophies like this Dream Stream brown to catching 8-inch greenbacks in Rocky Mountain National Park. No other state offers the diversity of Colorado. JAY NICHOLS

In writing this book, I relied heavily on the expertise of others. I feel that it is impossible to know everything about fly fishing, and I learn something new every day on the water. There are several lifetimes of fishing in the state, and no one can do it all. This book is a community of knowledge, not just one angler's opinion, and I spent many hours interviewing local experts for it. In many ways, this book is as much theirs as it is mine, and I am forever grateful for their contributions.

Hatches and Hatch Charts

Colorado does not have as many complex hatches as some other states, but the hatches that it does have can be dense, especially midges, BWOs, and PMDs. Because Colorado's weather and water levels change drastically from year to year, the hatch charts and emergence times are only guidelines. Some years, hatches may come off earlier, some years later, and some years not at all. There are six insects that will come off every year like clockwork: midges, caddis, BWOs, PMDs, Tricos, and stoneflies. Other more elusive insects like the Green Drake are more temperamental based on water flows and weather, making it tough to always hit the hatch. Always check with the local shops listed in each section of this book for hatches and current stream conditions.

Here is a collection of hatches that I love and recommend you try to hit.

Midges on the Ark. One of Colorado's best year-round hatches is midges on the Arkansas River below Pueblo Reservoir. Since it lies lower in elevation, temperatures of 60 degrees are not uncommon there in the middle of winter. This warming trend produces large, long midge hatches, especially on overcast days.

BWOs on the Pan. The Fryingpan River offers great hatches in spring and fall on perfect dry-fly water. The Fryingpan has great, calm water settings through pockets, pools, and slicks as it flows into the Roaring Fork River. Located near the Continental Divide just northwest of towering Mount Elbert, the Roaring Fork valley has frequent storm systems that offer the constant cloud cover Blue-Winged Olives thrive in.

Caddis on the South Platte. While two of the strongest hatches in the state are on the Arkansas and the Roaring Fork rivers, I prefer the South Platte River, since it is a tailwater and water levels are more consistent when the hatch occurs. From Charlie Meyers SWA to Eleven Mile Canyon, and especially the new caddis activity at Deckers, you can effectively target every week of the hatch from April to early June and chances are good you will have fishable water conditions.

Salmonflies on the Gunnison. From May through June, you can watch aggressive trout take these giant bugs in the Black Canyon. Runoff won't destroy the opportunity because of both the Crystal and Gunnison Diversion Dams.

PMDs on the Roaring Fork. Most Colorado rivers have this hatch, but one of the best PMD fisheries I have ever seen is the Roaring Fork in midsummer from 10 a.m. to 1 p.m. Even if there are minimal adults riding the surface, an emerger or cripple sunk just below the surface is key.

Green Drakes on the Taylor. Blooming around the Pale Morning Duns, Green Drakes give anglers a chance to finally mimic a large insect in the land of small. The Taylor River is in my opinion one of the most productive fisheries for this big bug. From June through September, hatches are best on overcast days, as well as a few hours before nightfall.

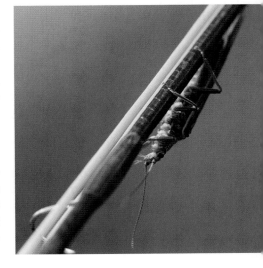

Sometimes anglers on big waters looking for big bugs overlook the smaller Golden Stones for the Salmonflies. Here is a close-up of an adult Golden Stone, an insect that plays a big role as a food supply in the Colorado River.
WILL BLANCHARD

Tricos on the Yampa. This is one of the thickest hatches in Colorado and one of the biggest, most dense Trico hatches I have ever experienced in the 23 years I have been fly fishing on the Yampa River. When the hatch begins in early July the adults are about a size 18. By the end of September, adults are a 24 or smaller.

Red Quills on the Williams Fork. Similar to Green Drakes, Red Quills give anglers the chance to fish larger mayfly imitations. This is also a sparse hatch that can be very short. One of my favorite locations to target this hatch is the Williams Fork and Colorado rivers in July and August.

In addition to great hatch fishing, depending on water and weather conditions, Colorado is perhaps the best place in the United States to catch a truly giant trout (over 10 pounds) on a year-round basis. The Taylor, Fryingpan, and Blue are excellent resident river trout fisheries where trout are known to exceed 30 inches and weigh up to 20 pounds. For migratory fish, the South Platte above Eleven Mile Reservoir, the Gunnison above Blue Mesa Reservoir, the Conejos above and below Platoro Reservoir, the White River in Meeker, and the Yampa River below Stagecoach Reservoir are some of best. With the exception of the Conejos, these are all year-round fisheries.

Fly Patterns

I firmly believe that presentation is more important than fly selection. Large trout are opportunistic feeders by nature, and the key to catching them is getting the fly to the fish's viewing lane while mimicking the size and silhouette of the natural. Instead of relying on the fly to catch the fish, I make sure every drift counts. This is why sight-fishing is so productive—the best indicator is the trout, not the one on your leader.

I don't personally believe that trout get conditioned to a fly. Instead, I think that trout see something unnatural in the presentation, rig, or the fly itself. Something like an RS2, which seems to always work, is very subtle. If you were to overpower that same imitation by adding a Krystal Flash wing case and tail, there is a good chance the trout would detect something unnatural, especially in low, clear water. At other times a little flash is what it takes to get the trout to bite.

I think some flies are more effective at catching anglers in fly shops than they are at catching fish. I call these bin flies. The flies that I have chosen for this book, while they do look good, have proven themselves on the water, day in and day out. These flies have been designed and tested by top anglers and by trout. Some of the flies in this book are more than a decade old while others are newer to the market. While I have listed different patterns for each chapter, all of the patterns in the book can be incorporated into one Colorado fly box that will provide a core group of flies that will serve you well on all waters in the state.

As a guide, I quickly learned to simplify, and this also includes fly selection. When I open up my box, I see twenty-five patterns (in three sizes) that I

The key to fishing streamers is being dedicated and having faith. The reward of fishing an Egg-Sucking Leech in the spring can be one of the largest trout you ever catch. LANDON MAYER

carry all the time. They are the Rojo Midge, Jujubee Midge, Griffith's Gnat, BWO Barr Emerger, Jujubaetis, Stalcup's Baetis, Mathew's BWO Sparkle Dun, Barr's Graphic Caddis, Breadcrust, Landon's Larva, Puterbaugh's Foam Caddis, Mercer's PoxyBack Little Yellow Stone, Barr's Tungstone, Pat's Rubber Legs, Crystal Stimulator, Rogue Stone, PMD Barr Emerger, Copper John, Mathews's PMD Sparkle Dun, Parachute Adams, Foam Flying Ant, Flashtail Mini Egg, Slumpbuster, Lawson's Conehead Sculpin, and Meat Whistle.

Many great anglers and fly designers such as John Barr, author of *Barr Flies*, also believe in a simplified, versatile system. By having one pattern that represents several different food forms, depending on the way that you fish or present it, you can simplify your fly selection and worry less about picking the right pattern and focus more on fishing technique. Many of the flies that I have confidence in are versatile enough to be fished in several different ways or to imitate several foods at once, such as John Barr's Copper John, which is a deadly pattern that serves three functions: attraction, imitation, and a substitute for split shot. Next time you are contemplating how to stock your box, consider these important insights that show how one of the best anglers that I know selects and fishes his flies: "When I am fishing a complex hatch with four to five insects hatching in the course of one morning," John Barr explains, "using my Vis-A-Dun imitation can effectively catch trout while imitating different sizes on a two-fly rig to match the silhouette of the naturals. It is also effective in various colors. For example, during a Trico hatch I prefer to

Because of its great fishing, Colorado can be crowded. Get away from folks by fishing during the week and during the off-season. Any river that is five to six hours from a major population center such as the Rio Grande or the Animas can provide the solitude that some anglers crave. Headwaters along trails, like the Middle Fork of the South Platte or the North and South forks of the White, can also be great places to hide. Canyons like Cheesman (above) offer miles of solitude. LANDON MAYER

use black because it is visible above the surface while displaying the most important image below, which is the black body, not the wings. Lastly the Vis-A-Dun is a great indicator fly, allowing you to fish it while dropping an imitation off the back like a beetle without loosing track of your rig as it drifts to the trout."

Barr takes this same approach to fishing the Meat Whistle, which was first developed for bass but works equally well for trout, carp, pike, bonefish, permit, and countless other species, as long as you change the color and retrieve: "You can hop it to imitate the lifting and falling retreat of a crayfish, strip it quickly to resemble an escaping baitfish, or skitter it along the rocks on the bottom of the river like a sculpin."

Maps and Access

Researching this book, I fished as much of the rivers as possible and interviewed local shops and guides to note prime access areas. However, the maps have several limitations: First, some rivers, such as the Rio Grande and the Arkansas, are so large that listing a pullout every 50 yards would have been impossible. Second, many of the maps cover a large area, so detail is limited. I advise you to use multiple maps as well as local knowledge from a guide or fly shop (see the Other Resources section in this chapter). For the sake of simplicity, blue icons signify both boat launch and wading access, and yellow icons wading access only.

The maps in the book are best used along with other references such as the DeLorme *Colorado Atlas and Gazetteer*. Most important, always stop by the local fly shop for directions and advice on spots that are fishing best. The maps are included here to accompany the text, orient the reader to the general area, and

Colorado offers an amazing array of backcountry fishing experiences. Whenever you are traveling in Rocky Mountain National Park, pay close attention to the trail signs. LANDON MAYER

Town stretches of water often have the best fishing, especially during the off-season.
MICHELLE MAYER

On rivers like the South Platte, you can find solitude and willing fish simply by walking. Respect private property, be courteous to other river users, and pick up all trash to make the fishing experience enjoyable for all. LANDON MAYER

show major access points. Some access areas described in the text may not appear on the maps.

Colorado has a long history of water rights and access disputes when it comes to its treasured rivers. From the late 1800s through most of the 1900s, rivers were considered completely public; however, in 1983 an opinion to a 1977 case determined that trespassing included the banks of rivers on private property but not the water's surface. As a result, Colorado does not allow angler access to the high-water mark as some states do. Anglers must either wade-fish on public land or float through the private land without touching the banks or bottom of the river, which includes anchoring.

Anglers should always observe posted "no trespassing" signs, whether on or off the river. Some rivers, such as the Fryingpan, have a lot of private water in between public access points, so you must look for indications of private land (most owners either post signs or erect fences). Fines can be hefty if the landowner catches you and calls the authorities. On the flip side, some rivers, such as the South Platte in South Park, offer so many consecutive miles of public water that you would almost think that no one lives in the county.

Other Resources

In addition to this book, it's important to have a copy of the DeLorme *Colorado Atlas and Gazetteer*. I also recommend the Colorado Department of Transportation website, cotrip.org, for real-time road conditions and closures so that you can plan alternate routes during rough weather. Additionally, websites such as wildlife.state.co.us and nps.gov provide current regulations for state and national parks, respectively. For camping accommodations, especially during peak travel season in the summer, forestcamping.com can help you plan your trip.

Some of the other guidebooks that you may find helpful were written by many of the anglers who contributed to this book.

A Fly-Fishing Guide to the South Platte River by Pat Dorsey, Pruett Publishing, 2007

Fly Fishing the Arkansas: An Angler's Guide and Journal by Bill Edrington, Xlibris, 2003

Fly Fishing Rocky Mountain National Park by Todd Hosman, Streamside Press, 2003

Fly Fishing Colorado by Jackson Streit, California Bill's Automotive Handbooks, 2004

Flyfisher's Guide to Colorado by Marty Bartholomew, Wilderness Adventures Press, 2008

Tactics, Tips, and Techniques for Pressured Trout

There are a few key things to keep in mind if you want to catch pressured trout in Colorado. For more on techniques, see my *Sight Fishing for Trout* and *How to Catch the Biggest Trout of Your Life*, but here is my bare-bones advice, including some on stalking and sight-fishing.

Select apparel that matches the backdrop above you instead of matching the landscape on the river's edge. Since trout have a cone of vision that is 45 degrees from the water's surface, you want to mimic what they naturally see. For example, on a bluebird day wear a blue jacket or shirt; if you are fishing in front of giant snowdrifts wear white; if you are fishing in a canyon wear earth tones.

Look before you fish. In pressured waters, larger fish find shelter on the river's edge. Scan the edges of banks, overhanging willows, and rocks before you take a step.

Start hunting trout by locating water that has cover, oxygen, and food. Without cover trout will not feel secure or even have a chance at survival from predators above. The most obvious cover is deep water and structure, but riffles, shadows, weather, and off-colored water all provide cover. This is the first and most important thing to look for.

Whenever you handle a trophy trout like this Conejos River brown, caught below the Pinnacles, always wet your hands first. LANDON MAYER

Trout need oxygen to survive, too. Trout and insects thrive in healthy oxygenated water such as cold water, deep runs, seams, drop-offs at the heads of deep runs, riffles, and pocketwater.

Trout are lazy by nature when it comes to food supply. The easier it is to consume the meal, the less energy they burn, so trout want food delivered to their viewing lanes. Look for water like the edges of seams, in front of rocks, tailouts of deep pools, and eddies.

Look for viewing lanes in the water—windows on the surface that are free of glare—to detect movements, silhouettes, or the white of the trout's mouth. On sunny days, position yourself with the sun at your back or directly above you, creating viewing lanes across, up, or downstream. In cloudy conditions, place yourself in front of the dark sky, allowing the black or gray clouds to reflect off the water's surface.

Move upstream from below the fish. Give yourself three areas to cast from when approaching the trout—upstream, downstream, or perpendicular. Determine where you can remain out of view while getting the best drift. Additionally, avoid high banks and fish as close to the water's surface as possible.

Make every presentation appear natural. Hunt the trout by staying low and wading quietly. Use fluorocarbon, natural-colored, small indicators, and eliminate split shot if possible to prevent the trout from detecting unnatural objects.

Start light when you are using nymphs, and then add weight as needed to reach the fish's depth. This will give the fish a chance to move up in the water column to take your fly and prevent you from snagging the river bottom or disturbing your drift, which can spook trout (especially the fish holding in the long riffled runs between holes).

Take the time to watch the insects and the water the trout is holding in before you present a dry. Match the motion of the natural with your fly. If the fly is moving or fluttering on the surface when the fish take, moving your fly will result in more takes. If the fish are feeding with sipping rises, don't skitter your fly.

Water speed also affects the way in which a trout will rise. Try to imagine what the trout sees as it is looking up at the water's surface while the silhouette of an insect drifts by. This will give you a better understanding of how a fish will react and rise to consume its meal. If the water is slick or slow moving, the silhouette of the fly will stay in the same plane or lane. The trout will consume its food slowly because the insect does not appear to be escaping. If the water the trout is holding in is moving fast, the trout's reaction will be more aggressive to ensure that its meal will not escape.

Change up your streamer retrieves. In addition to casting across the river, try casting up- and across-stream at a 45-degree angle, mimicking a head-on

When stalking pressured trout, keep low and try to blend in with your environment.
LANDON MAYER

approach while you retrieve the fly back to the bank you are standing on. This allows you to present streamers to the narrow waterways in Colorado without spooking the trout by lining their backs.

Lift on the fish to ensure a proper hook set. Do this by smoothly accelerating your rod to an abrupt stop in front of your shoulder, which prevents your rod from overflexing and sending all the pressure through to your tippet, breaking the fish off. When the headshakes follow, you can drop your arm to compensate and let the reel do its job.

Force the trout to headshake to land the fish quickly. Stay as close to the trout as possible while remaining perpendicular to it. From this position, bend the rod, applying maximum pressure from the butt section.

Release your trout by holding the fish stationary while it is facing upstream in a slow current. Do not rock the fish back and forth. Instead, increase the amount of oxygen in the water by splashing your hand in the water 6 inches above the trout's mouth.

Etiquette

With great fishing often comes great crowds, and lots of people means that some forget their manners. I always make a point to be polite and thoughtful toward others on the water. A bad encounter on the water can ruin your day.

An Animas River rainbow released. To ensure a proper release, always revive the trout in oxygenated water. LANDON MAYER

Being able to cast 70 feet with tight loops will get you nowhere on rivers like the South Platte or Fryingpan. Most casts are with 10 feet of fly line or less out of the rod tip—mastering the short game is essential. I teach clients to cast with a straight arm, keeping the fly line, leader, and tippet taut through the motion so that the flies land straight on the water, allowing them to become the first thing visible to the trout after a mend.
LANDON MAYER

First, give others 100 feet or more to fish. If you are within this range, ask politely whether they mind if you fish up- or downstream of them. That kind gesture alone can make someone's day.

When walking along the bank, give anglers a wide berth. There is nothing worse than casting to a pod of selective trout rising to Tricos when out of nowhere the water explodes as you look up and see an angler walking next to the bank directly above the trout you worked so hard to approach. I usually walk far enough away from the bank that I cannot see the water the anglers are casting too.

In the spring and fall, leave spawning trout alone. Concentrate on deep runs, river structure, or water that does not have the 1- to 3-inch cobblestone that the fish need to successfully reproduce. If you do land a trout that has the markings of battle, or is dropping eggs, return it to the water immediately and move on to new water. Concentrate on deep water and structure in the early spring (one to two months before spawning) for staging trout—these are the most aggressive and largest fish that have not lost weight from the rigors of spawning.

Clothing and Gear

Colorado has some of the most unpredictable weather in the West. You can see rain, snow, sunshine, and tornados in the beginning of July. Because many rivers in Colorado have a lot of pressure in the summer, winter is one of the best times to fish the waters in this book without crowds. Tailwaters are the name of the game because they supply a constant water temperature around 40 degrees. This prevents them from freezing and leaves trout actively feeding. Some of the best fishing in the state is during the winter, but dress warmly for air temperatures that are often below zero.

For fall, winter, and spring, start with a proper base layer of polypropylene or merino wool and a fleece midlayer. These two layers will help secure heat while also wicking moisture away from your body. Quality chest waders like Simms G3 or G4 waders will complete the insulation process. For slippery rocks, I like lightweight Vibram studded boots like the G4 Guide Boot. A Windstopper shell followed by a heavy Gore-Tex jacket will keep you warm and dry in extreme cold conditions. Shed layers as the day becomes warmer. Good socks, such as Smartwool, are a must.

In the summer, I wet-wade, using a pair of neoprene booties over wool socks. Because of mosquitoes, I don't wear shorts. Instead, I wear a pair of quick-drying pants that cover my legs. Always pack a waterproof shell. In the summer, you also need protection from the sun, which means sun gloves for your hands, a Tilly hat with wide brim, or a Buff, a lightweight piece of mate-

Jeff Lyons holds a healthy male brown trout from the Yampa River below Stagecoach Reservoir. Most of the tailwaters in Colorado hold large trout that are able to feed all year long. Temperatures in the tailwaters hold around 40 degrees in the winter and below 70 degrees in the summer. JEFF LYONS

An angler fishes the tailwater below Olympus Dam on the Big T. LANDON MAYER

rial similar to a neck gaiter that you can wear underneath the bottom of your sunglasses and lift over the back of your head. In addition to sun protection, a dark-colored Buff will also reduce glare. Don't forget plenty of sunscreen.

At all times of the year, polarized sunglasses are essential. I recommend copper or brown, which are dark enough for light days and light enough for dark days.

Colorado's Other Gamefish

In addition to trout species such as browns, rainbows, cuttbows, cutthroat, and brook trout (also greenback, splake, and Mackinaw), Colorado is also home to numerous other freshwater species that take a fly, such as mountain whitefish, pike, carp, and bass.

Mountain Whitefish

Indigenous to the White and Yampa rivers, mountain whitefish were introduced into the Cache la Poudre and Roaring Fork rivers and other waterways as well. Some anglers like them; others do not. Known to hold in deep runs in great numbers, these aggressive feeders readily take flies and range from 12 to 20 inches and up to 4 pounds.

With a healthy supply of freestone streams, Colorado offers anglers great float fishing. In low water, rafts are the way to go. ANGUS DRUMMOND

Pike

Pike were introduced into Colorado reservoirs in the 1950s to control populations of nuisance fish, such as sucker fish, in many stillwaters and a few rivers. But they reproduce so fast and damage populations of trout, so there is now no bag limit to try to reduce the negative effective these predators can have on a fishery. In the spring and fall when they cruise shallow shorelines or slow-moving river water, anglers can have a shot at these toothy critters on waters like Williams Fork Reservoir, Stagecoach Reservoir, Eleven Mile Reservoir, Spinney Mountain Reservoir, and the Rio Grande River.

Pike in Colorado can run anywhere from 25 to 35 inches, with some fish as heavy as 40 pounds or more. The current state record northern pike was caught in 2006 at Stagecoach Reservoir and came in at 30 pounds 11 ounces and 46 1/2 inches. These predators eat everything from crayfish to baitfish and even cannibalize their own. The best patterns to land these monsters are #2-6 rust, olive, and black Meat Whistles and #2-6 black Bunny Leeches.

Carp

Known as the poor man's bonefish, these fish can make any reel sing. Common and grass carp swim in reservoirs, lakes, ponds, and rivers and range in size from 5 to 25 pounds or more and 20 to 40-plus inches. As of 2010, the heaviest fish ever caught in the state was a 51-pound carp in Prospect Park Lake.

Read what Brad Befus and Barry Reynolds, authors of *Carp on the Fly*, have to say about carp fishing in the South Platte River chapter.

CHAPTER 1

Colorado's Fly Fishing

I was born and raised in Colorado and caught my first trout in the Gunnison valley when I was ten years old. My dad was a passionate angler, which gave me the opportunity to see Colorado's best trout streams at an early age. I am forever grateful for his guidance and streamside companionship.

From the beginning, I knew there was something special about fly fishing in Colorado, a state that has a wide array of angling possibilities from technical, clear tailwaters to large, untamed freestones. The terrain varies depending on the geographic locale—many streams meander through lush valleys, some sweep through rich ranchland, others carve their way through majestic, boulder-strewn canyons. In all scenarios, the common denominator is fly fishing at its best.

There is an estimated 9,000 miles of trout streams in Colorado, and many of those covered in this book are catch-and-release or designated by the Colorado Wildlife Commission as Gold Medal. Gold Medal trout streams contain more than 60 pounds of trout per acre, with 12 trout per acre larger than 14 inches. Gold Medal streams provide an angler the best opportunity to catch large trout. Colorado has approximately 170 miles of streams designated Gold Medal. Many of these quality waters are not stocked in routine management unless harsh environmental factors cause extreme die-off.

Colorado is known for its exceptional tailwaters, those streams that flow from beneath manmade impoundments. Tailwaters provide anglers with consistent, four-season fisheries and have many benefits compared to unregulated trout streams, called freestones. Tailwaters have stable water temperatures, a phenomenon biologists refer to as winter warm, summer cool, because of the warm releases during the winter and cool outflows during the summer. Other advantages to a tailwater include clear water even during runoff, weed-rich substrates, high levels of nutrients, healthy aquatic life, consistent hatches, stable stream banks, and large populations of trout.

Sight-fishing with miniscule nymphs is common on many of Colorado's premier tailraces. My favorite places to sight-fish include Cheesman Canyon, Spinney Mountain Ranch (newly renamed the Charlie Meyers SWA), Taylor, and Fryingpan. Keeping your flies in front of larger fish, as opposed to blind-fishing and fishing the water methodically, increases your odds of catching them. I really enjoy the hunt that is sight fishing. Anglers will also find reliable dry-fly fishing on tailwaters with adult midges, Blue-Winged Olives, Pale Morning Duns, Red Quills, Green Drakes, and Tricos.

Late March and early April brings excellent Blue-Winged Olive hatches on most of the tailwaters throughout the state. Inclement weather typically produces the best hatches. High humidity levels delay the emerging process of the mayfly duns, making them more available to trout, whereas bright and sunny conditions accelerate their development and the duns get off the water quickly. Some of the best Blue-Winged Olive hatches occur on the South Platte in Cheesman Canyon, a world-class fishery only an hour south of Denver. (Make sure your fly box is stuffed with a bunch of #20 Mathews' Sparkle Duns.)

Midsummer brings both Pale Morning Duns and Green Drakes. You'll find excellent Pale Morning Dun hatches statewide. An assortment of #16-18 Pale Morning Duns, Compara-duns, and parachute patterns will fool these risers. Flows can make or break your dry-fly experience with Pale Morning Dun imitations. For instance, if the flows are high, the fish will key on emerging

Ross Purnell sets on a trout that hammered a streamer at the Elk River confluence.
LANDON MAYER

Colorado is a four-season fishery, and die-hard anglers can catch trout through the winter and early spring, when pressure is light. The Eagle River above Wolcott can produce some great clear-water action in late spring when air temperatures can reach 70 degrees and trout go on a feeding frenzy. ANGUS DRUMMOND

nymphs as opposed to mayfly duns. If the flows are low and clear, it is entirely possible to experience one of the best Pale Morning Dun hatches of your life. The Colorado River near Parshall has one of the best Pale Morning Dun hatches in the state.

Don't forget to mark the Green Drake hatch on your calendar starting in mid-July. This can be some of the most explosive mayfly fishing of the season. One of the distinct advantages to this hatch is the mayfly's size. The duns are typically a size 10 or 12, which is a real advantage for those who struggle to see small flies.

My favorite place to fish the Green Drake hatch is on the Taylor River above Almont. The hatch progresses slightly upriver each day, so being in the right place at the right time is one of the key ingredients to success. A #10-12 Colorado Hen Wing Green Drake or a #10-12 Mathews' Green Drake Sparkle Dun is what I recommend for matching the hatch. You'll find good Green Drake hatches on the Gunnison and Roaring Fork rivers, too.

In late summer, the Trico hatch will bring the best out of any serious dry-fly angler. To be successful during this hatch you will need to use 9- to 12-foot leaders terminating in 7X with Trico imitations ranging between #22 and 26. This will be some of the most technical dry-fly fishing you'll encounter in Colorado. It's no wonder that the Trico hatch has been dubbed the "white-winged curse." You'll find consistent hatches of Tricos at the Spinney Mountain Ranch, Eleven Mile Canyon, the Colorado River below the Williams Fork confluence, and as Landon mentions, the Yampa. The duns hatch about 7 a.m., followed by the spinnerfall, which occurs between 9:30 and 11:30 a.m. Make sure you have plenty of #24 Stalcup's CDC Trico Compara-duns. This fly is relatively easy to see, even in small sizes.

Don't forget about the Red Quills on the Fryingpan, Blue, and Williams Fork. This hatch fills the void between the Pale Morning Duns and the Blue-Winged Olive hatches. Typically this hatch begins in early August and extends through the latter part of September. Unlike many of the other mayfly hatches, which occur during the morning or midafternoon hours, this hatch takes place in late afternoon or early evening. Many anglers head home too early and miss this hatch altogether. My favorite Red Quill pattern is A. K.'s Red Quill in size 16.

Autumn brings reliable Blue-Winged Olive hatches statewide. Scores of rising trout fatten up on mayfly duns in preparation for a long, harsh winter. With diminishing irrigation demand and stable weather, the flows are often the most consistent of the season. This in itself produces optimum conditions for consistent dry-fly fishing. Fly selection is similar to the spring hatches, but at this time of the year, you will need #22-24 patterns.

Several tailwaters also offer some good streamer fishing in the fall. Brown trout become super aggressive as they prepare to spawn. One of my favorite streams to fish streamers is on the Williams Fork during October. Don't leave home without olive and rust Barr's Slumpbusters and olive Conehead Woolly Buggers.

Tailwaters like the Fryingpan, Taylor, and Blue provide anglers with the opportunity to target huge Mysis-fed resident trout. Trout exceeding 10 pounds are not uncommon in these rivers. Occasionally anglers land fish over 15 pounds in these watersheds. Other world-class tailwaters like the South Platte below Spinney Reservoir provide anglers with the opportunity to target migrating, lake-run fish during the shoulder seasons. These pre-spawn rainbows, cutthroats, and cuttbows in the spring and brown trout in fall offer anglers the opportunity to catch a trophy trout. Each season, trout over 10 pounds are caught on this section of the South Platte, referred to as the "Dream Stream."

During the autumn season, mature four-year-old kokanee salmon, a land-locked sockeye, migrate into South Platte above Eleven Mile Reservoir, Colorado River above Granby, Gunnison above Blue Mesa Reservoir, and Blue River above Green Mountain Reservoir in search of areas to spawn. They start entering the rivers as early as the second week of August. Their migration varies from stream to stream, however. On the Blue River, they routinely show up around the third week of September. Check local fly shops for up-to-date information. Unfortunately their spawning success is minimal due to the ice-cold water; therefore, the Colorado

Green Drakes are the largest mayfly in the state (#10-14). Best rivers to fish this hatch on include the Fryingpan, Roaring Fork, and Taylor. NICK WILLIAMS

Division of Wildlife maintains several field locations to strip the eggs from the females and artificially inseminate the roe. Later, the fingerling kokanee salmon are stocked into nearby reservoirs and streams, and the process repeats itself every four years.

Similar to their sockeye cousins in Alaska and British Columbia, kokanee dig bowl-like depressions called redds in the substrate to deposit their eggs. Kokanee can be fooled with an assortment of bright-colored flies, including egg patterns, Prince Nymphs, red Copper Johns, and pink San Juan Worms. Downstream from the redds you'll find concentrations of trout that are feeding on eggs that get swept out of the redd. I have had some memorable days with my buddies on the Gunnison River, catching 16- to 20-inch rainbows below pods of kokanee salmon, in what I call a poor man's Alaska.

Colorado also has many noted freestone streams like the Animas, Rio Grande, Gunnison, Arkansas, Eagle, and Roaring Fork, to name only a few. Freestone rivers are unregulated trout streams unimpeded by dams. These fisheries are known for their robust populations of rainbows and browns and excellent hatches. They are not as stable as tailwaters, and flows and clarity can change dramatically from an afternoon rain shower.

In addition to walk-and-wade trips, anglers routinely float these rivers with inflatable rafts or drift boats. One of my favorite float trips is the Gunnison River. Floating these rivers allows anglers to cover more water and exploit a wide range of tactics. Anglers can either short-line or long-line with conventional nymphing rigs, fish attractor dry flies, or fish dry-and-dropper rigs near the banks. Dry-and-dropper rigs are effective in skinny water, where conventional nymphing rigs tend to spook trout and get hung up. Yet another option is to strip streamers tight to the bank, covering all the likely areas such as deadfall, shaded areas, and undercut banks. If you opt to fish streamers, you'll catch fewer fish, but the ones you hook will be bigger than average.

Freestone rivers have a more diversified aquatic life compared to tailwaters—anglers will find midges, Blue-Winged Olives, Pale Morning Duns,

Green Drakes, Red Quills, Tricos, caddis, Yellow Sallies, *Pteronarcys*, and Golden Stoneflies. You'll find reliable Yellow Sally hatches on almost any freestone in Colorado. A #14-16 yellow Stimulator is deadly fished in 18-24 inches of water throughout the month of July.

The Arkansas River has one of the best Mother's Day Caddis hatches in the West. I make it a point to hit this hatch every season. The hatch typically begins late April and extends into the first week of May. Many variables can affect this hatch—water temperatures, flows, weather—so I recommend checking with a local fly shop for up-to-date information before your departure. The Animas, Eagle, Gunnison, Roaring Fork, and the South Platte's caddis hatches are not shabby either, so don't rule them out.

The Arkansas River also has a great Blue-Winged Olive hatch, which for some reason is overshadowed by the caddis hatch—a huge oversight because it is every bit as impressive as the caddis hatch and more enjoyable because of the lighter crowds. Once again, inclement weather produces the best hatches. The Arkansas has a reliable late-summer Red Quill hatch too, lasting until the third week of September.

Jonathan Keisling holds a great rainbow on the Blue River. Many anglers benefited from Jonathan's teaching on this, and other, rivers. PAT DORSEY

Spring runoff is the most challenging time of the season as freestone rivers start to become off-colored in late April and early May from snowmelt. Flows fluctuate depending on Mother Nature's moods—a few warm days and the river blows out—but conditions can change quickly. If a cold snap hits the area, runoff stalls and the rivers recede and clear for a short period. Flows will frequently spike up and down this time of year, until warm weather and runoff finally prevail.

As a whole, most freestone streams are unfishable for a short period (three to five weeks), but spring runoff generally peaks by Father's Day. Once the river peaks, the river's edges begin to clear and it becomes fishable, especially with stoneflies, dark streamers, leeches, and brightly colored flies. One of my favorite dirty-water flies is a pink San Juan Worm. I have fooled countless trout with it when conditions seemed almost hopeless. Concentrate your efforts along the edges, fishing the softer currents.

During the height of spring runoff, many anglers, including myself, typically switch gears and fish tailwaters. Tailwaters experience runoff too, but not like freestones. While the flows are much higher than their normal historic flow regimes, the flows are clear and controlled. These higher flows can actually produce some of the best fishing of the year as larger food organisms such

Browns were first introduced to Colorado in the 1890s and are now abundant. With a naturally aggressive nature these trout thrive in many rivers in the state. With populations supplied by stocking and natural reproduction, locations like the South Platte River can host browns exceeding 30 inches. In the spring, when the irises bloom, it is caddis time, and you have a shot at catching these fish on the surface. JAY NICHOLS

Officially named the state fish of Colorado in 1994, brightly colored greenback cutthroat are true gems. Some of the best locations to catch these prizes are in Rocky Mountain National Park. In the Roaring River, for instance, these trout will average 6 to 12 inches, though larger specimens are caught, and rise eagerly to bite-size terrestrial patterns such as Charlie Craven's Baby Boy Hopper (above). JAY NICHOLS

Hooking steel like this rainbow from Antero Reservoir will make your reel hit new pitches. Colorado stillwaters offer anglers a chance to connect with rainbow trout that in some stillwaters can grow an inch a month. LANDON MAYER

as aquatic worms, scuds, stoneflies, and crane flies get washed away from the substrate and cause a feeding frenzy.

The post runoff period on a freestone can provide some of the best fishing of the year. If you like fishing attractor dry flies, you should plan your fishing vacation to Colorado for the latter part of the summer. I cannot even begin to tell you how many trout I have caught on Renegades, Royal Wulffs, House and Lots, and Limeades on the Gunnison River and other nearby freestones during late July, August, and early September. Dry-and-dropper rigs are another effective strategy for this time of year. After chucking lead all summer long, fishing with attractors or dry-and-dropper rigs is a nice break.

Colorado anglers will have the opportunity to target several varieties of gamefish: rainbow, cutthroat, cuttbow, brown, brook trout, kokanee salmon, and mountain whitefish. It is not entirely impossible to have a grand slam—landing all five species of trout in one day. I had a grand slam a couple summers ago on the Blue River above Green Mountain Reservoir. Needless to say, it was a special day!

Colorado was hit hard by whirling disease in the mid-1990s, but with the introduction of the Hofer rainbow in many watersheds the once-decimated

In addition to the greenback, other species of cutthroats, such as Colorado River cutts, Rio Grande cutts, and Snake River cutts (above), swim in the state's waters. Snake River cutthroats are found in the highest numbers on the South Platte River above Eleven Mile Canyon Reservoir. Because they are so aggressive, these fish will strike large imitations such as Mike Lawson's Conehead Sculpin. LANDON MAYER

The best thing about beautiful brookies is they are not shy about eating dry flies. Introduced to Colorado in the late 1800s, brook trout often become overpopulated and can outcompete other trout. They are typically found in higher-elevation lakes, beaver dams, and streams. ROSS PURNELL

Kokanee salmon play a big role in keeping the rivers and reservoirs in Colorado healthy. After they die, their decaying carcasses supply nutrients to waterways. PAT DORSEY

rainbow populations are bouncing back. Circumstantial evidence from electroshocking data collected by the Colorado Division of Wildlife show several year-classes of rainbow present in their samples, suggesting that Hofer rainbows are indeed reproducing on their own.

Many environmental affairs and water issues have surfaced in the past twenty years. The water in our rivers and reservoirs supplies major metropolitan areas with water as well as serving agricultural needs such as irrigating crops and pasture land and watering livestock.

In many cases, the river you have come to know and love is nothing more than a water conduit. Water-rights attorneys have made lucrative careers out of battling over water rights, determining who will get water and when. Recreational activities such as rafting, kayaking, boating, and other water sports are also important to Colorado tourism. Despite all odds, these rivers still remain excellent trout fisheries, in spite of the heavy demands placed on them.

What you hold in your hands is an invaluable source of knowledge. I wish I had this book when I was growing up; it would have shortened my learning curve dramatically. I learned how to fish the rivers in Colorado through trial and error. It was a long, drawn-out process, trust me! But make no mistake about it—there is no substitution for time on the water if you want to become a proficient angler. Fly fishing requires continual learning at all levels and abilities. The more you know about each river, the fish and their behavior, hatches and fly patterns, seasonal strategies, and techniques and tactics, the better chances you have of success.

That's why I feel this book is so important; it will complement your time on the water, reinforce what you already know, and provide you with a wealth of knowledge that will increase your productivity on the stream. Detailed maps pinpoint public access points, removing any doubt whether you are on public water. It is your responsibility to know these property boundaries—permission is required to fish on all private land. The thorough discussions of hatches, fly patterns, and effective tactics included in each chapter come from spending decades on the water.

Pat Dorsey
Parker, Colorado

COLORADO'S
BEST FLY FISHING
NORTHEASTERN

Trout hold near the river's edge to find relief from the high flows of the Cache La Poudre, Big Thompson, and Roaring rivers. Imitations like a Fat Albert hopper produce aggressive strikes from eager fish. LANDON MAYER

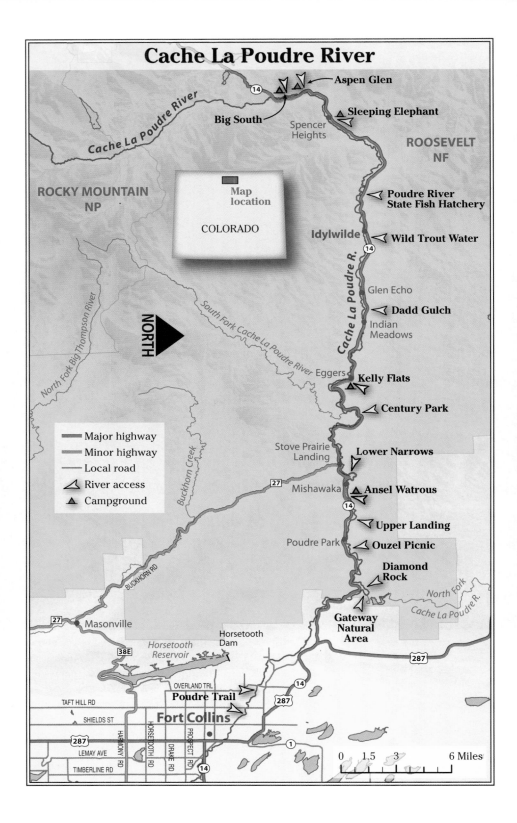

Cache La Poudre River

Aspen Glen

Big South

Sleeping Elephant

Spencer Heights

ROOSEVELT NF

ROCKY MOUNTAIN NP

Map location

COLORADO

Poudre River State Fish Hatchery

Idylwilde

Wild Trout Water

Glen Echo

Dadd Gulch

Indian Meadows

NORTH

Eggers

Kelly Flats

Century Park

Major highway
Minor highway
Local road
River access
Campground

Stove Prairie Landing

Lower Narrows

Mishawaka

Ansel Watrous

Upper Landing

Poudre Park

Ouzel Picnic

Diamond Rock

Gateway Natural Area

North Fork Cache La Poudre R.

Masonville

Horsetooth Reservoir

Horsetooth Dam

OVERLAND TRL

Poudre Trail

TAFT HILL RD

SHIELDS ST

Fort Collins

HARMONY RD

HORSETOOTH RD

DRAKE RD

PROSPECT RD

LEMAY AVE

TIMBERLINE RD

0   1.5   3   6 Miles

CHAPTER 2

Cache La Poudre River

For many attending Colorado State University in Fort Collins, the Poudre and its miles of water offer a terrific fishery close by. Although this intimate water (averaging around 40 feet wide in most spots) does not hold some of the larger trout that you will find on other Colorado waters, it provides great dry-fly fishing nearly year-round in a beautiful canyon with lots of fish that are eager to rise to Elk-Hair Caddis or large foam hoppers in the summer. Friend and former client Brandon T. Kramer, who explored miles of the river while attending the university, couldn't have said it any better: "The Poudre offers more public water than you can shake a stick at."

Though I have had lots of great trips to the Poudre, in fall 2009 I found a new appreciation for this waterway after fishing with Kramer and my better half, Michelle, during really bad weather. Once we suited up, the air temperatures dropped again, making it a balmy 20 degrees with snow on the horizon. The water was frozen below the hatchery, with a few flowing deep runs and shallow riffles above. We went for it, thinking that we might only squeeze in an hour before the storm hit. After 20 minutes we spotted a few lethargic fish unwilling to move. Then, in a small riffle just above a deep bend, Kramer spotted a few spooky, but feeding redsides. He gave it a good 20 minutes and turned to me, shivering: "Why don't you take a stab at them?"

I thought that was a great idea to keep my blood circulating through my body. I removed the indicator and weight from the rig and tied on two plastic bead midges that would not snag the river bottom. I crawled into position, cast, and watched one tilt to the left and slightly open its mouth. I set, and to my surprise, I saw the girth on the fish as the large muscle swam down into the deep run surrounded by ice and broke the surface. Seven minutes later, with some spills on the ice and having to cross the river, I was able to land the 25-inch bruiser with some help from Kramer on the net.

According to most sources, the Cache La Poudre River was named after a group of travelers in the early 1800s were caught in a freak snowstorm that

Trout like this are not just a chance of a lifetime, but a lifetime of chances—once you understand their behavior. With cloudy cold skies and shallow water I was able to find this cuttbow midging just below the surface just downstream from the wild trout waters in November; I caught it on a Dorsey's Flashback Mercury Black Beauty. MICHELLE MAYER

had to "cache la poudre" or "hide the powder" in order to lighten their load, returning to retrieve the gunpowder in the spring. While the worry of hidden gunpowder is no longer a concern, the river holds other hidden treasures—the healthy supply of rainbow, brown, and cuttbows ranging from 12 to 16 inches, some much larger, that still thrive in the long stretches of this scenic river.

Angler, fly tier, and author of *River Journal: North Platte* Eric Pettine says that he loves every part of the Poudre, from its birth in Rocky Mountain National Park and its descent from Cameron Pass down the Poudre Canyon to its emergence onto the high plains just north of Fort Collins. Part of his love affair is because of the amazing beauty and diversity it offers: "It is the only Colorado River designated 'Wild and Scenic.' The headwaters of the South Fork of the Poudre are so small you could catch the river in two hands. As it descends, the river gathers snowmelt and mountain spring waters quickly enough to support a rich brook trout fishery accessible within a couple of miles of easy hiking. In another couple of miles, cutthroat trout join the brookies. A bit farther down, rainbows are swimming in the mix. Finally, the South Fork pours into the main flow of the Poudre River below Cameron Pass and becomes a rainbow and brown trout fishery."

With its headwaters beginning in Rocky Mountain National Park (RMNP), the Poudre is one of the larger freestone rivers draining out of the Rockies onto the plains of northern Colorado. If you choose to take a backcountry adventure to the headwaters, follow the directions to RMNP (see the RMNP chapter) and follow US 34 West to the Poudre River Trail just before Milner Pass. This is a high mountain trail that requires overnight permits, has no road access, and is frequently inaccessible, as US 34 closes in this area from October through May and intermittently during summer.

Canyon Stretch

While the canyon fishes year-round, the river runs west to east, so little light hits the water and the river will be filled with ice shelves and frozen areas from November to March. During this cold spell, the best ticket is midge larvae and pupae with the occasional adult if the weather warms enough to supply a hatch. As the water warms and rays of light hit the canyon, the river comes to life with insect and trout activity through October, with a break due to high water during runoff. When the heavy flows drop to around 800 cfs, the following summer and fall will produce good numbers of hatches.

"The Poudre is fishable as soon as the ice goes off the river, usually in April," Pettine states. "I often wait for the water to warm to 48 degrees. At that temperature the fishing will turn on. I have never found another river where good fishing is so temperature-dependent. Early on, the fishing is mainly nymphs. The river has a full complement of aquatic insects, from large stoneflies to caddis and mayflies. My favorite nymph for this time of year is

The only river in the state designated as a "Wild and Scenic River" by the National Park Service, the Poudre offers miles of quality water and good numbers of trout willing to eat year-round. An angler on the high bank in the Canyon stretch helps the angler on the low bank stalk a fish. LANDON MAYER

a brown stonefly in a size 10. Since I usually fish with a dropper, I add something that imitates a caddis larva. Although a good one is the Tungsten Pyrite Caddis, many combinations of flies will work."

Pettine says that he "works the edge of the river from the bank using a brown stonefly with schlappen hackle twice the length of the fly body" to target trout that move to the margins of the river at high water to intercept the stonefly nymphs that are working their way out of the water. "This fishing is totally missed by most anglers," he says. He adds that anglers should stay out of the water at this time: "It is unwise—if not downright foolish—to risk wade fishing during high water. We have drowning fatalities, mostly whitewater enthusiasts, every spring and early summer on our swollen Colorado rivers, and the Poudre is no exception."

In June 2012, the High Park Fire, one of the largest in Colorado history, destroyed over 87,000 acres of land in Poudre Canyon. Despite this, fishing has remained fairly good, but contact local fly shops before your trip as conditions can change.

The canyon also has hatches of Green Drakes, caddis, and BWOs and Red Quills in the summer. Terrestrial imitations like #16-20 black Foam Beetles, #16-18 Baby Boy Crickets, #18-20 red/black Flying Ant imitations, and #14-16 green or yellow Fat Alberts work well for the trout lying in wait below overhanging vegetation. In the faster water, searching dry flies like #14-16

Amy's Ants, # 14-18 Kaufmann's Crystal Stimulators, and #16-18 Black Ants can be very effective fished in pocketwater, eddies, and edges.

The first access along CO 14 is approximately 50 miles upstream at the Big South Campground. The water has large rock structures that provide good holding water, and pine trees lining the river's edge provide cover. As a side note, Joe Wright Creek flows downstream from Joe Wright Reservoir, through Chambers Lake, and merges with the Cache la Poudre near Big South Campground. This prime dry-fly fishery opens July 31.

A mile downstream from Big South Campground, the next access is past Chambers Lake at Aspenglen Campground. At this point the river is very narrow, with multiple pullouts for a couple more miles down to Sleeping Elephant Campground. River access beyond Sleeping Elephant Campground is predominately through dirt pullouts every 50 to 100 feet, unmarked with the exception of Roaring Creek Hiking Trail and Big Bend, for 5 miles, to just below the Poudre River Fish Hatchery.

The 4 miles of water below the hatchery (past Idylwilde), provides some of the largest trout in the river. If you want to catch some of these big boys,

The fall months supply anglers with good conditions on the Poudre River when the water has dropped from the high flows of summer. ROSS PURNELL

Located east of Cameron Pass along CO 14, Joe Wright Reservoir has 152 surface acres of water for anglers to explore. In this lake, one of the only in the state that has grayling, fishing is by artificial flies and lures only, and no gas-powered vehicles are allowed. Grayling are not as selective as trout, and anything from a Parachute Adams to a Stimulator works great, especially if you use a nymph dropper. There is a good supply of rainbow and cuttbows, so the chance of landing multiple species is good.

With a small mouth positioned on the lower part of its head, a grayling has to come down on top of the fly to consume it, so you must wait for the grayling's head to go back under the water before you set. It is not uncommon for the fish to miss the dry on its first attempt.

Concentrate your efforts on the reservoir's edge after mid to late July, when the grayling are done spawning and are feeding heavily in the warming shallows. There is also less wind on the edges of large bodies of water, allowing food sources to remain on the surface longer. If the topwater bite is not on, tandem nymphs under a large indicator or buoyant hopper are the ticket once you figure out the depth at which the fish are feeding.

In addition to the largest population of grayling in the state, the reservoir has a great supply of the Eagle Lake strain of cutthroat trout as well as Mackinaw trout and tiger muskies, which were introduced to keep the growing grayling populations under control. To catch these reservoir predators, use imitations that look like the grayling and trout. Large black or black/purple Bunny Leeches and white/green Clouser Minnows are good imitations from ice-off through July on the edges where the grayling spawn and these predators come in to feed. ■

Grayling will feed heavily on the surface as they cruise shorelines or hang on the edge of rivers, and you often only need a Parachute Adams to catch them. Joe Wright Reservoir and Crosho Lake are two prime spots for this species. LANDON MAYER

Deep long pools like the ones below the hatchery are prime areas for large trout to feed at the head of the run or drop-off point. The two sections of the river designated "Wild Trout Water" (catch-and-release only) are from Pingree Park Road upstream to the town of Rustic, approximately 5 miles, and from the Black Hollow Creek confluence 4 miles upstream to Big Bend Campground, just past the Poudre River Fish Hatchery. NICK WILLIAMS

fish to specific targets instead of blind casting. As the water warms in the early spring and then cools in the fall while dropping in flow, more trout become apparent in the deep drop-offs, riffled runs, braids, and clear water, often feeding on *Baetis*. Because of the turbulent water, you can get into a great position to make a presentation because the trout cannot detect you as well.

There are several campgrounds from Mishawaka to Joe Wright Reservoir, including the Narrows and Sleeping Elephant, which have access near the river. Around mile marker 84, below the water treatment plant, the pullouts are marked with fence signs that announce the "Wild Trout Water" designation given to this section. Moving downstream is the National Forest Visitor Center and Norman Fry Drive with pullouts on the side of the bridge. These pullouts again continue to the town of Rustic, where the Wild Trout Water officially ends.

From here, there is a patch of private property to mile marker 92, where the pullouts again become accessible until the road veers away from the

Poudre. The next access is at Dadd Gulch just below Indian Springs. Eggers is next, with camping downstream at Kelly Flats Campground.

At mile marker 99, there is river access at Mountain Park with camping and a trailhead, and beyond that are Century Park and Dutch George with the same. At this point most of the access is via marked campgrounds, trailheads, or use areas as the river becomes more developed. Stove Prairie Landing is next, with various pull-offs on your left to the point where no-parking signs appear on both sides of the river. Lower Narrows, Ansel Watrous, and Upper Landing are also well-marked access points.

Ouzel picnic area, another 3 miles downstream from Ansel Watrous, also has access, with Diamond Rock 3 more miles down providing a long stretch of public parking on the left, as well as public facilities, before you leave Roosevelt National Forest. From here, Hewlett Gulch marks some of the last access, as private development takes over until you reach Greyrock National Recreational Trail on your left. The last good stretch begins at Gateway Natural Area, which allows access to Seaman Reservoir and various pull-offs to Picnic Rock a mile down.

Eric Pettine says, "In recent years, largely due to the inspiration of local fishing guides such as Cory Engen and Chris Schrantz, there are an increasing number of float fishermen on the 3½-mile stretch from the Pump House to Picnic Rock. The float is water dependent, but fly fishers don't need as much water for their sport as do whitewater enthusiasts. As with any fishing float, the best technique is to work the banks with dry flies and small streamers."

Some of the largest brown trout are located in Fort Collins where they can feed more easily throughout the year in the slower water. LANDON MAYER

CACHE LA POUDRE RIVER

	JAN	FEB	MAR	APR	MAY	JUN	JUL	AUG	SEP	OCT	NOV	DEC
Midge (*Chironomidae*)					■	■	■				■	
#18-24 olive Jujubee Midge, Mercury Midge, Flashback Mercury Black Beauty, Rick's Transparent Pupa, Griffith's Gnat												
Blue-Winged Olive (*Baetis* spp.)					■	■			■	■		
#16-22 WD-40, Flashback Pheasant Tail, Stalcup's Baetis, BLM Baetis, RS2, Loop Wing Emerger, Vis-A-Dun												
Caddis (*Brachycentrus* and *Hydropsyche* spp.)						■	■	■				
#16-20 Larry's High-Vis Caddis, olive Rick's Transparent Pupa, Graphic Caddis, Landon's Larva, Buckskin, Lawson's E-Z Caddis, Tak's Splitwing Caddis												
Golden Stonefly (*Perlidae*)						■	■					
#8-14 Hotwire Prince, 20 Incher, Tungstone, Pat's Rubber Legs, Tak's Go2 Prince, Stimulator												
Green Drake (*Drunella grandis*)							■					
#12-16 Mercer's GB Poxyback Green Drake, Copper John, Lawson's Green Drake, Green Drake Cripple												
Red Quill (*Rhithrogena* sp.)							■					
#14-18 Copper John, Pheasant Tail, A. K.'s Red Quill, Adams												
Terrestrials								■	■			
#10-18 Ant Misbehavin, Schlotter's Foam Flying Ant, High-Vis Parachute Hopper, Amy's Ant												
Streamers					■					■	■	
#6-12 Beadhead Crystal Bugger, Articulated Leech, Slumpbuster, Lawson's Conehead Sculpin												
Worms and Eggs			■	■	■	■	■	■	■	■	■	
Micro Worm, Flashtail Mini Egg, Nuke Egg, Otter's Egg												

Town Stretch

Eric Pettine describes the often-overlooked public water through Fort Collins as mostly pools with "some surprisingly large trout, mostly browns." In town, the gradient is not as steep as in the canyon and the water flows are slower, providing deeper runs that are often home to larger predatory browns looking to ambush the next meal. If the trout are not on the rise, larger nymphs and streamers can trigger takes. "Be warned that there are few fish in this stretch, and they are surprisingly hard to fool—especially the lunker browns, who are accustomed to dining on an abundance of crayfish here," says Pettine.

Access is easy via the Poudre River Trail, which follows the river for approximately 10 miles from any major intersection, with some of the more common points being Lee Martinez Park or the crossing at Shields. This area holds some of the larger browns in the river, the most popular section being from Lions Park to Lee Martinez. To access Lions Park, take a right off CO 14 onto Overland Trail. Parking is just past the bridge over the Poudre on your right. For Lee Martinez Park, continue on Overland, take a left onto Mulberry, another left onto Remington, and enter the park from the south. "Although many people fish the Poudre in the canyon, few people stop to see what the

Fishing the Poudre in Fort Collins can offer big rewards. In low light, brown trout go on the hunt. MICHELLE MAYER

in-town section has to offer," says Grant Houx of St. Peter's Fly Shop. "On the northwest side of town, all major roads that travel north and south through Ft. Collins cross the Poudre, and almost all of them allow for public access. As you proceed southeast (downstream) you will find that all the major east/west roads cross the river."

Houx continues, "The Poudre River in town is a diverse fishery. You will find both trout and warmwater species, depending on where you are. The water temperatures in the northwest side of town are more favorable for trout habitat, and—more importantly—insect diversity. Some of the largest trout in the river reside in town, but they are few and far between. The majority of the population of trout in town consists of browns between 10 and 12 inches, with the occasional rainbow."

Loop Wing Emerger

Hook: #18-24 Tiemco 100
Thread: Gray 8/0 or 14/0
Tail: Pheasant tail fibers
Abdomen: Light olive biot
Wing case: Natural mallard CDC
Thorax: Olive dry-fly dubbing

High-Vis Caddis

Hook: #16-20 Tiemco 100
Thread: Gray 8/0
Abdomen: Medium gray rabbit
Wing: Speckled gray Spirit River
            Aire-Flow Stonefly Wing
Post: Hot pink/orange Poly Yarn
Hackle: Grizzly
Thorax: Medium gray rabbit

Vis-A-Dun (BWO)

Hook: #16-24 Tiemco 100
Thread: Iron gray 8/0 Uni-Thread
Tail: Watery dun hackle fibers
Wing: Light gray Poly Yarn
Abdomen: BWO Superfine
Hackle: Light dun rooster
Thorax: BWO Superfine
Head: BWO Superfine
Note: The PMD variation uses PMD
            Superfine.

Jujubee Midge (Olive)

Hook: #16-22 Tiemco 2488
Thread: White 10/0 Gudebrod or
            74-denier Lagartun
Abdomen: Two strands of olive Super Hair
            and one strand of black
Thorax: Black 8/0 Uni-Thread
Wing case: White Fluoro Fibre

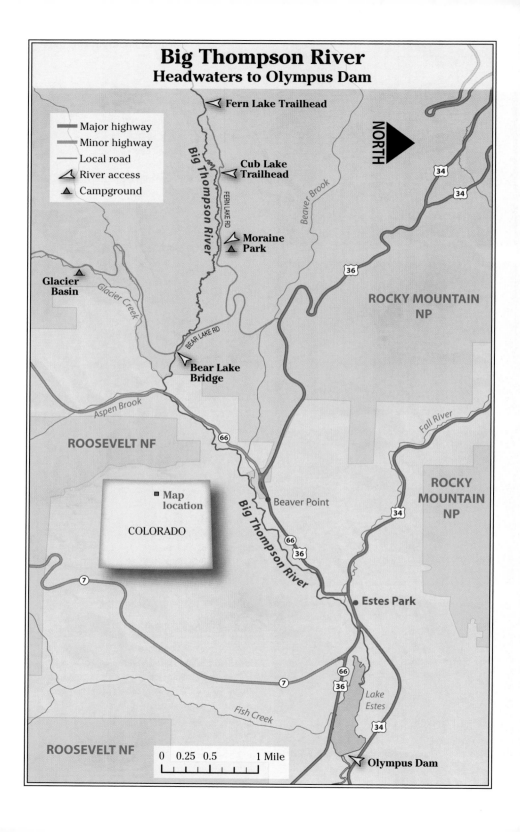

Big Thompson River
Headwaters to Olympus Dam

Fern Lake Trailhead

NORTH

Major highway
Minor highway
Local road
River access
Campground

Cub Lake
Trailhead

Big Thompson River

Beaver Brook

FERN LAKE RD

34

34

Moraine
Park

36

Glacier
Basin

Glacier Creek

BEAR LAKE RD

ROCKY MOUNTAIN
NP

Bear Lake
Bridge

Aspen Brook

Fall River

ROOSEVELT NF

66

Map
location

COLORADO

Beaver Point

Big Thompson River

66
36

34

ROCKY
MOUNTAIN
NP

7

34

Estes Park

66
36

7

Lake
Estes

Fish Creek

ROOSEVELT NF

0   0.25   0.5   1 Mile

34

Olympus Dam

CHAPTER 3

Big Thompson River

The Big T is one of the largest rivers on the Front Range, due in part to the enormous number of drainages that come together to form it. The other factor is the 13-mile, 9-foot-diameter Alva B. Adams Tunnel constructed as part of the Colorado-Big Thompson Project of the 1930s, which brings water from Shadow Mountain Reservoir on the Western Slope, through the Continental Divide, and into the Big Thompson River. While originally constructed for irrigation, this project now supplies water to the Front Range for household consumption.

Named for David Thompson, an English surveyor who mapped the river and surrounding areas in the 1800s, the Big T is born in Forest Canyon in Rocky Mountain National Park (in Larimer County), and flows east through Moraine Park to the town of Estes Park. There, Olympus Dam holds water in Lake Estes and creates the tailwater that eventually flows into Big Thompson Canyon. The top-releasing Olympus Dam supplies warmer surface water from Lake Estes, warming the river below it. Because of the influx of warmer water, hatches begin earlier, but you must be mindful of the temperatures in the summer so that you do not fish when it is too warm.

Most anglers break the river up into two sections: the upper Big T around Moraine Park, and the lower river from Olympus Dam to Loveland. I also divide the lower river into the mile-long tailwater below the dam and the canyon section downstream, which fishes more like a freestone. While the Big T is located in some gorgeous country, the one downside is traffic during the summer, especially in the water just below Olympus Dam.

The Upper River

My favorite time to hit the upper river is in the fall. The leaves are changing, the summer crowds dwindle daily, and the sounds of bugling elk all add to the experience of what Mike Kruise, owner of the Laughing Grizzly Fly Shop in Longmont, describes as "glacially-sculpted scenery with first-class fishing for wild trout."

Kruise continues: "Above Moraine Park, the Big Thompson flows out of Forest Canyon, paralleling Fern Lake Trail. This section is a typical mountain freestone stream with great populations of browns, brookies, a few rainbows, and greenback cutthroats from the Fern Lake trailhead upstream to the pool. High water during runoff makes this stretch tough to fish, but it provides great pocketwater fishing from the end of runoff until late fall."

After reaching Moraine Park, a 2-mile-long flat meadow, the river begins to slow down, giving the trout a chance to hold and feed. According to Kruise, "Brown trout to 14 inches dominate this stretch, with a few brook trout and the occasional rainbow." Moraine Park can be accessed at the Bear Lake Road bridge and the best water is from here upstream to the footbridge at the Cub Lake Trailhead. The road runs along the river, but access is best by foot through the meadow. There are plenty of riffled runs, pools, and backwaters that will hold trout, and Kruise recommends double nymph rigs in the spring through runoff. In the summer you can switch to dry flies with droppers to take advantage of the hatches: "Summer sees hatches of PMDs, Red Quills,

In addition to year-round fishing, the tailwater is also popular for its stunningly beautiful trout. Fly designer John Barr says, "Every trout you hook in the tailwaters of the Big T is more unique than the one before." In addition to rainbows, the Big T has healthy populations of brown, brook, and cutthroat trout along its entirety. LANDON MAYER

The headwaters of the Big Thompson supply cover in the form of shade and structure where trout feed without pressure. During the summer, fish terrestrial patterns on the edges, focusing near overhanging vegetation and shade. A #14-16 Takahopper, #14-16 Tak's Drowned Hopper, #12-16 Green-Legged Fat Albert, #12-14 BC Hopper, or # 18-20 ants in various colors all work well. ROSS PURNELL

caddis, and small stoneflies. Terrestrials provide great action as well," Kruise says. No matter what you are drifting below the surface, make sure you replace any indicators with flies like a #12-14 Amy's Ant or BC Hopper to make your rig look as natural as possible. Because this area is so open, the trout are wary. In addition to crouching and walking slowly, you should keep your false casts to a minimum—less movement equals more fish.

As the river cuts through a wide meadow populated by a large herd of elk, deep undercut banks provide a home for larger trout that will take a weighted streamer like a #8-12 tungsten-cone Slumpbuster. Kruise says, "Really large (over 24 inches) browns hide under the banks and are rarely caught, except by dedicated after-dark anglers." To reach these challenging areas, use weighted caddis larvae, stoneflies, and leeches such as a #16-18 Pine Squirrel Leech, #12-14 Slumpbuster, #14-16 Hotwire Prince Nymph, #14-16 Barr's Tungstone, or #14-16 brown Pat's Rubber Legs.

To get to the upper river, enter the park through US 36 (Beaver Meadows entrance) and take your first left onto Bear Lake Road. Just past the Moraine Park Visitor Center is the right-hand turn to the Fern Lake Trailhead, where the headwaters can be accessed from its confluence with Fern Creek. Farther downstream, access can be found through the Cub Lake Trailhead, which crosses the river on its way to the lake.

The Lower River

Directly below Olympus Dam, the water is wide with a giant turbulent pool for trout to hold and feed. Many of the trout find shelter from the heavy current on the edges of the run and slow sections of the numerous seams. The mystery of what holds below the surface demands at least a few casts before moving on, but I only fish it if I think no one else has.

Just a few hundred feet below the dam the river starts to look like classic tailwater, with structure such as boulders, logs, and weirs throughout. This section is one of my favorite sight-fishing areas in the state, because you are able to scan the narrow river (in places no more than 10 feet) more effectively than a wider stretch of water with a lot of glare. From late fall through early spring the water is low and clear and the lightly pressured fish are easier to see.

The water below the dam fishes well year-round, and the fish can grow large (one fish caught in 2009 was 27 inches). From the dam to Waltonia, fishing is catch-and-release with artificials only. Water flows below the dam can fluctuate as much as 700-plus cfs in the summer and drop to below 200 cfs in late summer. The best flows are when the water is at its lowest or on the drop.

Avid angler Eric Pettine loves starting his season on the tailwater: "January on the Big T is a wasteland of ice. What does not freeze is the 1/2-mile long tailwater below Lake Estes, from which the river issues. Consequently, there are a few hardy (and probably mentally challenged) fly fishers who choose to open the season on January 1 here. I can seldom resist the first day of the new year on this water, because there are usually trout rising to midges there. The possibility of taking a fish on a dry fly to start the season is irresistible. There are usually elk grazing in the area; the surrounding mountains are white with snow to water the river in the coming spring; and once you are sufficiently frostbitten, the town of Estes Park is right there to provide a great breakfast and lots of hot coffee."

According to Pettine, "Good patterns for fishing this tailwater are #20-24 red Craven's Jujubee Midge and a #20-24 blue/red Secret Nymph. For the dry midge, there are a variety of patterns, though I like the #18 Eric's Midge with an orange post for easy visibility. I will fish this and often drop a #22 or 24 without the post off the larger fly. This makes a good combination because the #24 is almost impossible to see." In the lower stretches of the river you

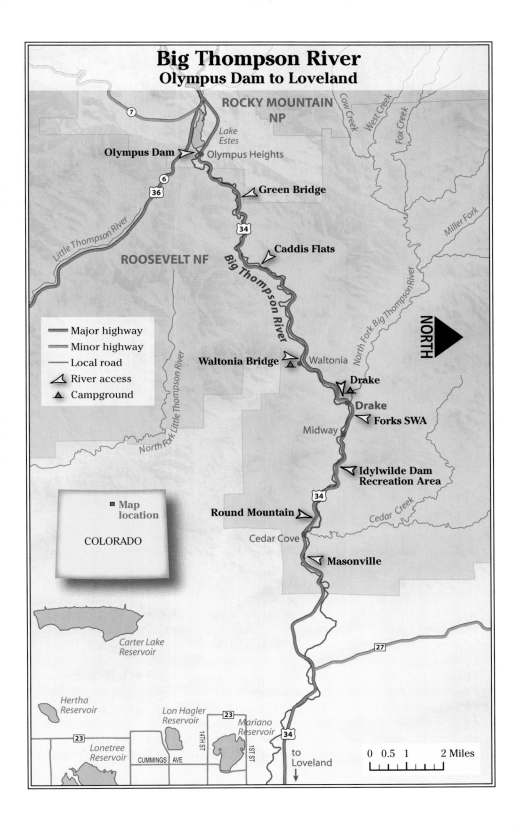

Big Thompson River
Olympus Dam to Loveland

ROCKY MOUNTAIN NP

Cow Creek

West Creek

Fox Creek

7

Lake Estes

Olympus Dam ▷ Olympus Heights

6

36

◁ Green Bridge

Little Thompson River

34

ROOSEVELT NF

Caddis Flats ◁

Big Thompson River

Miller Fork

North Fork Big Thompson River

Major highway
Minor highway
Local road
◁ River access
▲ Campground

North Fork Little Thompson River

Waltonia Bridge ▷ ▲ Waltonia

North Fork Little Thompson River

Drake
◁
▲ Drake
Forks SWA ◁

Midway

Idylwilde Dam ◁ Recreation Area

Cedar Creek

NORTH

■ Map location

COLORADO

34

Round Mountain ◁

Cedar Cove

◁ Masonville

Carter Lake Reservoir

27

Hertha Reservoir

Lon Hagler Reservoir

23

Mariano Reservoir

23

14TH ST

1ST ST

Lonetree Reservoir

CUMMINGS AVE

34

to Loveland ↓

0   0.5   1   2 Miles

Colorado is a four-season playground for anglers, and many, such as this angler fishing below Olympus Dam, spend their powder days on the water instead of the slopes.
LANDON MAYER

will see some good activity during the summer of caddis, Blue-Winged Olives, and stoneflies after runoff. In addition to *Acroneuria*, Golden Stones make up a good deal of the trouts' diet and #14-18 Prince Nymphs, #14-18 red or black Copper Johns, #14-16 Go2 Princes, and #8-16 Kaufmann's Golden Stonefly nymphs are good imitations for the stones. Insects farther downstream from the dam are generally one size larger.

To access the tailwater below Olympus Dam, take US 34 East from Estes Park. Just after you leave town, turn right onto Mall Road and gain access to the dam parking lot by crossing the river and taking your first right on an unmarked road. Parking is at the end of this road. While the next public access starts on the left side around mile marker 65, the banks are fairly steep, and as private property dominates until Rock Canyon Road, it is better to access the river from the large pullout at this location. Approximately a mile downstream of the dam is Roosevelt National Forest, with plenty of public access and river to explore.

Where the water flows through national forest, the current's speed picks up considerably, so locate fish by targeting areas where fish can get a break. Pettine advises: "While technically the rest of the river through the Big T

Jay Nichols fishes pocketwater in Big Thompson Canyon. The diversity of water, scenery, and great fishing, all within an easy drive, make the Big T a special river. According to author Eric Pettine—and this corroborates my own experience—Big T trout aren't that selective to pattern and fishing is not that technical: "Though I have tied and tried a variety of flies over fifty years, I think the question of fly selection is more a matter of what fly a trout won't take than what they will. I always put my money on the angler rather than on the fly." LANDON MAYER

Canyon is a tailwater, it fishes more like a freestoner. The water from the top of the canyon to the small town of Drake drops precipitously and forms classic pocketwater that is best fished with a size 10 brown stonefly with a dropper in the spring. As the summer progresses, your favorite hopper or a stimulator with your favorite nymph dropper is usually good enough to catch fish."

While the tailwater can fish well year-round, the canyon stretch fishes best after mid-July, when runoff subsides. Moving downstream, good stretches include Green Bridge near mile marker 66 and Caddis Flats between mile markers 69 and 70. There are stretches of private land mixed in, which are also clearly marked. The mix of public and private access continues past mile marker 72, where the river enters Big Thompson Canyon.

Waltonia Bridge has access for 1/2 mile via a large pullout between mile markers 73 and 74. The gradient becomes very steep through the next several pullouts as you approach the town of Drake, which is about 2 miles east of Waltonia Bridge with access between mile markers 74 and 75 and a campground.

At mile marker 76 you can access Forks State Wildlife Area on your right through either the parking lot or a pull-off just downstream. After another stretch of private land, Idylwilde Dam Recreation Area provides easy access before the gradient again becomes steep. After a few more pullouts that offer

Though the canyon locks up with ice in the winter, cold-weather fishing is great below the dam with midge patterns such as black Jujubee Midges. LANDON MAYER

BIG THOMPSON RIVER

	JAN	FEB	MAR	APR	MAY	JUN	JUL	AUG	SEP	OCT	NOV	DEC
Midge (*Chironomidae*)	███	███	███	███	███	███				███	███	███
#18-24 Tyler's Holiday Midge, Tak's Mini Bow-Tie Buzzer, Zebra Midge, Jujubee Midge, Yamauchi's Blackfly Larva, Griffith's Gnat												
Blue-Winged Olive (*Baetis* spp.)					███	███			███	███		
#18-22 Mercer's Micro May, Flashback Pheasant Tail, Flashback Barr Emerger, Jujubaetis, Parachute Adams, Cannon's Snowshoe Dun												
Caddis (*Brachycentrus* and *Hydropsyche* spp.)						███	███					
#16-20 Lawson's Electric Caddis, Deep Sparkle Pupa, Landon's Larva, Barr's Graphic Caddis, Garcia's Mother's Day Caddis, Tak's Splitwing Caddis, Tak's Go2 Caddis, black Puterbaugh's Foam Caddis												
Golden Stonefly (*Perlidae*)						███	███					
#8-14 Barr's Tungstone, Pat's Rubber Legs, 20 Incher, Madam X												
Pale Morning Dun (*Ephemerella* spp.)						███	███					
#16-20 yellow Copper John, BTS PMD, Burk's Crystal Hunchback, Dorsey's Mercury PMD, Sparkle Dun												
Green Drake (*Drunella grandis*)							███	███				
#12-16 Lawson's Green Drake Nymph, Barr's Tung Teaser, Furimsky's Foam Drake, Lawson's Cripple												
Red Quill (*Rhithrogena* sp.)							███	███	███	███		
#14-18 Copper John, Pheasant Tail, A. K.'s Red Quill, Parachute Adams												
Terrestrials							███	███	███			
#12-16 Charlie Boy Hopper, Stimulator, Kingfisher's Red Legged Hopper, tan Chernobyl Ant, Takahopper												
Worms and Eggs	███	███	███	███	███	███	███	███	███	███	███	███
#8-12 Micro Worm, Flashtail Mini Egg, Nuke Egg, Otter's Egg												

access for those who don't mind the steep terrain, there are larger pullouts by mile marker 78, with the river veering away from the road around Round Mountain. The city of Loveland has marked river access with a couple more pullouts before the gradient again becomes too steep for most anglers. With a final access point at the Masonville sign, the river then widens and flows out into the Front Range.

Though the best water is from the dam to Drake, fly-tier extraordinaire Rick Takahashi says, "The lower section of the river from Drake down through the town of Loveland can be highly productive. Be cautious of private land, which is not always well-marked, but there are plenty of pull-offs next to the road that can provide some excellent action." The lowest sections of productive water fish the best as runoff subsides and the cooler water of fall arrives. BWO, caddis, and some stonefly activity is best on the lower end. With river temps reaching 70-plus in the summer, the trout become lethargic and begin to migrate upriver to cooler water.

In the summer, afternoon storms can turn the water off-color after a heavy rain. It was one of these storms, albeit of a rare magnitude, that caused what some call Colorado's deadliest natural disaster. On July 31, 1976, eight

Rick Takahashi, coauthor of **Modern Midges,** *says that one of the best ways to locate larger trout on the Big T is to fish during the late fall and winter when midges are the main food supply. Fishing is great from November through March.* RICK TAKAHASHI

inches of rain fell in one hour, creating a raging wall of water 19 feet high. Sweeping 10-foot boulders in front of it, the water sped down the canyon slopes. Cars, campers, and buildings in its path had no chance of survival. During its fury, 139 people were killed and 6 declared missing.

Dorsey's Mercury PMD

Hook:	#16-18 Dai-Riki 270 or Tiemco 200R
Bead:	Silver-lined glass (extra small)
Thread:	Light cahill 8/0 Uni-Thread
Tail:	Brown saddle hackle fibers
Abdomen:	PMD Superfine
Wing:	Brown Z-lon
Thorax:	PMD Superfine
Legs:	Brown Z-lon
Head:	Thread colored with brown Sharpie

Copper John (Yellow)

Hook: #14-18 Tiemco 5262
Bead: Gold colored brass or tungsten, sized to hook
Weight: Lead wire
Thread: Black 70-denier Ultra Thread
Tail: Dark brown goose biot
Abdomen: Yellow Ultra Wire
Wing case: Black Thinskin and pearl Flashabou covered with epoxy
Legs: Mottled brown hen back

Zebra Midge (Black)

Hook: #18-24 Tiemco 2487/2488
Bead: Silver
Thread: Black 8/0 Uni-Thread
Body: Black 8/0 Uni-Thread
Rib: Fine silver wire

Cannon's Snowshoe Dun (PMD)

Hook: #16-20 Tiemco 101
Thread: Light cahill 8/0 Uni-Thread
Tail: Ginger Betts tailing fibers
Abdomen: Sulphur yellow goose biot or thread
Thorax: PMD Mad River Fine & Dry Dubbing
Wing: PMD snowshoe rabbit hair

Tyler's Holiday Midge

Hook: #18-26 Tiemco 200R
Bead: Red glass
Thread: White 70-denier Ultra Thread
Body: Red Ultra Wire ribbed over white Ultra Thread
Thorax: Pearl Ice Dub

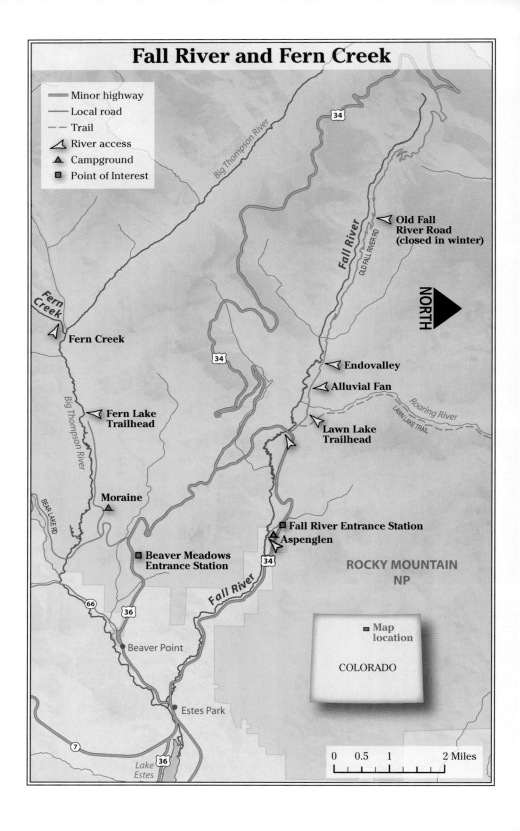

Fall River and Fern Creek

Minor highway
Local road
- - - Trail
◁ River access
▲ Campground
◼ Point of Interest

Big Thompson River

34

Fall River

OLD FALL RIVER RD

◁ Old Fall
River Road
(closed in winter)

NORTH

Fern Creek

◁ Fern Creek

34

◁ Endovalley

◁ Alluvial Fan

Roaring River

LAWN LAKE TRAIL

◁ Fern Lake
Trailhead

Big Thompson River

◁ Lawn Lake
Trailhead

BEAR LAKE RD

▲ Moraine

◼ Fall River Entrance Station

Aspenglen

◼ Beaver Meadows
Entrance Station

34

ROCKY MOUNTAIN
NP

66

36

Fall River

◼ Map
location

COLORADO

Beaver Point

7

36

Estes Park

Lake
Estes

0   0.5   1   2 Miles

CHAPTER 4

Rocky Mountain National Park

I n 1915, Rocky Mountain National Park became the tenth National Park in the United States. Its 400 miles include over 100 named peaks that tower above 10,000 feet, 355 miles of trails, 147 lakes, and countless creeks, beaver ponds, and rivers, including the headwaters of the Colorado, the Big Thompson, and the Cache La Poudre. There is enough water in this refuge to supply a lifetime of fly fishing, and it is the perfect destination for a day- or week-long adventure hiking the backcountry for greenback cutthroat, Colorado's native species of cutthroat trout. The key to getting the most out of every visit to the park is to enjoy it for the adventure and scenery, not just the superb fishing.

The park's endless water, native trout, and abundance of wildlife provide one of the state's great escapes for outdoor enthusiasts. Ross Purnell, editor of *Fly Fisherman* and longtime resident of Colorado, admits that the fish are small, and getting to them is often hard work, but says the experience is worth it for anglers who appreciate wildness: "If trophy-size trout and a short walk from the parking lot are what you're after, there are better places. But if you appreciate the sounds of bugling elk instead of roadside traffic, the adventure of alpine lakes fringed with snow in July, twisted pines wracked by wind and ice, small streams bubbling through flowered meadows, gem-like greenback cutthroat trout, and the majestic scenery of some of the highest peaks in the Rockies, then this place is worth a visit."

Though the park gets a lot of traffic in the height of summer, the farther in you hike, bike, or camp, the fewer anglers you will encounter. On the other hand, many of the trout are more than willing to take the fly. With proper presentation, the action can last all day for brown, brook, rainbow, and cutthroat trout. Though summer has great weather conditions and hatches, it is also the most crowded season, making September (after summer vacations are over)

Hillary Drummond gets ready to fish Fern Creek below Fern Falls. The long runs and pools provide anglers with great dry-fly fishing. ANGUS DRUMMOND

A larger than average greenback cutthroat. By 1937, they were almost extinct; small pop-
ulations from the South Fork Poudre River and Como Creek provided biologists with
naturally-reproducing brood stock for hatcheries. They are now more prolific on the east
side of the park, due to water levels, habitat, and reduced competition from brown and
rainbow trout. ROSS PURNELL

my personal favorite time of year. With less traffic, the majestic sounds of
large bugling bull elk echo through the meadows, and the lush colors of red,
orange, and yellow paint their way up the lush landscapes of the towering
peaks. If you want to beat summer crowds, also consider that June can offer
good fishing, especially at lower-elevation waters such as the headwaters of
the Colorado and Fall rivers (because of snow in the mountains, July is a safer
bet for high-elevation lakes and creeks).

The best way to get to the park year-round is by taking US 36 to Estes
Park, where you can enter the park through the Beaver Meadows Entrance
or take US 34 West to the Fall River Entrance. During the summer, people
access the west side of the park from US 34, but US 34 is closed from October to May and intermittently throughout the summer, so it is always wise
to find out if you can use the entire road before your trip by checking road
closures through the Colorado Department of Transportation's website,
cotrip.org.

To cover all the park's waters in one chapter is impossible, so I will only
focus on what I think are the best opportunities, including those for the native

greenback cutthroat. These include stillwater fishing in remote mountain lakes, as well as small-stream opportunities.

Planning Your Trip

When planning your trip, keep in mind some of these important considerations, from the National Park Service website:

"As you plan your hike, keep in mind that park elevations range from 7,500 to over 12,000 feet. Even very fit individuals coming from lower elevations may experience altitude problems. Symptoms include headaches, shortness of breath, insomnia and rapid heartbeat. After a few days your body will have made some physiological adjustments to higher elevations, but full acclimation may take weeks. To minimize symptoms drink plenty of fluids, avoid alcohol, don't skip meals and get plenty of rest.

"Although you may not feel thirsty, the 'thinner' air at high elevations actually results in increased water evaporation from your lungs. Again, drinking extra water may prevent a bad headache or other altitude symptoms.

"Ultraviolet light is stronger in the mountains because there is less atmosphere for the sunlight to pass through. Wear sunscreen, a hat, sun glasses and consider wearing a long sleeved shirt if you are out in the sun for an extended period."

Also, definitely obtain a copy of the Rocky Mountain National Park *Backcountry Camping Guide* if you are planning a multiple-day trip. Versions with and without maps can be downloaded from www.nps.gov/romo/planyour visit/backcntry_guide.htm. The entire RMNP website is a valuable resource and one of the first things you should consult when planning a trip. Armed with its info, along with the recommended maps and reading on that site, you should be prepared for a trip of a lifetime.

If you camp in the backcountry, you must obtain a permit. The following info is abridged from the Backcountry Camping Guide:

You can pick one up at the Headquarters Backcountry Office (beside the Beaver Meadows Visitor Center on US 36 west of Estes Park, CO) or at the Kawuneeche Visitor Center (US 34, north of Grand Lake).To minimize impact on the park's resources, the number of permits issued is limited. You may obtain day-of-trip permits in person year-round. You may make reservations by mail or in person anytime after March 1 for a permit for that calendar year. You may only make reservations by phone from March 1 to May 15 and anytime after October 1 for a permit for that calendar year. Write: Rocky Mountain National Park, Backcountry Office, 1000 W. Hwy 36, Estes Park, CO 80517. Call: (970) 586-1242. June through September, campers may stay in the backcountry for a maximum of 7 nights. October through May, campers may stay in the backcountry a maximum of 14 nights with no more than a total of 21 nights per year. In the backcountry, you must camp at a designated site.

The hike amplifies the fishing experience in the RMNP backcountry. As Todd Hosman says: "The park creates an amazing habitat for trout, and all the more so when you consider that most park waters lie at elevations between 7,500 to 11,000 feet above sea level, typically in rugged terrain. Further, the trout are wild and self-sustaining, not stocked."
ROSS PURNELL

While there are too many mountain lakes to describe all in detail, here are a few that you might want to check out the next time you are in the park. I encourage you to explore on your own.

Waterproof maps are available at park offices and visitor centers. You can also purchase a great waterproof *Trails Illustrated* map published by *National Geographic* online for $10 at maps.nationalgeographic.com. This detailed map shows major hiking trails and backcountry camping sites.

Certain waters in the park that have restored native fish populations are open year-round during daylight hours, except as indicated. Use barbless hooks only on these waters. Any and all fish species taken must be immediately returned to the water unharmed. No bait is permitted for anglers of any age in catch-and-release areas.

According to the NPS website (January 2011), the greenback cutthroat waters open for catch-and-release fishing are Arrowhead Lake, Big Crystal Lake, Caddis Lake (Lower Fay Lake), Cony Creek, Dream Lake, Fern Lake and Creek, Forest Canyon (above the Pool), Hidden Valley Beaver Ponds and Hidden Valley Creek, Hutcheson Lakes, Lake Husted, Lake Louise, Lawn Lake, Lily Lake, Loomis Lake, Lost Lake, North Fork of the Big Thompson above Lost Falls, Odessa Lake, Ouzel Creek and Ouzel Lake, Pear Lake and Creek, Roaring River, Sandbeach Lake and Creek, Spruce Lake, and West Creek.

High Country Lakes

The work it takes to get to the high country is well worth the effort. Sight fishing to shoreline-cruising trout is one of the main attractions of the park, and unlike many trout in lower-elevation lakes, high-country stillwater trout are often eager to take flies on the surface because of the scarcity of food. But you have to keep a few tactics in mind to be successful.

To start, go to a high vantage point and watch. Look for feeding trout, watch their patterns, and then proceed with caution because the water is crystal clear and trout can see your every move. Limit your casts, stay on the edge without wading if you can, and keep low. Finally, place the fly in the lane the trout is feeding in, but not too close. Even if you cast short or too far, you can correct if the trout is not close to the imitation. Never beat the water directly in front of the trout with the flies. Leading the fish allows your fly to settle without disturbing the trout.

If you are having trouble hooking up, try this: As soon as the trout sees your fly, encourage its interest by twitching it with a 2- to 4-inch strip of fly line. A simple lift and drop of a dropper fly, or skating the dry fly a bit, will often trigger an attack. These trout, which mostly range from 8 to 14 inches, are lightning-fast on the take, and your nerves can often get the best of you.

Attractor patterns work well for a lot of the trout in Rocky Mountain National Park, but lakes often demand patterns that are a little more imitative. "The flat, glassy lakes demand flush-floating patterns such as #12-18 Parachute Adams, #14-18 CDC and Elk, and #14-18 thorax-style mayfly imitations with the hackle trimmed flat on the bottom," Ross Purnell explains. "I've never seen a full-blown mayfly hatch on a lake above 9,000 feet, but mayflies are always around, and the trout recognize them."

Purnell continues, "Midges are the most important aquatic insects, and sometimes actually produce a real hatch with selective feeding. I bring my San Juan River fly box to RMNP, as the flies are often similar. Midge pupae are sizes 14-18 early in the season, and by August and September become nearly microscopic. Adult midges are correspondingly small and are usually black, cream, or tan. A simple thread body with a single turn of hackle is as good as anything else I've tried."

Timber Lake

For a real Colorado high-mountain backpacking adventure to fish for native greenbacks, try Timber Lake via the Timber Lake Trailhead, located on the west side of the park off US 34 just before the Colorado River Trailhead. Tim-

In calm water on lakes and ponds, low-riding terrestrials such as #14-18 beetles, small #10-12 grasshoppers, and #16-18 Baby Boy Crickets work well. Size 14-18 red, tan, and black flying ant patterns are also very effective. Kirk Bien, co-owner of Kirk's Fly Shop and Mountain Adventures, explains, "Ants are constantly getting blown off trees, rocks, and cliffs and landing on the water." ROSS PURNELL

ber Lake sits at over 11,000 feet in a protected basin below Mt. Ida and the Continental Divide. This less-traveled trail offers a small measure of solitude and several pleasant backcountry campsites near the lake. The trail is 9.6 miles round-trip, and these trout do not see a lot of pressure.

Sprague Lake

Farther down Bear Lake Road past Glacier Basin sits Sprague Lake. It is worth a visit before heading to Glacier Gorge, as it is easy to access. It contains brookies, browns, and rainbows with virtually no approach time, and it has handicap access. The backdrop is stunning, and clear spots on the bank make casting easy. While there is a pristine backdrop, trout here see more pressure.

A slight breeze creates enough disturbance on the water to prevent the trout from seeing you. Remember, the higher in elevation you go, the fewer mayflies, hoppers, and caddis you will see. This is when midges, attractors, and streamers work best. In lower elevations there is a healthy supply of caddis, mayflies, stones, and hoppers. ROSS PURNELL

Fern Lake and Fern Creek

From the trailhead in Moraine Park, Fern Lake is a rugged 4-mile hike. To get to the trailhead take US 36 into the park via the Beaver Meadows Entrance. Just past the entrance, take a left onto Bear Lake Road. The trailhead is at the end of the first road on your right. Less than 3 miles up the creek, you will come to Fern Falls, which adds to the scenery of this adventure. Fern Creek is lined with vegetation, making it challenging to cast in these tight quarters. Fern Lake is crystal clear, with cruising native greenback cutthroats willing to take a well-presented fly.

Glacier Creek/Glass Lake

This diverse, beautiful creek has brookies, browns, and rainbows, and there are cutthroats and greenbacks in the lake. An approximate 5-mile day hike will bring you to the lake at 10,827 feet. Access is from Glacier Gorge Trail located off Bear Road on the east side of the park near Bear Lake.

Rivers and Streams

Leave the waders at home, grab your lightweight wading boots, neoprene or wool socks, a lanyard for your neck, and a small box full of your favorite attractor dry flies and you are ready for the many rivers and streams in the park. And after you have had your fill of catching fish—all on dry flies, if that is your preference—you can really take the time to enjoy the breathtaking surroundings and give your arm a rest.

Todd Hosman, author of *Fly Fishing Rocky Mountain National Park*, says: "Three of Colorado's major rivers—Big Thompson, Cache la Poudre, and North Fork of the Colorado—originate in the high country of the park, where each measures only about as broad as a Catskill trout stream. Compared to grand rivers like the Yellowstone and Missouri, every moving water in the park is small. Not that there's any shortage of fishing destinations; in fact, my guidebook details more than a hundred. Regardless, fly anglers should realize that, with the exception of a handful of high mountain lakes, they must contend with small streams and short-line presentations."

While these trout are, on average, a lot smaller than those in other waters in the state (averaging 8 to 12 inches), it is a dry-fly paradise with some very aggressive trout. The fish closer to the main roads and trails are more wary than others, making a hike to untouched water a must. If you do have to fish pressured water, concentrate on the stream on the opposite side from the trail and pockets that are large enough to hold trout but small enough to be overlooked for bigger pools (even if the space is only 15 inches wide). Any high floating attractors such as a #16-18 Royal Wulff, GTH Variant, yellow Humpy, #16-20 Elk-Hair Caddis, #16-18 Limeade, #16-18 Crystal Stimulator, #14-16

It is not always the size of a fish that makes it a trophy. This Fall River brown was holding in slow water and required a long cast and long leader. LANDON MAYER

Baby Boy Hopper, or #16-18 Parachute Adams work well. Remember to keep the flies on the small side so the fish can fit them in their mouths. Even with smaller attractors on the menu, a 10-inch trout will literally have to pounce on the fly to fit it in its mouth. It is vital that you count to two or three and wait for the fish to descend before setting the hook. If you practice this, I promise that your hook-up ratio will double.

Not having to match the hatch can be a pleasant change of pace, and instead of laying out lots of line, you will often be reaching out and dapping flies in likely-looking pockets. To accomplish this presentation, simply lift your rod to lift the flies above the water's surface and then drop or flip your leader to place the imitation into the prime run the fish is feeding in. This will get your rig into tight spots that may only have an open window of a few feet. Generally, if it looks fishy, it will hold a trout.

Kirk and Laurie Bien, owners of Kirk's Fly Shop and Mountain Adventures, like to fish the spots that other anglers avoid in order to catch trout in some of the pressured streams: "We are constantly fishing downed logs in many streams. Most fishermen stay away from these spots because of snags, but wherever there are logs there is more bug life—hence more fish. We also just like to move a lot, since most of the time all you have to do is just find the fish and you will catch them."

Colorado River

Flowing through the Kawuneeche Valley with the Never Summer Mountains rising to the west, the headwaters of the Colorado are accessible from US 34 on the west side of the park at pull-offs like Never Summer Ranch and Timber Creek Campground (see the Colorado River chapter for more detail on access). In the park, the narrow river has classic riffles with deep undercut banks and a healthy population of brown and brook trout. It is a great place to introduce someone to fly fishing.

From November through March, the main food supply (like on most rivers) is midges (#20-24 red, black, or olive Rojo Midges or adult imitations like #20-26 Griffith's Gnats) and Blue-Winged Olives. Once the promise of spring rolls around and the snow begins to melt, scuds also become important trout food. Supplied by high alpine lakes that have been rumored to host gulping 5-pound brookies, these crustaceans are washed into the Colorado and create a nutritious diet for the trout. The key to remember with imitation scuds

When you are targeting deep plunge pools, always cover the water at the tail end of the run first. Trout will often move a good distance to take a fly. ROSS PURNELL

is that when they are orange, they are dead. When they are a transparent olive, tan, or gray, they are alive. Orange #16-20 scuds work well when the rise of water begins washing all the dried-up scuds onto the banks or nestling them in the rocks downstream. As the water levels increase and stay steady, living scuds begin to wash downstream from the supplying lakes or reservoirs. In late June this river comes alive, with virtually every food supply becoming available for the trout, from caddis to stones and Pale Morning Duns to Red Quills. Cover your bases with a hopper/dropper rig and switch to single dry flies if the fish are really feeding on top.

Fall River

In 1982, Lawn Lake Dam gave way and a wall of water raced down the Roaring River and crashed through the Fall River in the Horseshoe Park wetlands, packing enough power to wipe out lodges along Fall River Road and

Dapping dry flies in pocketwater lets you fish for trout holding in pockets that are only a foot long. For example, the Roaring River, off of Lawn Lake Trail, is littered with giant rocks and boulders, creating deep coolwater pockets and runs where native cutthroat thrive. LANDON MAYER

flood downtown Estes Park. By all accounts, Fall River died in 1982 and studies predicted that the river would take generations to return to its productive state.

Well, the good news is that Mother Nature can also be kind, and the river is now thriving again like it did before the flood. This is a classic mountain river, with narrow boulder-filled pools on the upper stretch on Old Fall River Road giving way to beautiful riffled runs in a stunning meadow as you descend toward the valley past Chasm Falls. It supports good numbers of browns, brookies, greenbacks, and rainbows.

To access this river, use the Fall River entrance on US 34 to enter the park and drive along Trail Ridge Road to Old Fall River Road. Old Fall River Road follows the river to its headwaters; however, this is summer access only. Access on this stretch of Old Fall River Road is marked by pullouts until you hit Endovalley, which marks the beginning of year-round access. There is a huge fence around this area with gates well marked on the south side of the road. Park in either Endovalley or Alluvial Fan.

Farther downstream you can cross Trail Ridge Road and park across the road at a small paved area that has one trail to the river or continue down to the last right after the entrance and enter Aspenglen Campground. For the campground, use the pullout just off the bridge or set up camp and walk back up.

Fall River trout are often wary, so try to remain out of view. Look for impressions in the soft silt bottom made by the fish holding in feeding lanes that wash out the river bottom. Once you have located the fish, use long leaders and cast far enough above the target so the ring left after the fly lands in the water (the disturbance) is not felt or seen by the trout.

Roaring River

The flood of '82 that ripped into the park also devastated this river, and it seemed doomed until greenback cutthroat were planted in it. With no threat of a stray rainbow messing with the gene pool, it is now thriving with naturally-reproducing native cutthroat.

To access this river—a small mountain stream, really—take Fall River Road to Lawn Lake Trailhead, which is the first trail on the right after the turn onto Fall River Road. Parking is well marked, and regulations are in the lot. From the Lawn Lake Trailhead, around 8,500 feet, the path to the river climbs about 800 feet in 1 1/2 miles. With loose terrain at your feet and numerous switchbacks, this and other trails in the park can make you feel like you have walked over a mile to move 200 feet. This is why many do not often get off the beaten path.

After a quarter mile of switchbacks you reach the Roaring River, which is narrow enough in some spots that you can jump across it. While most of the trail runs along the river, some spots require you to descend. In the fast water,

Michelle Mayer

There is nothing better than backpacking into an area that has high mountain lakes, spring creeks, and most importantly, no footprints. Unfortunately, this means that everything I need to survive not only the trip, but any potential emergency, needs to fit on my back.

The general rule in backpacking is to never carry more than 25 percent of your body weight. This means food, clothing, shelter, and of course, fishing gear. While it may sound easy, you would be surprised at how heavy substandard gear is, and most importantly, you will definitely feel it about 2 miles down the trail. Many a trip has been cut short because someone did not bring the proper equipment—even worse, it sometimes ends up costing someone their lives. You have to decide what is important versus how much it weighs and how much it costs. The lighter and higher-quality a piece of gear is, the more expensive it becomes. That being said, you can pay now or pay later. My suggestion is to find good pieces on sale rather than skimp on something that may potentially be the difference between bailing during bad mountain weather or staying to catch that native cutthroat sitting in the next creek.

Packs

The bottom line: Find the lightest waterproof internal frame pack with a capacity between 3,000 and 3,500 cubic inches. Waterproof material is superior in strength, making it more durable. This level of pack is also lighter (under 4 pounds), as it is usually designed for four-season mountaineering. I don't personally believe in a lot of bells and whistles, as these tend to make the pack weigh more.

Fit is extremely important and varies by manufacturer. Pay attention to torso length and how many points of adjustment the pack has. Ideally, a pack distributes weight square onto your hips and balances the load perfectly parallel to your body. This requires a minimum of 8 points of adjustment. When you have decided on a pack, take it home, load it with everything you will require for your trip (equally distributed inside the pack), and stand next to a mirror. Make adjustments to the torso first, waist second, and then each adjustment that pivots the load, to the point where you achieve no stress in your lower back or between your shoulder blades. When you take your first trip, you may have to adjust after a couple of miles, but after that you should be good to go.

Boots

I am a big fan of Gore-Tex and Vibram. All good boots also contain a metal shank in the heel to absorb the shock that hiking with a heavy load on your back produces. High-quality boots are worth every penny, as inferior boots will degrade much more quickly. These boots need to be broken in, which can

(continued from page 53)

cons to each fabric. Merino wool is warmer in the winter, cooler in the summer, and will not retain odor. It does, however, cost more and takes longer to dry. Synthetics, on the other hand, cost less and are more durable. Unfortunately, any odor they pick up usually stays on them forever, and I find they feel clammy in cold wet weather.

Layers consist of base, mid, and outer layers, plus a waterproof shell. This system is designed for outdoor activity by allowing your body heat to pass to your outer layer and return back to you while wicking moisture. The human body generates an incredible amount of heat; using this heat efficiently is the key. Too many layers make you less efficient, as does an inferior fabric like cotton, which disperses the heat.

I wear a merino wool base layer (top and bottom), fleece or quick-dry pants, Windstopper fleece zip tee, merino/poly-blend socks, Schoeller fabric jacket, and Gore-Tex hard shell. This way I can sweat into the base layer without permanently stinking it up, but as wool is not windproof, I have the rest in synthetic and can pull clothing off as conditions warrant.

Sleeping Bag/Pad

Sleeping bags can seem like extremely complicated purchases. I have two, a down one strictly for backpacking, and a synthetic for sleeping in the back of my truck on the river. My backpacking bag is down for a very simple reason: Down has a lower temperature rating per pound than synthetic. As weight is extremely important, I can get a 15-degree 800-fill mummy bag to come in at around $2^1/2$ pounds, which is a hard feat for a synthetic. Synthetic dries more quickly, though, and down bags are more expensive, but I think they are worth every penny. I also have a high-end sleeping pad that keeps me warm on the cold ground; it weighs $1^1/2$ pounds. The sleeping pad is a must even if you purchase a cheap foam one to keep you warm.

Tent

Many companies make two-person, three-season backpacking tents that have a trail weight of $3^1/2$ pounds. If you want to go really high-end, you can choose a single wall that will hold up in four seasons, but the price doubles. Splitting the tent and poles between backpackers can help distribute the weight, but for most, the tent is not a problem. Pay attention to how much wind a tent can withstand—high mountain adventures can put you in some pretty hardcore thunderstorms where wind gusts can exceed 70 mph. Additionally, make sure that your tent is always anchored properly, and during adverse conditions, internally guy it to add to its stability.

In the fall, elk bugles echo through the park. While you always have the opportunity to see wildlife on any river in the state, this protected land is a healthy reminder that it is not a crime to stop fishing and just simply enjoy where you are. SCOTTIE MILLER

take a little time, so carrying moleskin in your pack is a must. I recommend stiff boots with a lot of arch and ankle support. Rough terrain can wreak havoc on your feet and twist your ankles into some unnatural positions. Good support minimizes this. Yes, they take longer to break in, but once they do, they are your friends for a very long time.

Clothing

From your toes to your head, there are two rules in high country backpacking—layer, layer, layer, and never, ever wear cotton. There are only two fabrics suitable for the outdoors: merino wool and synthetics. There are pros and

(continued on page 54)

Food, Water, and Cookware

Food can take up an awful lot of space, but freeze-dried food is by far the lightest to pack and takes the least number of cubic inches. I choose the highest-calorie freeze-dried meals and eat flour tortillas with everything. Powerbars and the tuna fish (or chicken) that manufacturers now package in foil pouches instead of cans are great during the day after a packet of oatmeal and powdered coffee for breakfast. My cookware consists of one pan for boiling, one tin cup, a micro-stove with a four-season cartridge, and a spork. I filter water from the creek and keep it in a bladder in the hydration pocket of my pack. Some people leave out the filter to cut weight and use purifying tablets instead, but keep in mind that if you do this you must find water that contains very little debris. Ideally, you pump out of a spring source or clear, fast-running creek on the trail, not a lake or pool in a creek. While there are some bottles with the filter built in, I find that the capacity is too small (my bladder holds three liters) and they don't filter out debris very well. Remember, never drink water without treating it in some fashion—even in an emergency, you need to at least boil the water.

Fishing Gear

I seldom bring waders on a trip. Typically on summer backpacking trips wet wading is not a problem, and most fish can be brought in without a net. I always bring wading sandals so I can keep my boots dry. Additionally, the sandals typically have felt on the soles to keep me from slipping around in the high mountain creeks/lakes. My rod breaks down into four pieces, is placed in its sock, and strapped to the side of my pack. I also carry my reel, two fly boxes (one with dry flies, one with nymphs/streamers), extra leaders, and my lanyard (for attaching items like my tippet, clippers, hemostats, weight, or indicators).

In addition to the basic gear listed above, I always carry a standard first-aid kit, a good multitool, stadium binoculars, an emergency bag (very important!), some climbing tape, and a headlamp that has the ability to flash. You never know what may happen, so being well-versed in wilderness survival and having a CPR course under your belt can be invaluable.

If this seems like an awful lot to consider, don't worry—the rewards are immense. Imagine being able to hike to the most remote section of any wilderness with everything you need on your back. There is no schedule, no traffic, and no demands. Just that pristine high mountain lake surrounded by snow-capped 14,000-foot peaks. The sky is the deepest blue you have ever seen, and the sun is intensely beating down on your face. As you take in all of this grandeur, something catches your attention out of the corner of your eye and you realize that native cutthroat you came all the way up here to hunt . . . just rose. ■

your drifts should be short and strategic—you will often have to use a bow-and-arrow cast or just fish the leader while constantly rock-hopping to get a good presentation. This technique is effective all the way to Lawn Lake, but unstable ground makes careful steps necessary. Some of the larger fish are higher up near Lawn Lake, where the trout see less traffic.

Mill Creek

Also off Bear Lake Road, this creek can be accessed from a picnic pullout past Moraine Park Visitor Center or by parking at Hollowell Park Trailhead and hiking upstream. This popular creek has less of a gradient than other creeks, and the wood debris creates great cover for the brookies, browns, and rainbows that call it home.

East Inlet Creek

Located on the west side of the park, this creek is on the West Portal of Grand Lake. The access is from the lake before the Grand Lake Entrance Sta-

"Though only 8 or 9 inches long, greenbacks are extraordinarily beautiful—especially to anglers who cherish wilderness," says author Todd Hosman. Remember to use barbless hooks and return these fish to the water as quickly as possible. This Roaring River fish ate a Crystal Stimulator. LANDON MAYER

ROCKY MOUNTAIN NATIONAL PARK

	JAN	FEB	MAR	APR	MAY	JUN	JUL	AUG	SEP	OCT	NOV	DEC

Midge (*Chironomidae*)

#18-24 Tyler's Holiday Midge, Yamauchi's Blackfly Larva, Rojo Midge, Tak's Mini Bow-Tie Buzzer, Zebra Midge, Jujubee Midge, Griffith's Gnat

Blue-Winged Olive (*Baetis* spp.)

#18-22 Mercer's Micro May, Flashback Pheasant Tail, Jujubaetis, Flashback Barr Emerger, Cannon's Snowshoe Dun, Parachute Adams

Caddis
(*Brachycentrus* and *Hydropsyche*)

#16-20 Lawson's Electric Caddis, Deep Sparkle Pupa, Graphic Caddis, Garcia's Mother's Day Caddis, Tak's Splitwing Caddis, Go2 Caddis Nymph, black Puterbaugh's Foam Caddis, Breadcrust

Stonefly (*Perlidae*)

#8-14 Barr's Tungstone, Pat's Rubber Legs, 20 Incher, Rubber Leg Copper John, Poxyback Stonefly, Madam X, Crystal Stimulator

Pale Morning Dun
(*Ephemerella* spp.)

#16-20 yellow Copper John, BTS PMD, Burk's Crystal Hunchback, Mercury PMD, Beadhead Barr Emerger, Pheasant Tail, Sparkle Dun

Green Drake (*Drunella grandis*)

#12-16 Lawson's Green Drake Nymph, Barr's Tung Teaser, Furimsky's Foam Drake, Lawson's Cripple, olive Parachute Adams

Red Quill (*Rhithrogena* sp.)

#14-18 red Copper John, Pheasant Tail, A. K.'s Red Quill, Parachute Adams

Terrestrials and Attractors

#12-16 Charlie Boy Hopper, Stimulator, Kingfisher's Red Legged Hopper, tan Chernobyl Ant, Takahopper, Fat Albert, black/red Foam Ant, black Foam Beetle, Stout's Para Cricket, Schlotter's Foam Flying Ant, Royal Wulff, GTH Variant, Limeade, red Micro Worm, San Juan Worm, Nuke Egg

tion and can be reached on the East Inlet Trailhead, where the pressure is not as great as it is on the east side of the park. The creek sits in a meadow where you can follow it off-trail, and contains brookies, browns, and cutthroat trout. For 7.8 miles, the trail follows a fast-flowing creek through a pristine U-shaped valley. If you want to get an overnight backcountry permit, you can travel almost 10 miles upstream and hit Spirit Lake. The lake is in a meadow-like setting, with the rugged profile of the Continental Divide directly behind it. Few hikers get as far as Spirit Lake, so you will probably have it all to yourself.

Onahu Creek

Also on the west side, this tributary of the Colorado has some of the easiest access in the park for brookies, browns, and cutts. Onahu Trailhead is well marked from US 34 and sits in a beautiful meadow on the east side of the road. Try this one the next time you are on your way to fish the Colorado headwaters.

Craven's Baby Boy Hopper (Cricket)

Hook:	#12-16 Tiemco 2499 SP-BL
Thread:	Black 14/0 Gordon Griffith's
Body:	Black Fly Foam (2 mm) over binder strip
Legs:	Black round rubber (medium)
Wing:	Fine natural deer hock hair

Foam Beetle (Black)

Hook:	#8-20 Tiemco 100 SP-BL
Thread:	Black
Shell:	Black foam (2 mm or 3 mm)
Body:	Peacock herl
Legs:	Black Krystal Flash
Hot Spot:	Orange 2 mm foam

Trigger Nymph (BWO)

Hook:	#18-22 Tiemco 3761
Bead:	Gold or copper
Thread:	Olive dun 8/0
Tail:	Lemon wood duck/pheasant tail fibers
Wing:	Olive Ice Dub
Abdomen:	BWO turkey biot
Thorax:	BWO Superfine
Legs:	Mottled brown partridge hackle fibers

Craven's GTH Variant

Hook:	#10-18 Tiemco 100 SP-BL
Thread:	White 74-denier Lagartun
Wing:	White calf body hair
Tag:	Opal Mirage Tinsel (medium)
Tail:	White calf body hair
Abdomen:	Fl. green 70-denier Ultra Thread
Thorax:	Black peacock Ice Dub
Hackle:	Brown and grizzly mixed

COLORADO'S
BEST FLY FISHING
SOUTHEASTERN

Rivers in the southeastern part of the state, such as the Rio Grande and Conejos, offer anglers the chance to hunt for trout that do not get as much fishing pressure as fish in other rivers. ANGUS DRUMMOND

Conejos River

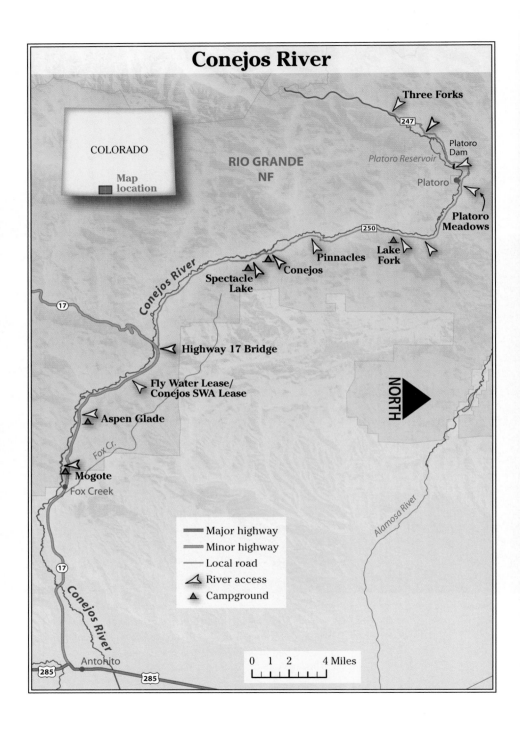

COLORADO

Map location

RIO GRANDE NF

Three Forks

247

Platoro Reservoir

Platoro Dam

Platoro

Platoro Meadows

250

Conejos River

Pinnacles

Lake Fork

Conejos

Spectacle Lake

17

NORTH

Highway 17 Bridge

Fly Water Lease/
Conejos SWA Lease

Aspen Glade

Fox Cr.

Mogote

Fox Creek

Alamosa River

▬▬▬	Major highway
▬▬▬	Minor highway
▬▬▬	Local road
◁	River access
▲	Campground

17

Conejos River

285   285   Antonito

0 1 2   4 Miles

CHAPTER 5

Conejos River

S tarting from the snowmelt along the Continental Divide, the 60-mile-long Conejos (Spanish for "rabbit") passes through Platoro Reservoir and continues southeast through Rio Grande National Forest before getting to the town of Conejos and eventually flowing into the Rio Grande. Where it drains through the scenic San Juan Mountains west of the San Luis Valley, this river supplies anglers with a wealth of quality public fly-fishing water with some large trout, including Rio Grande cutthroat.

With the largest and most diverse supply of insects out of all the rivers in Colorado, the river offers an abundance of food for hungry trout. The water is full of mayflies—Blue-Winged Olives, Green Drakes, Gray Drakes, Pale Morning Duns, and Mahogany Duns—as well as a mix of stoneflies, caddis, midges, and terrestrials. With such a wide variety of insects, you will often have to adapt to different hatches and conditions. "The river always keeps you guessing," says Devan Ence, co-owner of Potamoi Anglers Fly Shop.

In addition to the challenge of matching the many hatches, the other hard thing about figuring out the Conejos is that water levels can fluctuate drastically throughout the year, making it imperative that you consider flows while planning a trip. To regulate the water supply for the 81,000 acres of land irrigated by the Conejos Water Conservancy District, flows can reach 1,000 cfs and higher according to demand and then drop to a staggering low of 7 cfs in late fall through the winter. Like in my home waters on the South Platte, the fish in the Conejos move for survival. "The trout on the Conejos are similar to other trout that migrate from large bodies of water to survive and spawn," Ence explains. "They move far distances on a yearly schedule to survive. Their journey during the low water will lead them down to the Meadows and the plentiful water of the Rio Grande River. Once spring arrives and the water levels rise, the trout will return to the water they call home for the summer and early fall."

Make sure you check the water flows before a trip to the river. When flows are high, areas such as the Pinnacles below Platoro Reservoir can be

The Pinnacles below Platoro Reservoir is accessed by a steep trail. Trout hold in the heavy currents through this stretch. LANDON MAYER

impossible water to cross and dangerous to wade. Once the flows are stable and begin to drop, you can expect more success because the fish have the ability to stabilize in feeding lanes. During extreme low flows, trout in the river above Platoro Reservoir cannot find refuge. Check with local shops to find out what the water conditions are.

The prime seasons are midsummer through late fall, from June through October. Fall on the Conejos is a magic time, with views of blazing aspens that rival any location in Colorado. Late in October the water levels begin to drop rapidly, making it difficult for the trout to find cover. While summers can be rough with extremely low water, the trade-off is typically unpressured trout that are willing to take the fly.

To reach the Conejos from the Front Range, take I-25 South to Walsenburg. At Walsenburg, take US 160 West to Alamosa and then US 285 South to Antonito. Go through Antonito and take CO 17 West. From the Western Slope, head out on US 50 East to Saguache, continue on US 285 South to Antonito, then take CO 17 West. At this point, CO 17 runs along the river. The Conejos follows CO 17 until FR 250 (Conejos River Road). To continue to the headwaters, turn north onto FR 250 toward Platoro and Platoro Reservoir. This section has many unmarked pullouts as the river and road run alongside one another.

Headwaters

Parking is located where FR 247 dead-ends, marking the trailhead for the Three Forks area. El Rito Azul, the Middle Fork of the Conejos, and the North Fork of the Conejos all come together to create the upper Conejos. All of these tributaries are worth fishing if you have the time.

According to Ence, the main types of water in the Three Forks area are rif-fled runs and pocketwater with browns, rainbows, brookies, and native Rio Grande cutts. Fish sizes range from 8 to 10 inches, with a few larger speci-mens. "In this section you will find most of your success with a dry-and-dropper system. Early in the year smaller #14-16 Para Wulffs and a variety of smaller caddis and mayfly nymphs will bring you the most success. During higher water you will find great success with a big stimulator on top, and a few different types of stonefly nymphs or The Worm will be great options. Later in the year, you find fish willing to take big hopper patterns."

The water changes to deeper water and riffled runs as it flows into Pla-toro Reservoir. "The inlet," Ence says, "always has fish cruising near it that will take suspended nymphs and eat streamers." During most of the year, the main species of fish in this stretch are brown and rainbow trout. The aver-age fish size is 12 to 14 inches, with some fish much larger. According to Ence, the time to target larger fish is during the fall when larger browns

The upper Conejos River above Platoro Reservoir provides good fishing in a meadow setting. Trout will migrate upstream from the reservoir, offering anglers the opportunity to catch some large fish. ANGUS DRUMMOND

migrate out of the reservoir and take streamers. During the spring, the road above Platoro Reservoir (10,000 feet-plus in elevation) is closed to cars due to heavy snowfall.

Elk Creek

A tributary of the Conejos, Elk Creek has large trout in a pristine setting. With browns, rainbows, cuttbows, and cutthroat ranging from 10 to over 20 inches long, the rugged endurance it takes to travel along this 10-mile-long fishery is worth the challenge to reach these fish that are eager to take a fly.

From the trailhead at Elk Creek Campground off FR 250 toward the reservoir, the water flows through the wilderness of the San Luis Valley alongside the steep and sometimes rugged trail. The starting elevation is 7,200 feet and climbs at a steady grade that can lead you to lakes at 10,200 feet. Though there is plenty of pocketwater in the small canyons, the meadow fishing is the main attraction. Camping spots are available in the second meadow; water can be pumped and filtered from spring-fed feeder creeks along the way. The best places to camp are in the second meadow, so it is suggested that you use this meadow as a base camp to access the other meadows.

The parking for the trailhead is by the Elk Creek Campground restrooms. There is a sign-in sheet at the beginning of the trail. It is approximately 3 miles to the first meadow (camping is at the top of the meadow) with good fishing in the canyon along the way. The first meadow is only about half a mile long, and since it is the one closest to the trailhead, it sees more pressure than the other meadows.

From here, the trail becomes steeper as it leads you another 4 miles into the south San Juan Wildlife Area to the second meadow, where approximately 6 river miles of snaking water and the largest size and numbers of trout, compared to other sections of the creek, await you. Here, two granite rock structures descending toward the middle of the vast landscape split the meadow into two sections. The first supplies shallower water with more width and slick surfaces ideal for dry flies, and the second stretch, where the water narrows, has deeper plunge pools and heavy, undercut banks.

After the second meadow, the creek's edge is lined with vegetation and growth, making the approach to these trout more challenging. Thinking about each step before you cast will help you present the fly without spooking the target. While gradually climbing, the creek begins to narrow before reaching the third meadow about a mile up the trail, creating some challenging casting areas. Having a spotter in these situations is helpful to direct you in making the right cast. In addition, presenting the fly from a position downstream of the trout allows you to remain undetected. This narrow water continues as you enter the fourth meadow, another 2 miles up the trail. Even though the stream is small and runs thin in spots, it still provides enough holding water for unusually large trout throughout the creek. Dipping Lakes are at the top and provide great fishing.

The best times to fish Elk Creek are in June, July, August, and September. As the water warms, Elk Creek has great hatches, allowing the trout to reach their potential size every year. Midges hatch in June, followed by dense hatches of caddis and some of the largest Pale Morning Duns I have ever seen from late June through August. Additionally, Blue-Winged Olives hatch primarily in September and on cloud-covered days during the summer. Elk Creek also provides great opportunities for terrestrials such as grasshoppers, ants, and beetles.

Below Platoro Reservoir

Below Platoro, the river looks like a meadow stream, with a healthy supply of riffles, runs, pools, and pocketwater for 8 miles. Directly below the dam the main diet for the trout is midges and *Baetis*, and it is not uncommon for trout to ignore the surface—even in a thick hatch—for food below. According to Ence, you should stick below the surface unless you see steadily feeding trout on the surface, though later in the year "you will find fish willing to eat big hoppers off the surface." From here to the South Fork you must fish with artificial flies and lures only, with a possession and size limit of two fish 16 inches.

As you are heading down from Platoro Reservoir on FR 250, you will see a sign for Conejos Cabins and a road that goes to the right. Follow this road and stay to the right to access the tailwater below the dam. Parking is on the left-hand side of the road before you get to the gate. From here you can walk downstream to the first house on the river (approximately a quarter mile down) and fish all the way to the dam from there.

About 1 1/2 miles down from the dam, the river transforms from a tailwater-type fishery to more of a freestone river with insects that like deep, fast-moving water, such as stoneflies and Green Drakes, in large numbers. "As you leave the willows behind and continue heading downstream, you see Platoro Meadows," Ence says. "There is a variety of water here—long deep pools, riffled runs, and more flatwater sections. The meadows can produce some very large fish, but the fishing tends to be a bit more challenging. A lot more stealth is required here. Fish average around 14 inches, with some much larger. You will find mostly brown trout here with a few rainbows scattered throughout. Nymphing in the meadow will provide the best success for many anglers—have a lot of red in your box in the early season—but when the fish get on top . . . it will blow your mind."

Once you are back on FR 250, you will pass Platoro Lodge where public access begins and the first big pull-off overlooks the water on the right-hand side of the road. Heading farther downstream, multiple pull-offs on the right-hand side of the road provide access to the river. The upper part of the

Devan Ence helps his client (left) land a brown of a lifetime. DEVAN ENCE

meadows has been improved by Trout Unlimited—the bottom of these improvements is marked with a decently-sized sign talking about the project, making another great access point with a pull-off on the right-hand side of the road. About a quarter mile farther downstream, there is another pull-off on the left-hand side of the road and two more pull-offs down from there on the right-hand side, near wooden signs for "artificial flies and lures only."

From here to Lake Fork Campground, there are many pullouts as well as easy public access to the river in the fishermen's parking area within the campground itself. Farther downstream you will see a road going off to the right, with two very large wooden posts that used to have a sign hanging from them that has long since disappeared. If you take that road, it will cross the river and you will see a parking spot on the right after the bridge.

From the bottom of the meadow to the top of the Pinnacles, there is lots of pocketwater full of eager browns (and a few rainbows), averaging in size from 8 to 14 inches, with a few larger.

Pinnacles

The top of the Pinnacles begins at Trail Creek Campground on FR 250, which provides access to the top of the Pinnacles all the way to the Lake Fork access. The next access is the camera overlook. Be sure you use the switchbacks on this steep trail. Other access includes Saddle Creek and South Fork. Downstream from South Fork Trailhead is private property. "Water here is pocketwater, riffled runs, and deep runs with some great seam lines," Ence says. "This section has a lot of brown trout, some rainbow trout, and a few scattered brook trout and cutthroat trout. The average fish size is 12 to 14 inches, with some fish over 20 inches. The best techniques are nymphing and dry-and-dropper fishing, and on nastier days you find fish will take streamers very well. If the flow out of Platoro is over 190 cfs, do not go into the Pinnacles. It is not worth risking your life, since there is plenty of other great water to be had at those flows."

From South Fork Trailhead to CO 17 there is a lot of private water. The next public access is just past the private property on the downstream side of the South Fork Trailhead. It is a pull-off on the right-hand side of the road, near a two-sided cedar post fence, which marks the parking area (the fence is not very big but very visible). You can fish downstream from there up to the fence line that marks the boundary for the bottom of the private property.

Continuing downstream is the Conejos Campground. You can fish upstream and downstream from this access point. Farther down is Spectacle Lake Campground, the third forest service campground you will come to on FR 250, where the access is very easy and the water is public upstream and downstream. After one more pullout, you will hit another fence line and for the most part, it is private property from there all the way down to CO 17.

Lower Stretch

The first public access point on CO 17 is at the highway bridge before Cumbres Pass. You can fish downstream for half a mile or so from the parking spot on the left-hand side of the highway before you hit private property, and fish upstream until the cable that crosses the river marking the property boundary for Rainbow Trout Ranch.

Farther down CO 17, the next public access point that you come to is the fly water, 4 miles of fly-fishing-only water the state has leased from a ranch owner. There are multiple access points for this section of river, all very well marked with stiles (ladders that go over the fence) and signs. After the fly-fishing-only stretch, the next public access point

Skwala stoneflies hatch in good numbers on the Conejos River in mid-March. Imitate them with a #8-10 Beadhead Red Fox Squirrel Nymph and a dark brown #10 Stimulator.
DEVAN ENCE

During high water, this river can feel intimidating at times, especially the sections below Platoro Dam like the Pinnacles. It is fast, often deep, and hard to wade, so use caution. For many, the first approach—unless you see rising trout—will be nymphing with heavy flies such as #14-16 Barr's Tungstones, #12-16 20 Inchers, and #14-18 Hotwire Prince Nymphs.

Ence likes to use a version of the right-angle leader when nymphing, which consists of a 3-foot section of 2X to 3X fluorocarbon attached to a Thingamabobber with a clinch knot. Then he attaches 3 to 5 feet (the distance he wants it to sink) of 4X to 5X tippet material to the Thingamobobber, to which he attaches his flies. The thin-diameter tippet sinks faster than the tapered leader and maintains a 90-degree angle to the flies, allowing the same depth throughout the presentation. "Instead of extending my leader length for depth, I keep the distance from my split shot at 4 feet on average, then add weight to keep my flies drifting below the indicator. The trout on the Conejos are notorious suspended feeders even in the highest flows." This throws many anglers off, because they are thinking heavy and deep in big fast water.

In low water, non-weighted flies or rigs without split shot can be effective. The main goal when flows are low is to achieve a drift without snagging river bottom or cutting the drift in half. A good way to do this is replacing the metal bead with plastic for a slower sink rate. You can also drop a nymph only 1 to 2 feet below a dry to keep it riding shallow through the drift. ■

In addition to numerous fish, the Conejos also has some trophies, such as this rainbow Devan Ence is holding. To be effective on this river, you need the trout to tell you (through trial and error) what they want, especially in the lower flows of summer, when the complex hatches can show an angler five or six insects hatching in the course of one day. DEVAN ENCE

you come to is the fishermen's parking at Aspen Glade Campground. Other access includes the Conejos River SWA (fishing easement) from the Aspen Glade Campground upstream to Menkhaven Ranch (about 4 miles), which has special regulations of fishing with artificial flies and lures only, with a possession and size limit of two fish at least 16 inches long, and some portions from South Fork to Menkhaven Ranch.

Before you go up the hill to Conejos Ranch, the river comes back alongside the road right where you can pull off, although there is only half a mile of

CONEJOS RIVER

	JAN	FEB	MAR	APR	MAY	JUN	JUL	AUG	SEP	OCT	NOV	DEC

Midge (*Chironomidae*)
#18-24 claret Shuckin Midge, Griffith's Gnat, Rojo Midge, Barr's Pure Midge Larva, Holiday Midge, Brooks' Sprout Midge

Skwala Stonefly (*Skwala parallela*)
#10-12 Tungsten Rubber Legs Prince Nymph, Tungsten Golden Stone, black Stimulator, Jimmy Legs

Caddis
(*Brachycentrus* and *Hydropsyche* spp.)
#16-20 Net Builder Caddis, Buckskin, Pettis' Pulsating Caddis, Peacock Caddis, black Puterbaugh's Foam Caddis

Salmonfly (*Pteronarcys californica*)
#4-10 Pat's Rubber Legs, 20 Incher, Rogue Foam Stone

Golden Stonefly (*Perlidae*)
#6-12 Pat's Rubber Legs, Rubber Leg Prince, Tungstone, Stimulator

Yellow Sally (*Isoperla* sp.)
#14-16 Tungsten Yellow Sally, Poxyback Hare's Ear, Stimulator

Red Quill (*Rhithrogena* sp.)
#14-18 Copper John, Pheasant Tail, A. K.'s Red Quill, Parachute Adams

Gray Drake (*Siphlonurus occidentalis*)
#10-12 Tungsten Pheasant Tail, Poxyback Hare's Ear, Tungsten Rubber Legs Prince Nymph, Parawulff Adams, Modular Gray Drake

Brown Drake (*Ephemera simulans*)
#12-18 Mercer's Poxyback Emerger, Befus' Wired Stonefly, Lawson's Brown Drake

Callibaetis (*Callibaetis* sp.)
#14-16 Pheasant Tail, Poxyback Hare's Ear, Extended Body Callibaetis

Green Drake (*Drunella grandis*)
#10-12 green Copper John, Tung Teaser, Tungsten Rubber Legs Prince Nymph, Gilled Pheasant Tail, Poxyback Hare's Ear, Brooks' Sprout Flav, Green Drake Emerger, Lawson's Cripple, Modular Green Drake, Meaty Green Drake, Colorado Green Drake, Parawulff Green Drake

Pale Morning Dun
(*Ephemerella* spp.)
#14-18 Juju PMD, red Pheasant Tail, Poxyback Hare's Ear, Gilled Pheasant Tail, Extended Body PMD, #16-18 Barr Emerger, Befus' Para Emerger, Lawson's Halfback Emerger, Lawson's Cripple

Slate Drake (*Isonychia bicolor*)
#10-12 Tungsten Rubber Legs Prince Nymph, Poxyback Hare's Ear, Tungsten Pheasant Tail, Modular Gray Drake, Parawulff Adams

Late Golden Stone (Nocturnal)
(*Perlidae*)
#4-10 Jimmy Legs, Tungsten Golden Stone, golden Jumbo John, golden Tungstone, yellow Gimmie Stimi, golden In the Zone Stone

Blue-Winged Olive (*Baetis* spp.)
#18-22 Barr Emerger, Flashback Pheasant Tail, RS2, Russell's Pablo's Cripple, Lawson's No Hackle, Vis-A-Dun

Terrestrials
#10-18 Disco Beetle, Flying Ant, Boy Baby Cricket, BC Hopper, Fat Albert

Streamers
#6-12 Circus Peanut, Meat Whistle, Lawson's Conehead Sculpin, Egg Sucking Leech

Worms and Eggs
Micro Worm, Flashtail Mini Egg, Nuke Egg, Otter's Egg

An angler high-sticks a good run on the lower section of the Conejos River. LANDON MAYER

public access downstream before Conejos Ranch. The last public access point is Mogote Campground, half a mile downstream from the ranch, which offers over 2 miles of public water (access is in the fishermen's parking in the campground). "This section has mostly brown trout, with some really large rainbow trout and some cutthroat trout mixed in," says Ence. As with most of the river, fishing subsurface with nymphs and streamers is your best bet, though Ence says that "dry-fly fishing can be amazing during some of the major hatches."

BC Hopper

Hook:	#4-10 Tiemco 5262
Thread:	Tan 3/0 monocord
Body:	Tan foam (3 mm) over binder strip
Legs:	Tan round rubber
Underwing:	Mottled tan Web Wing
Flash:	Rootbeer Krystal Flash
Overwing:	Elk hair
Bullet head:	Natural deer hair
Front legs:	Tan round rubber
Indicator:	Pink McFlylon

Griffith's Gnat

Hook: #16-26 Tiemco 101
Thread: Black 8/0 or 10/0
Hackle: Grizzly
Body: Peacock herl

Cripple Green Drake

Hook: #8-12 Tiemco 100
Thread: Olive Uni-Thread
Tail: Olive marabou
Wing: Brown deer hair
Hackle: Grizzly dyed olive
Abdomen: Light olive marabou
Thorax: Olive dubbing

Tungstone (Tan)

Hook: #6-14 Tiemco 5263
Bead: Gold tungsten
Thread: Yellow 6/0 Danville
Weight: Lead wire
Tail: Ginger goose biot
Rib: 3X monofilament
Flash: Pearl Lateral Scale
Shellback: Golden stone mottled oak Thin Skin
Abdomen: Tan Wapsi Sow Scud dubbing
Wing case: Golden stone mottled oak Thin Skin
Thorax: Tan Wapsi Sow Scud dubbing
Legs: Gold-dyed grizzly hen saddle

Benton's Shuckin Midge (Claret)

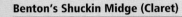

Hook: #20-22 Tiemco 2487
Bead: Black metal
Thread: Claret 8/0 Uni-Thread
Tail: Red Antron
Body: Tying thread
Collar: Claret beaver dubbing

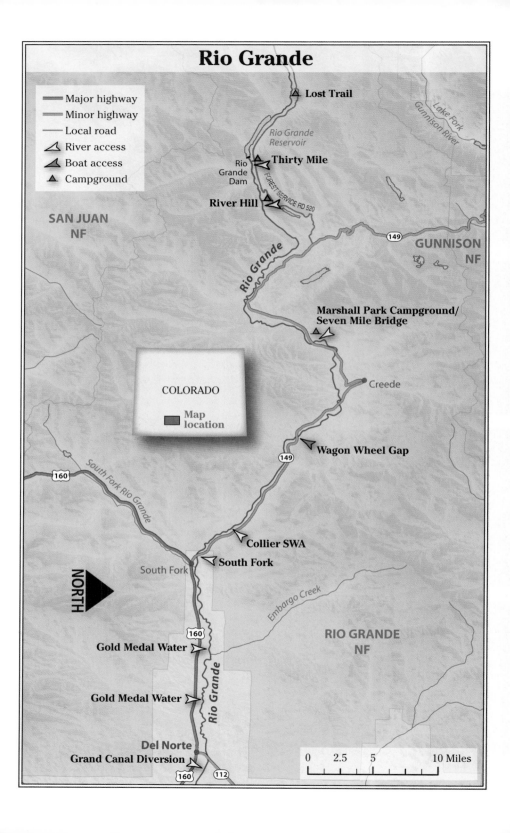

Rio Grande

Legend:
- Major highway
- Minor highway
- Local road
- River access
- Boat access
- Campground

Lost Trail

Rio Grande Reservoir

Thirty Mile

Rio Grande Dam

River Hill

FOREST SERVICE RD 520

SAN JUAN NF

Lake Fork Gunnison River

149

GUNNISON NF

Rio Grande

Marshall Park Campground/
Seven Mile Bridge

COLORADO

Map location

Creede

Wagon Wheel Gap

149

160

South Fork Rio Grande

Collier SWA

South Fork

South Fork

NORTH

Embargo Creek

RIO GRANDE NF

160

Gold Medal Water

Rio Grande

Gold Medal Water

Del Norte

Grand Canal Diversion

160   112

0   2.5   5   10 Miles

CHAPTER 6

Rio Grande

S panish for "Big River," the Rio Grande flows 1,885 miles, making it the fifth-longest river in North America. Flowing through the San Luis Valley in Rio Grande National Forest, this river system has miles of quality fishing in the southwest corner of the state. Best known for its large browns, the Rio has an abundance of rainbows, cutts, and the occasional brook trout near its headwaters that form at the base of Canby Mountain, just east of the Continental Divide.

To see the river at its best, look to the Salmonfly hatch in mid to late summer, as well as a host of terrific hatches for about a four- to five-week window from mid-June to mid-July that provides fairly consistent and predictable fishing, primarily because you can cover lots of water and locate edge-dwelling trout that will feed in high water. Because of the abundance of top-water activity, including great hatches of Pale Morning Duns, BWOs, and caddis, the fish are looking up through the summer and fall, giving rise to a unique method of fishing that I have not seen on any other river in the state: popper fishing for large browns.

From the Front Range, take I-25 South to Walsenburg and US 160 West through Alamosa to South Fork. From South Fork, veer right onto CO 149 and connect to FR 520. From the Western Slope, take US 50 East to Saguache, US 285 South to Del Norte, and then US 160 South to South Fork.

Upper River (Headwaters to Wagon Wheel Gap)

To fish the headwaters, take FR 520 past Lost Trail Campground, above Rio Grande Reservoir. The good fishing starts around 2 miles past the campground, and you need a four-wheel-drive vehicle to get there. Here the river is 8 feet wide or more, with willows lining the edge, supplying good holding water and cover for 12- to 14-inch browns and cutthroats, as well as 10- to 12-inch brook trout.

Public access below the reservoir begins off of FR 520 at Thirty Mile Campground and continues 2 miles to River Hill Campground. Parking is

The Rio Grande is one of the best rivers in the state to hit good fishing during a Salmonfly hatch. These prehistoric-looking bugs cling to the vegetation overhanging the water, drawing trout in close—so close that they hug the river's edge to within inches of the bank, waiting for one to fall. WILL BLANCHARD

located at each campground with pullouts in between. From River Hill Campground, the river cuts through Box Canyon and meanders away from the road. The canyon is made from rough terrain and inaccessible in high water. When water levels drop, it is still difficult to maneuver. While there is a primitive boat launch at River Hill, it's for experienced kayakers only, as the water can frequently run Class VI. Special regulations from the lower boundary of River Hill to the west fence of Masonic Park are with artificial flies and lures only with a possession and size limit of two browns 12 inches with all rainbows being returned to the water immediately.

Five miles after River Hill, turn right on CO 149 to reach public land at Marshall Park Campground 6 miles west of Creede. For a full-day, 15-mile float, you can put in at Seven Mile Bridge, at the Marshall Park Campground, and taking out at Wagon Wheel Gap. The Class I to II rapids and 40-foot-wide river in this section make it an enjoyable float. You can also float an additional 9 miles from South Fork, past Wagon Wheel Gap to the Hannah Lane takeout. Flows average around 1,200 to 1,600 cfs during prime floating time (the river usually clears from runoff around June 15).

John Flick, co-owner of Duranglers Flies and Supplies, tells anglers not to get on the water too early. "It is a cold valley. It takes the sun, even in the summer, to get the water warm enough to get the bugs going. Sleep in and take your time getting to the river. In general, the 'bite' doesn't usually start till 10:30 a.m. or so. Fish skinny water—you'll be amazed at the size of fish holding in literally inches of water."

In addition to floating the river, you can also get to a lot of the best water by foot in low flows. One of my favorite areas to target in low water is Wagon Wheel Gap, between Creede and South Fork. The river here provides identifiable drop-offs and runs that are easy to detect by reading the water up-

Near Creede, towering walls line the river's edge. In addition to holding water behind rocks, hunt for trout along the edges of the river and in areas of color change, such as deep green or blue runs. Vegetation on the bottom of the river can also attract fish, providing both camouflage and a home to trout food. LANDON MAYER

Most anglers think of bass or saltwater when referring to poppers. For those big thrillseekers, you can even cast #6-12 poppers with rubber legs against the bank and chug them back to the boat with long pauses between movements. Seeing it work on the Rio is something you will never forget.

Will Blanchard is a true believer in this out-of-the-box style of topwater action: "If the fish are high in the water column and aggressive, it will only take a few casts into the right water to get the popper destroyed by a Rio Grande brownie. More times than not, the fish will miss the popper. After a little coaching on popper placement, speed of retrieve, and the hook set, the last hour of the day can be a riot. The takes are ferocious. It is dry-fly streamer fishing. Things can go crazy with two, and on occasion three, different fish attacking the popper at the same time. It can be unreal. We have also seen these aggressive browns chase the bug as it gurgles across the surface for over 30 feet before attacking. The faster the popper moves, the faster and more aggressive the fish will get. Sometimes the fish will have started the chase at the bank but take the fly at the boat with half the leader in the rod. Dry-fly fishing is one thing on the Rio, but the popper fishing is something to see." ■

Yes, you can catch trout on the Rio Grande River with surface poppers. This is one of the most exciting topwater takes you can experience on the fly. WILL BLANCHARD

and downstream. Starting in September, you will have the lowest water conditions until December.

One thing to keep in mind when planning a trip is the annual Rio Grande raft races, which have been held between Creede and South Fork along CO 149 on the second weekend of June each year since 1960. When the chaos of the event takes place, the trout will also take a break from all the commotion, making it a mandatory time-out for anglers in this stretch of the river.

Wagon Wheel Gap to Del Norte

The lower stretches of the river have brown and rainbow trout from 14 to 18 inches, but larger beasts always lurk around this large waterway. Additionally, there is a 22$\frac{1}{2}$-mile stretch of Gold Medal water from the CO 149 bridge at South Fork to the Rio Grande Canal diversion structure at Del Norte where special regulations are with artificial flies and lures only with a possession and size limit of two browns 16 inches, with all rainbows being returned to the water immediately.

Heading downstream on CO 149 from Wagon Wheel to South Fork, you can get access at Palisades Campground (approximately 3 miles from Wagon Wheel Gap) or any of the well-marked pullouts. At South Fork, you can continue to follow the river downstream by taking US 160 toward Del Norte. The access past South Fork includes Collier State Wildlife Area and the Gold Medal water between South Fork and Del Norte. Off US 160, you can take both CR 18 at Grainger Road and US 17 heading north at Hannah Lane.

At the Grand Canal diversion, the river looks like a classic freestone with a lot of rocks, long riffles, and many pools. The width of the river can range to 40-plus feet across at some points. Some of the runs are very deep, while the braids and riffles can be extremely shallow. This is great for fishing the river during the off-season, because it gives you the advantage of sight fishing water that is normally high and dirty with few-to-no crowds. On other rivers you typically have riffled runs that gradually descend in depth to a deep pool; however, on this section of the Rio Grande, you can have a riffled run that is 2 feet deep and 30 feet long that flows abruptly into a 15-feet-deep pool. It has a slick surface with aqua-blue water, allowing you see the dark silhouettes of trout feeding below.

Angus Drummond searches the long even water on the Rio Grande near Wagon Wheel Gap access. From Rio Grande Reservoir to the town of Del Norte is Gold Medal water and some of the best fishing in the state. LANDON MAYER

Hatches and Techniques

With a healthy supply of insects during the summer, the river produces some of the most diverse and prolific hatches in the region, John Flick says, and hatches can be amazing for a four- to five-week period. "Although there are some *Baetis* hatching in April, the 'bug cafeteria' doesn't usually open till about the second week in June. However, once it opens, get ready. Beginning with giant Salmonflies, the hatch then goes to Golden Stones, then Green Drakes, then small brown stones, then PMDs. All the while, caddis are thick too! Since the fish have been frozen in time for half the year, they too are ready. They feed hard and heavy on these hatches, and key in on just which bug they have decided to eat for the day."

During high water when the trout hold next to the banks, you can wade-fish from shore with some success, but fishing from a boat is the best way to cover water effectively. Flick explains, "During early summer, floating is still

To see the river at its best, look to the Salmonfly hatch in mid to late summer, as well as a host of terrific hatches for about a four- to five-week window from mid-June to mid-July that provides fairly consistent and predictable fishing. In the summer, fish the shadows, as this angler is doing near Collier SWA. LANDON MAYER

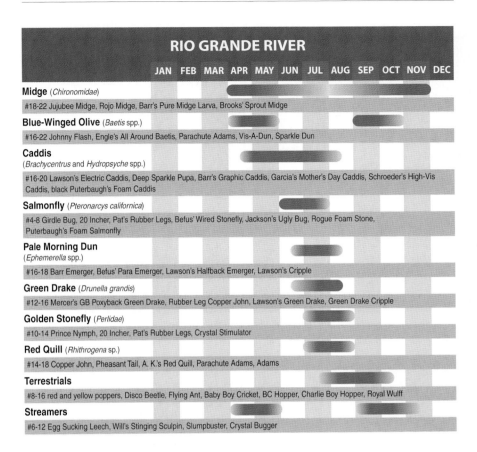

RIO GRANDE RIVER	JAN	FEB	MAR	APR	MAY	JUN	JUL	AUG	SEP	OCT	NOV	DEC

Midge (*Chironomidae*)
#18-22 Jujubee Midge, Rojo Midge, Barr's Pure Midge Larva, Brooks' Sprout Midge

Blue-Winged Olive (*Baetis* spp.)
#16-22 Johnny Flash, Engle's All Around Baetis, Parachute Adams, Vis-A-Dun, Sparkle Dun

Caddis
(*Brachycentrus* and *Hydropsyche* spp.)
#16-20 Lawson's Electric Caddis, Deep Sparkle Pupa, Barr's Graphic Caddis, Garcia's Mother's Day Caddis, Schroeder's High-Vis Caddis, black Puterbaugh's Foam Caddis

Salmonfly (*Pteronarcys californica*)
#4-8 Girdle Bug, 20 Incher, Pat's Rubber Legs, Befus' Wired Stonefly, Jackson's Ugly Bug, Rogue Foam Stone, Puterbaugh's Foam Salmonfly

Pale Morning Dun
(*Ephemerella* spp.)
#16-18 Barr Emerger, Befus' Para Emerger, Lawson's Halfback Emerger, Lawson's Cripple

Green Drake (*Drunella grandis*)
#12-16 Mercer's GB Poyback Green Drake, Rubber Leg Copper John, Lawson's Green Drake, Green Drake Cripple

Golden Stonefly (*Perlidae*)
#10-14 Prince Nymph, 20 Incher, Pat's Rubber Legs, Crystal Stimulator

Red Quill (*Rhithrogena* sp.)
#14-18 Copper John, Pheasant Tail, A. K.'s Red Quill, Parachute Adams, Adams

Terrestrials
#8-16 red and yellow poppers, Disco Beetle, Flying Ant, Baby Boy Cricket, BC Hopper, Charlie Boy Hopper, Royal Wulff

Streamers
#6-12 Egg Sucking Leech, Will's Stinging Sculpin, Slumpbuster, Crystal Bugger

the best way to approach the river since it is usually still high and hard to wade. The fish will stack within a foot of the bank and eat like they have never eaten before, so casting dry flies from the boat to the bank is truly 'money in the bank' during this time." Streamers stripped from the bank are also a great way to target the edge-dwelling trout.

When the fish are close to the bank, Flick says that fishing one dry fly is better than fishing two flies. "I see all these anglers with droppers and nymph rigs during one the most amazing bug spectacles in the state. They are not catching any more fish. In fact, many times, fewer fish. These fish hold within inches of the bank. No angler can put his dry fly close enough to catch these fish if he has on a dropper. Impossible."

As the water levels begin to drop, you can begin to cover the water more effectively on foot through the late summer and fall. "Float fishing the Rio is a fantastic way to see it," Will Blanchard, owner of Animas Valley Anglers, says, "but when flows drop, there are numerous public access points to hit by foot. There is also considerable private water, so make sure you are not

This angler prepares to drift another dry along the edge of a deep seam in water with a heavy current. WILL BLANCHARD

From a boat, you can cover miles and miles of water in one day. If you are fishing this river for the first time, I recommend hiring a guide with a boat to show you the river's potential—and help you land its bruiser fish. WILL BLANCHARD

When you are fishing small pocketwater on tributaries like the South Fork of the Rio Grande, you should keep a low profile and wade carefully. Eliminating strike indicators and split shot will make your presentation appear more natural in winter's clear water.
ANGUS DRUMMOND

trespassing. Same goes for float fishing—landowners are very open to anglers floating through their properties, but respect their property. No anchoring, beaching, or getting out to wade." If you are wading, don't be afraid to get in the car and travel to different access areas to get into the best fishing.

In addition to the Salmonflies during June and July, Golden Stones and Brown Stones are active on the Rio Grande. Accompanying the stoneflies is caddis from June through August, and Green Drakes and Pale Morning Duns become the main diet as the water levels begin to drop in July and August. The trout will never starve on this waterway.

South Fork Rio Grande

For numbers, not size, this main tributary to the Rio Grande is worth the trip after runoff. The topwater action on this tributary can be awesome, with a healthy supply of rainbows, browns, and brookies, especially in the dog days of August when the trout cannot refuse a hopper such as a #12-16 Dave's Hopper, BC Hopper, Red Legged Hopper, or Charlie Boy slamming down on the water's surface. At other times of the year, an abundance of caddis, Green Drakes, PMDs, stones, BWOs, and midges keep trout looking up.

The South Fork is located on US 160 toward Wolf Creek Pass. The water follows US 160 until the intersection of FR 410, which it will follow to Big Meadows Reservoir. It flows toward the town of South Fork where it merges with the main stem. Big Meadows Campground provides access to the water just below the dam, with Columbine and Park Creek Campgrounds providing additional access 3 to 5 miles downstream. There is also access at the Highway Springs campground, but from that point to the town of South Fork the water is private.

Wired Stonefly (Dark)

Hook: #8-#16 Tiemco 200R
Thread: Olive 70-denier Ultra Thread
Tail: Two dyed brown goose biots
Abdomen: Copper and black Ultra Wire
Wing case: Mottled brown Medallion
            Sheeting
Legs: Dyed brown goose biots
Thorax: Peacock herl

Charlie Boy Hopper (Tan)

Hook: #8-10 Tiemco 100 SP-BL
            or #4-8 Tiemco 5262
Thread: Tan 3/0 Danville Monocord
Body: Tan Thin Fly Foam (2 mm) over
            thin piece of foam
Legs: Tan round rubber (medium) with
            brown and red bands
Wing: Natural deer hair

Cripple Dun PMD

Hook: #14-20 Tiemco 100 or 5212
Thread: Pale olive 8/0
Tail: Brown Z-lon and marabou,
            tied sparse
Rib: Fine red/copper wire
Wing: Deer hair
Hackle: Light gray dun
Abdomen: Ring-necked pheasant tail fibers
Thorax: PMD Superfine

Slumpbuster (Natural)

Hook: #6-12 Tiemco 5263
Thread: Tan 70-denier Ultra Thread
Cone: Gold tungsten
Ribbing: Gold Ultra Wire
Body: Gold Mini-Flat Braid
Wing: Natural pine squirrel Zonker Strip
Collar: Natural pine squirrel

COLORADO'S
BEST FLY FISHING
CENTRAL

In low light you can see trout holding in the river with the sun reflecting off their bodies. This is one of the best ways to hunt large trout before dark, when they begin actively feeding. JAY NICHOLS

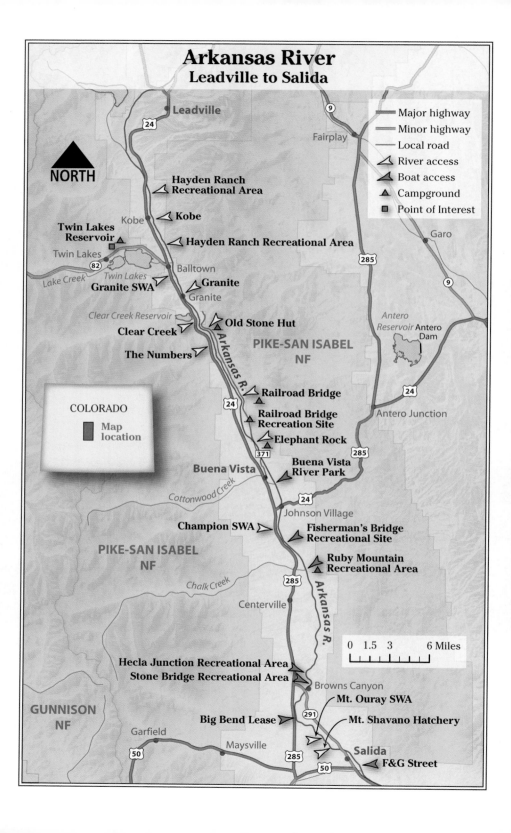

Arkansas River
Leadville to Salida

NORTH

Legend:
- Major highway
- Minor highway
- Local road
- River access
- Boat access
- Campground
- Point of Interest

Leadville

24

9

Fairplay

Hayden Ranch
Recreational Area

Kobe

Kobe

Hayden Ranch Recreational Area

Garo

Twin Lakes
Reservoir

285

Twin Lakes

82

Balltown

Granite SWA

Lake Creek

Twin Lakes

Granite

Granite

Clear Creek Reservoir

Old Stone Hut

PIKE-SAN ISABEL
NF

Antero
Reservoir Antero
Dam

Clear Creek

The Numbers

9

Arkansas R.

24

COLORADO

Map
location

Railroad Bridge

24

Railroad Bridge
Recreation Site

Antero Junction

Elephant Rock

371

285

Buena Vista
River Park

Buena Vista

24

Cottonwood Creek

Johnson Village

Champion SWA

Fisherman's Bridge
Recreational Site

PIKE-SAN ISABEL
NF

Ruby Mountain
Recreational Area

Chalk Creek

285

Centerville

Arkansas R.

0 1.5 3   6 Miles

Hecla Junction Recreational Area

Stone Bridge Recreational Area

Browns Canyon

GUNNISON
NF

Mt. Ouray SWA

Big Bend Lease

291

Mt. Shavano Hatchery

Garfield

Maysville

Salida

50

285

50

F&G Street

CHAPTER 7

Arkansas River

D ropping 4,600 feet in elevation from its headwaters in Leadville (elevation 10,152 feet) to Pueblo (elevation 4,662 feet), the Arkansas River has some of the fastest fly fishing in the West, making this an exciting and challenging river for floating and wading anglers. From small, boulder-filled runs near the town of Leadville to the tailwater below Pueblo Reservoir, the river provides a wide range of fishing situations and settings in which to pursue good numbers of trout, primarily browns, that average 10 to 14 inches.

Without question, the main attraction on this river is the annual blizzard caddis hatch from mid-April through May. Also called the Mother's Day hatch, these caddis really begin hatching around April 15 and should probably be called the Tax Day hatch instead. However, early-season hatches of Blue-Winged Olives in the stretch between Salida and Cañon City can be just as good, if not better, at this time of year—as long as the skies are overcast. And with warm temperatures due to the low elevation, combined with the tailwater below Pueblo, this river is one of few that supplies abundant mayfly and midge activity year-round. In the middle of December or January, it is not uncommon to see huge hatches of Blue-Winged Olives covering the water's surface, creating the perfect break for the cabin fever blues the long winter season can bring.

Bill Edrington, owner of Royal Gorge Anglers and author of *Fly Fishing the Arkansas*, has fished the river for over 50 years and started a fly shop in 1990 on the river. "I thought the Arkansas was one of the best dry-fly rivers I had ever fished and believed it was totally underrated," Edrington states. "Now hundreds of fly fishers agree with me." Despite the fact that the word is out about the river's great fishing—and it sees more pressure than it used to—Edrington belives that the river is resilient: "The good thing about the Arkansas is that no matter how many people fish it in one day, the next day starts over as if nothing had happened. This is the most resilient river, with the strongest gene pool of fish, I have ever strung a rod on. I love it as much now as I did 50 years ago."

Trout Unlimited and local shops like Anglers Addiction and ArkAnglers improved trout habitat from below Pueblo Reservoir through Pueblo, with boulders, weirs, and rock clusters supplying oxygenated water for trout. LANDON MAYER

But like most streams in the state, the Arkansas has had its fair share of knocks. Trout on this river have had to battle the effects of pollution from mining and must constantly fight fierce flows during high water. The end result is some stunted growth that is countered by the numbers of fish eager to take flies.

The Ark's steep grade and fast water will not leave any margin for error, making it a challenge for even the most experienced oarsmen. Anglers float in rafts and hard boats, with rafts being the best option for less experienced rowers or for low water. Less experienced rowers should consider taking a rowing class through one of the local outfitters like ArkAnglers, co-owned by Greg Felt and Rod Patch. When wading the river, fish the edges and be extremely careful. Studded boots and wading staffs will help you stay standing as you traverse the river's slick bottom. Stay away from the deep drop-offs, and only cross in the long riffled runs and shallow tailouts.

In high or off-colored water, concentrate on river edges where larger fish will still feed. Greg Felt, co-owner of ArkAnglers with Rob Patch, says, "At high water, brown trout either park along the bottom of deep, slow pools and eddies or move into edge-water pockets. Focus on the strip of water between the shoreline and the main current seam line. You can work it on foot like a small stream, not getting wet above the knees, or hit it from a boat."

Premier Hatches

The main attraction is the epic *Brachycentrus* caddis hatch. Some of the most productive water for this hatch is from Cañon City to Salida. While the dry-fly fishing can be very good, the most effective way to catch fish is to imitate the emerging, or pupating, caddis. "The greatest overlooked technique on this river," according to Bill Edrington, "is fishing wet flies on the swing. With over 70 species of caddis, caddis pupa, and larva constantly adrift in the current, using soft-hackle wets is an exceptional method of fishing."

Since there are several different sizes and colors of caddis on the river at the same time, try to be aware of what is hatching. Fly designer Larry Kingery explains, "There is a tiny black caddis that comes off at dark in the late summer that are challenging to fish. You can hardly see them, and there is a larger tan caddis coming off earlier in the evening, and the fish seem to switch. My best luck has been trailing a #20 Black Caddis behind a #16 or 18 tan." Effective flies include #14-18 Puterbaugh's Foam Caddis, #16-20 Larry's Caddis,

This beautiful brown could not resist a Kingfisher's Red Legged Hopper. The best patterns for the Ark ride low in the surface film. In the course of its 150 miles, the climates, insects, and flow of the river change quickly. The river passing through Cañon City has stonefly and caddis hatches throughout the summer. Farther downriver, the tailwater below Pueblo Reservoir is cooler with small mayflies and midges hatching in the slower water, providing year-round fishing. LANDON MAYER

#16-20 Lawson's Spent Caddis, #16-18 Larry's Beadhead Pupa, #16-18 tan or green Barr's Graphic Caddis, #14-18 Beadhead Hare's Ear, #16-18 Beadhead Breadcrust, and a #16-18 Swing Caddis.

The famous caddis hatches tend to overshadow some of the other hatches, but the early season *Baetis* (Blue-Winged Olive, or BWO) fishing can be as good if not better. "The *Baetis* hatch in late March and early April precedes the *Brachycentrus* caddis," Edrington says, "so people tend to concentrate their trips around that instead. I have had better days fishing a blanket BWO hatch the first week of April than fishing the caddis hatch two weeks later." Edrington also adds, "Another overlooked hatch is the Red Quill hatch in July and August. Even though it may be spotty, the fish never overlook them for something else." Pat Dorsey, author of *Tying and Fishing Tailwater Flies*, has reported seeing plenty of Red Quills in September as well.

Standard freestone fare, such as stoneflies and PMDs, are also important. From June through mid-July, Golden Stoneflies are abundant under the water—when they grow too large for their exoskeletons, they molt out of them and tumble downstream until they cling to a rock or structure on the river bottom and begin to migrate toward the banks. Yellow Sallies are a more reliable topwater hatch on the Arkansas in high water, and fish will take a #14-18 Striped Ape Stimmy or #14-18 tan Charlie Boy Hopper fished close to the bank.

In addition to hatch-matching patterns, you need the right flies for this swift water. Fly designer extraordinaire Charlie Craven says, "Recently, the Arkansas River in and around Salida has really influenced my fly pattern design. The Ark is a fast moving, pocketwater freestone with piles of eager fish. It's a perfect river to float and ply every seam, edge, and drop-off. This type of target-shooting style of fishing is my favorite, and the endless stream of fish holding areas really keeps my attention. Rivers like the Ark demand dry flies that float well and long and nymphs that sink fast and stay down in the quickly moving water. My Two Bit Hooker was developed as a specific answer to a small thin dropper fly on the Ark and has turned out to be a productive pattern in many other rivers that share the Arkansas' characteristics. My Charlie Boy Hopper is right at home in this same type of water, acting as an indicator for a pair of nymphs dangling below while pulling up fish interested in hoppers as well as Golden Stones. The varied insect life in this river as well as its gradient and broken character require different flies than slower moving waters, and it seems every day I spend on this great river inspires some new idea to bounce around in my brain."

Headwaters

While a boat trip down the headwaters might be exhilarating, I think this smaller water is best suited for wading. To get to the Arkansas headwaters, head south on US 24 East out of Leadville. As the Arkansas is dominated by private land from Turquoise Lake to Crystal Lakes, Hayden Meadows (or Hayden Ranch as it is called locally) provides the first real public access downstream of Leadville. The road is well marked on your left. After the turn

The Ark near Buena Vista rages in higher water, but the rest of the time it is one of my favorite areas to wade-fish. When floating the river, Taylor Edrington, co-owner of SoCo Guide Service, says, "Accuracy is key to present in often small pockets or edges. It is one cast for one drift." ANGUS DRUMMOND

you will cross a bridge, and parking is on the right-hand side of the dirt road (camping is located at Twin Lakes). Special regulations in this section from the US 24 river overpass to the lower boundary of Hayden Ranch are artificial flies and lures only with a possession and size limit of one fish 12 inches.

Approximately 3 miles down US 24, you can gain access directly off the highway at Kobe. This parking lot is also well marked and has a trail down to the river. While it is also technically a launch site, I would not launch here or at Granite but would instead launch farther down, after both Twin Lakes and Clear Creek add volume. From Twin Lakes, railroad tracks run parallel to the river and must be crossed to attain river access. About 1/2 mile above the turnoff to Twin Lakes (CO 82 West) is an unmarked pullout on the right side of the road that allows access and is worth a look as it is also part of the Hayden Ranch Recreational Area.

After Twin Lakes (to access the lakes themselves, head west on CO 82 toward Independence Pass; parking is on the left), the Arkansas gains volume from the creeks below Twin Lakes and Clear Creek Reservoir. There is pullout just north of the Chaffee County line into the Granite SWA, two pullouts before and after town, and then one in Granite that can be reached by turning left onto CR 397 into Granite and crossing the bridge over the Arkansas. A small dirt road on the left (which is also technically CR 397) will double back north on the east side of the river through Granite's residential section. After you clear the private land, you have reentered San Isabel National Forest (signs

The Ark's vibrant rainbows are not as common as the brown trout. Bright colors like this red Flashback Beadhead Pheasant Tail are great imitations. LANDON MAYER

show public land) and will see many dirt pullouts. Chances are good you can find solitude down here.

Continuing on US 24 East, the next access comes at Old Stone Hut, another well-marked pullout with camping. While it might seem tempting to use the pullouts at mile marker 195, it is best to access the river from the pullout near mile marker 198, Tiger Lily Creek, as it provides better trail access. The Numbers launch comes next, before the Arkansas meanders east and away from the highway, leaving San Isabel National Forest.

Near mile marker 201, Railroad Bridge access is reached by heading east on CR 371, and it is a good launching alternative when The Numbers is crowded. Along CR 371, camping is available at Railroad Bridge Campground and Railroad Bridge Recreation Site. This turn is well-marked off of US 24, and the county road hits the Arkansas within a couple of miles, continuing along its east side all the way to Buena Vista. The last pullout on US 2 before Buena Vista is located just north of mile marker 207.

Buena Vista to Salida

While the water here is big during runoff, it is a large creek the rest of the time and is much more wading friendly than the water downstream. It's one of my favorite areas to fish and some of the best dry-dropper fishing in the state can be found on this stretch of the Arkansas. To access the river, look for the two pullouts above Buena Vista and four pullouts below.

One of the most overlooked sections is just north of Buena Vista on the east side of the river. To get there, head east on Main Street in town and take a left onto North Colorado Avenue (Chaffee County Road 371). Double back to head north out of town until you clear the residential neighborhood and the road turns to dirt. Multiple pullouts provide river access over the railroad tracks on the west side. Additionally, BLM primitive camping on the ridge above Elephant Rock offers a view of the Collegiate Peaks just outside your tent.

After Johnson Village, US 24 veers east and you can follow the Ark on US 285 South to Salida for another 24 miles. Champion State Wildlife Area near mile marker 147 on US 285 is the first access after the highway change. The parking lot is well-marked on the east side of the highway. Fisherman's Bridge/Ruby Mountain is next and is also well-marked, followed by Hecla Junction off of CR 194, which winds down to the river after approximately 3 miles. The Browns Canyon launch can be accessed from here, but as this float is for more advanced rafters, a guide trip is strongly recommended (Contact local shops such as Royal Gorge Anglers or ArkAnglers for package deals). For camping, turn east onto CR 194 at Hecla Junction and drive to Browns Canyon. Farther down US 285, you can explore Big Bend Lease, which has a boat launch and over a mile of public access on the launch side, before doubling back and taking CO 291 toward Salida. The river becomes wider as it approaches Salida, and the pine trees and aspens are replaced by large granite walls and juniper bushes.

The first access on CO 291 is Stone Bridge in the Stone Bridge Recreational Area, which also has a boat launch and a well-marked parking lot. Just before CR 195, as the highway goes over the Arkansas, there is a parking lot located on the right. Mt. Ourey State Wildlife Area also provides three-quarters of a mile of access via the CR 166 bridge to the River Run Inn on the west side only. After crossing a green metal gate bridge, you will see Mt. Shavano State Hatchery and Rearing Unit on the right side of US 291. Take the paved road toward the hatchery to gain access to the river through multiple pullouts along the road.

You can fish the river in Salida by taking a left onto F Street and parking at Riverside Park. South of Salida, on CO 291, there is a pullout by a fairly prominent gravel pit that also provides access, as well as a pullout on the north side of the county bridge.

Salida to Cañon City

Though extremely popular, the easy-to-access stretch from Salida to Cañon City along US 50 supplies miles of river to fish. While it has big water during runoff, and is often riddled with rafts during high summer water, flows before May and after August drop to 500 cfs or below, making it prime for fly fishing.

Starting just east of Salida on US 50, the first access is reached by turning left onto CR 102 (artificials only from CR 102 to Badger Creek; rainbows must be returned to the water immediately). Just before the bridge, a parking lot is on the right-hand side. While there are unmarked pullouts located every 100 to 500 feet directly off the highway, you should always have a State Park Pass on your windshield during your trip to this stretch of the river. All major parking areas require the pass, which you can get at any major grocery store.

This section of the river flows through dry desert land with juniper bushes and cactus scattered throughout the terrain, with a mix of islands creating braids, long riffled runs, and numerous tailouts. It is popular with floaters because of the abundant access. If you are floating, you can get out at Vallie Bridge, or if you want to extend the trip, at Texas Creek. Continuing on US 50, access is just before Wellsville, with parking on the left. Just past

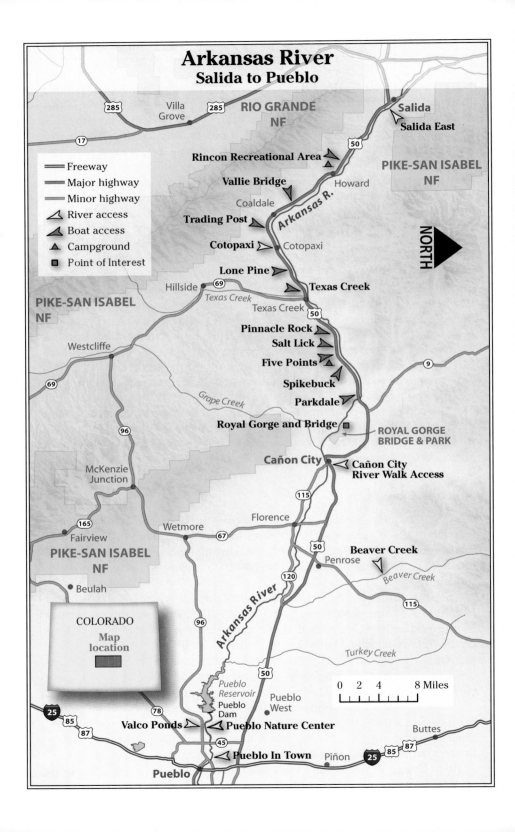

Arkansas River
Salida to Pueblo

285 Villa Grove 285

17

RIO GRANDE NF

Salida
Salida East

50

PIKE-SAN ISABEL NF

Rincon Recreational Area

Vallie Bridge
Howard

Coaldale

Arkansas R.

Trading Post

Cotopaxi Cotopaxi

Lone Pine

Hillside 69

Texas Creek

Texas Creek

Texas Creek 50

PIKE-SAN ISABEL NF

Pinnacle Rock
Salt Lick
Five Points

Westcliffe

9

69

Spikebuck

Grape Creek

Parkdale

Royal Gorge and Bridge

ROYAL GORGE BRIDGE & PARK

96

Cañon City

Cañon City River Walk Access

McKenzie Junction

115

Florence

165

Fairview Wetmore 67

50

PIKE-SAN ISABEL NF

Beaver Creek

Penrose

120

Beaver Creek

115

Beulah

Arkansas River

Turkey Creek

COLORADO
Map location

96

Pueblo Reservoir
Pueblo West

50

Pueblo Dam

0 2 4 8 Miles

25
85
87

78

Valco Ponds Pueblo Nature Center

45

Buttes

Pueblo In Town Piñon 25 85 87

Pueblo

Legend
- Freeway
- Major highway
- Minor highway
- River access
- Boat access
- Campground
- Point of Interest

NORTH

Swissvale is Rincon, which is well-marked. Vallie Bridge, Canyon Trading Post, and Lone Pine are next in order with a patch of access in Cotopaxi from town to the KOA Campground. All lots are well-marked and have restrooms.

Texas Creek, 26 miles west of Cañon City, is perhaps one of the most popular areas—wading is good here, and the creek itself fishes well during runoff. Near the junction of US 50 and CO 69 take a left at the road next to the Texas Creek Café. Cross the bridge—parking is on the right. While you are allowed to fish upstream, do not park on the left side of the road, which is private property. You can also continue down the road past the private property to additional parking and drop down to the river from the north. One of the best float trips on the river is from Texas Creek to Parkdale. If you don't want to float 20 miles, take out at Pinnacle Rock for a 7-mile float.

Maytag is next, with Pinnacle Rock, Salt Lick, Five Points, Spike Buck, and Parkdale to follow. Five Points has camping on the south side of the highway, but space is limited and it is a very popular area during rafting season. After Parkdale, the Arkansas takes a different path from the highway as it dives into the Royal Gorge. As travel along the railroad tracks is prohibited, the best way to fish the gorge is to book a trip with local guides.

Cañon City/River Walk

The Arkansas River Walk in Cañon City holds some of the largest trout in the river. Like many other stretches of water that flow through towns in Colorado, it is overlooked and provides the best opportunities for catching unpressured trout. Here, the grade subsides, making it easier for the trout to feed and grow a little larger than those that have to battle fast water throughout the year. Taylor Edrington likes the river walk for the large, overlooked trout: "Some of the largest trout I have landed have been in town up to 18 inches with no anglers in sight. If you travel to this fast waterway, don't pass up the chance to fish in town before you leave."

To get to the river walk, turn right (south) at Raynolds Avenue on the east side of town. Go through the four-way stop and cross the Arkansas River. Clearly marked parking is located on the left side of the road after you cross the river. While access is short downstream, the entire river walk upstream to 9th Street is fair game and offers approximately 7 miles of good water with lots of stream improvements. There is private property on the north side of the river, but you can access the river from the south side.

Pueblo Reservoir

Completed in 1974, Pueblo Reservoir is 135 feet deep and its surface measures 4,500 acres. Because of its depth and bottom release, water from 42 to 48 degrees provides cold temperatures during the summer and water warm enough to not freeze in the middle of winter. In addition, with an elevation of 4,695 feet, Pueblo is warmer than many other areas of the state (Pueblo, on average, is warmer than its neighboring city of Colorado Springs by 6 degrees or more),

Though often overlooked, the river walk in Cañon City provides great access and great fishing. Michelle Mayer looks for trout in a side channel—always a good bet to find a few willing fish. LANDON MAYER

and BWOs can hatch here in the middle of winter, while other rivers only have midge hatches. The cold water and consistent flows tame the Ark's otherwise temperamental characteristics, and this stretch holds trout over 20 inches.

Trout Unlimited and local shops like Anglers Addiction and ArkAnglers improved trout habitat from below the reservoir through Pueblo by adding boulders, weirs, and rock clusters that supply oxygenated breaks and runs for trout to hold. In my opinion, the only thing left to complete in this fishery section is to introduce catch-and-release regulations. This would add twice the numbers and growth to what is already abundant, but already every year has higher numbers of bigger holdover trout.

Jeremiah Johnson, District Wildlife Manager III in the Pueblo East district, knows firsthand the potential for size and numbers because of the stream improvements. "There are large number of fish in the Arkansas River that range from 6 inches up to and above 22 inches. One of the best stretches of river is from the Pueblo Nature Center upstream to the Valco Ponds. This stretch of river offers numerous runs, riffles, and pools that all hold large numbers of trout. The bigger trout in the river tend to hold in the long, deep runs where it is often difficult to make a good presentation. When we sampled (electro-fished) the river last summer, a large number of the big trout that we rolled were in the deep runs just below the hatchery outlet."

Fishing from the bridge at Valco Ponds downstream to Pueblo Boulevard (except at the Pueblo Nature Center) is with artificials only and all trout meas-

ARKANSAS RIVER

	JAN	FEB	MAR	APR	MAY	JUN	JUL	AUG	SEP	OCT	NOV	DEC

Midge (*Chironomidae*)
#18-24 Purple Thing, Black Beauty, Zebra Midge, Rojo Midge, Mercury Midge

Blue-Winged Olive (*Baetis* spp.)
#16-20 Larry's Black Ice, Beadhead Pheasant Tail, Mighty May, Trigger Nymph, Beadhead Barr Emerger, Parachute Adams, Vis-A-Dun, Sparkle Dun

Caddis
(*Brachycentrus* and *Hydropsyche* spp.)
#16-20 Elk-Hair Caddis, Larry's High-Vis Caddis, black Puterbaugh's Foam Caddis, green Copper John, Larry's Beadhead Pupa, Barr's Graphic Caddis, Devil Bug

Little Black Caddis
(*Amiocentrus aspilus*)
#18-22 Barr's Web Wing Caddis, Horodysky's Rip Cord Caddis, Peacock Caddis, Larry's Black Ice

Golden Stonefly (*Perlidae*)
#8-12 Larry's Arkansas Rubberleg Stone, Barr's Tungstone, Pat's Rubber Legs, Amy's Ant, Kaufmann's Foamulator

Pale Morning Dun
(*Ephemerella* spp.)
#16-18 Peterson's Bat Wing Emerger, Beadhead Barr Emerger, Mercer's Trigger Nymph, Flashback Pheasant Tail, Lawson's Cripple Dun, Two Bit Hooker

Terrestrials
#8-16 Larry's Striped Ape, Lawson's High-Vis Foam Beetle, Kingfisher's Red Legged Hopper, Fat Albert, Charlie Boy Hopper

Streamers
#6-12 Larry's Trick or Treat, Articulated Leech, Slumpbuster, Circus Peanut, Lead-Eyed Gonga

uring 16 inches or longer must be returned to the water immediately. To get to the nature center, turn onto 11th Street from CO 45. Parking is available at the nature center, but a State Parks Pass is required. For a free parking option, you can take the first right on West 8th Street from 11th Street. West 8th Street is a dirt road that accesses a long stretch of river below the Nature Center, and there is no fee for parking anywhere along that section of the river.

Additionally, there is access at Valco Ponds, which you can reach by continuing on CO 45 to Thatcher Avenue. Turn right on Thatcher Avenue and continue about 5 miles. You will see the ponds on your right. The Arkansas River runs right next to the ponds. Parking is available at the ponds and there is a self-service station in the parking lot, as well as restrooms. These three ponds have warmwater species like bass and catfish in them that will take a #6-12 Barr's Meat Whistle or #6-10 black foam popper in the evening. The toilet-flushing rise of a bass on the surface before dark is a true rush.

To get to the Valco Ponds, follow 11th Street until it dead-ends, turn right under the 11th Street Bridge, and pass directly under a "Whitlock Water Treatment Plant" sign. After going under the bridge, stay to the left to access the parking lot and restroom area. Parks passes are not required in this area.

Finally, one of the most overlooked access points is referred to as the City Park Diversion. To get there, take CO 45 south about 5 miles to Goodnight

Avenue. Follow Goodnight Avenue east through Pueblo City Park and around the Pueblo Zoo. Goodnight Avenue is one-way through the park. On the east side of the city park, Goodnight Avenue exits the park on a roundabout. Sometimes a gate is closed that forces you to exit the park—if this is the case, take Goodnight Avenue out of the park, make a U-turn, and come back into the park. Turn north on City Park Avenue and follow the street around past the maintenance facilities and the baseball park to the parking area. There is no parking pass required here, and the river is directly below the parking area. The hill going down to the river is steep, however, and can be difficult to traverse.

Beaver Creek

Many tributaries feed into the Arkansas, including Beaver, Texas, and Grape creeks, which all offer anglers the chance to travel off the beaten path to solitude and willing trout. Small waterways can change every year due to flows and weather conditions. The great thing about Beaver Creek is its consistency year after year. To get to it, head south on CO 115 to Penrose, just after Colorado Springs. From here, get onto US 50 West heading toward Cañon City, but turn right onto Phantom Canyon Road (US 67 North) before town. Take a right onto CO 123 and then a left onto CO 132. From the Western Slope, take US 50 East through Cañon City, go through town and take a left onto Phantom Canyon Road (US 67 North), and follow the same directions as for the Front Range.

Brook, brown, rainbow, and cutthroat trout thrive in the creek's cold waters. With a healthy supply of mayflies, caddis, midges, and terrestrials in the creek, dry-and-dropper rigs work best for the 10- to 15-inch trout. Make sure you check the weather and try to select a time frame when the area has not received any rain that will turn the water off-color. Since air temperatures can break 100 degrees in the summer, fish early and late in the day. I like to start the hike around 6:00 a.m. and then break for lunch, or get off the water by 2:00 p.m. before a storm rolls in.

Puterbaugh's Foam Caddis (Black)

Hook:	#14-18 Tiemco 100
Thread:	Black 8/0
Abdomen:	Black foam strip (2 mm)
Wing:	Natural elk hair (cow or yearling)
Hackle:	Brown rooster

Kingery's Striped Ape Stimmy

Hook:	#12-16 Tiemco 200R
Thread:	Hot orange 6/0
Tail:	Bleached elk
Abdomen:	Orange/yellow foam and brown hackle
Wing:	Bleached elk
Thorax:	Peacock Ice Dub or peacock herl and grizzly hackle

Kingery's Bead Head Pupa

Hook:	2X long nymph
Bead:	Gold
Thread:	Black
Abdomen:	Rabbit, Ice Dub, and Antron blend
Thorax:	Rabbit, Ice Dub, and Antron blend
Hackle:	Dark dun hen
Note:	Abdomen is a blend of 1/3 olive rabbit, 1/3 olive Ice Dub, and 1/3 olive Antron cut 3/8" long; thorax is same as abdomen, except Antron is cut double the length of the hook.

Arkansas Rubber Leg Stone

Hook:	#8-10 Daiichi 1750
Cone:	3/16" gold
Thread:	Tan 6/0
Tail and Legs:	Pumpkin blue/black Spirit River silicone legs
Body:	Variegated chenille, custom blend

Sparkle Dun (Baetis)

Hook:	#18-22 Tiemco 100
Thread:	Olive 6/0 Danville
Tail:	Light olive Z-lon
Abdomen:	BWO Superfine
Wing:	Deer hair
Thorax:	BWO Superfine

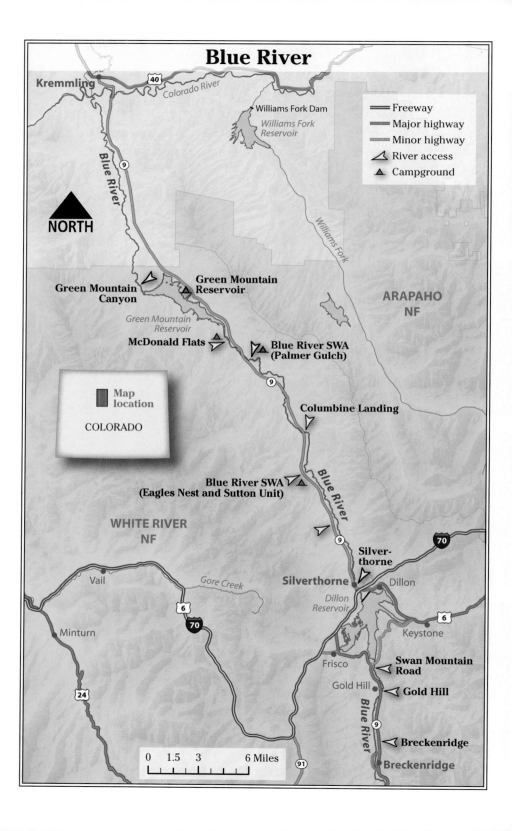

Blue River

Kremmling

40

Colorado River

→ Williams Fork Dam

Williams Fork Reservoir

Blue River

9

NORTH

ARAPAHO NF

Williams Fork

Green Mountain Canyon

Green Mountain Reservoir

Green Mountain Reservoir

McDonald Flats

Blue River SWA (Palmer Gulch)

9

Columbine Landing

Blue River

Blue River SWA (Eagles Nest and Sutton Unit)

WHITE RIVER NF

Vail

Gore Creek

6

70

Minturn

9

Silver-thorne

70

Silverthorne

Dillon

Dillon Reservoir

6

Keystone

24

Frisco

Swan Mountain Road

Gold Hill

Gold Hill

Blue River

9

Breckenridge

91

Breckenridge

══	Freeway
══	Major highway
══	Minor highway
◁	River access
▲	Campground

Map location

COLORADO

0   1.5   3   6 Miles

CHAPTER 8

Blue River

Not only is the Blue below Dillon Reservoir one of three Mysis shrimp fisheries in the state, which grows very large trout (15-plus pounds), its location provides access to skiing at Breckenridge, Keystone, and Arapahoe Basin, as well as shopping at the outlet malls in Silverthorne. On this four-season fishery, you can literally fish in the morning and be on the slopes in the afternoon. An angler can bring the entire family to this area and ensure that everyone has something to do while he or she sneaks off for some trout fishing. But it is not easy fishing. Though it is the only place that I know of where you can catch extremely large trout with a 7-Eleven in the backdrop, the wading is some of the toughest in the state, with rocks that feel like greased bowling balls, and the trout can be some of the hardest to locate because the river is riddled with red, green, and gray rocks, providing perfect camouflage for the browns, Snake River cutts, and rainbows that call the Blue River home.

Originating in southern Summit County west of the Continental Divide in the Ten Mile Range, the Blue River flows 75 miles through the ski resorts of Breckenridge, into Dillon Lake, and across Colorado's most heavily-traveled mountain thoroughfare (I-70) before feeding the Colorado River at Kremmling. To reach the Blue from either Denver or the Western Slope, take I-70 to CO 9 south at Dillon. Continue around Dillon Reservoir and south to Breckenridge. Colorado Springs residents can access this river by taking US 24 west and then taking CO 9 north, just past Hartsel, through Fairplay to Breckenridge.

Above Dillon Reservoir

The Blue starts small on CO 9 south of Breckenridge and flows for 10 miles before reaching Dillon Reservoir. Stream improvements such as weirs and rocks provide ample pools for wild brown trout and stocked rainbows ranging from 12 to 16 inches, which are often eager and cooperative even for beginner anglers. The river flows and drops into deep pool after deep pool, earning the name "the Steps" from the locals.

Angus Drummond holds a Blue River monster caught in town below Dillon Reservoir on a Mayer's Mysis. With clear water, the Blue River is one of the best tailwaters in the state to sight fish, especially in winter when the river runs around 50 cfs and crowds are slight. However, the trout can disappear in the large pastel red, green, blue, and gray round rocks and boulders along the river bottom. LANDON MAYER

The Blue is easily reached from South Park Avenue to CR 3 as the river runs along a bikeway running parallel to the highway. Parking for the bikeway can be reached from CO 9. There is also a stretch farther downstream, about two miles, at Gold Hill on CO 9, with parking well-marked at the trailhead. In this popular spot, a series of weirs creates nice holding water around the large granite rocks.

Continuing north on CO 9, the point at which the Blue enters Dillon Reservoir can also be very productive. To get there, take a right toward Keystone on CO 1 (Swan Mountain Road) and park at the pullout past the bridge. In-stream rocks and 2 to 3 inches of cobblestone on the river bottom provide refuge for trout when the reservoir's depths do not protect them. It is also prime spawning water; as such, the river is closed from October 1 to February 1. From the north inlet at CR 3 downstream to Dillon Reservoir, fishing is with artificial flies and lures only with a bag-and-possession limit of two fish at least 16 inches long.

On average the rainbows, browns, cuttbows, and cutthroats here range from 10 to 18 inches, though it was reported that a fish nearing the 30-inch mark was landed in this stretch in 2010. Classic freestone imitations—caddis, small stoneflies, BWOs, PMDs, and midges—are good imitations here. See the hatch chart in this chapter for patterns.

Below Dillon Reservoir

Below Dillon Reservoir the river is filled with Mysis shrimp. During runoff or an increase in flow, shrimp are flushed into the outflow, causing a feeding frenzy. Similar to the Fryingpan and Taylor rivers, this section is home to some of the state's largest trout. To get there, continue past Breckenridge on CO 9. After you get around the reservoir, turn right onto Stephens Way and then take another left onto River Road, where parking is clearly marked. You can also find parking by continuing straight on Stephens Way until it ends. From Dillon Dam downstream to the north city limits of Silverthorne, fishing is catch-and-release only. Below Silverthorne (from city limits to the CO 9 bridge), the regulations revert back to a two-fish, 16-inch limit.

This section was once a shallow sight-fishing paradise, but restoration work has dug out long deep runs to provide more holding water for trout and made it more difficult to fish to the giants in high flows. I still target the large Mysis-shrimp eaters in low water (between 100-300 cfs after high flows) or runoff, when the trout are pushed downstream from the unfishable 100-yard stretch below Dillon Dam, where some of the largest trout live and feed heavily on the Mysis shrimp sucked out of the bottom-release dam.

Against the red, green, and blue rocks, the red sides of rainbows or green backs of browns can melt away, making them seem impossible to locate at times. If you are not taking time to scan the bottom for silhouettes, fins, and movement, you could find yourself casting to rocks for half an hour. The trick to seeing fish on the Blue River is looking beyond the water's surface and

The Blue downstream of Silverthorne in morning light. Midges, BWOs, PMDs, Green Drakes, and Red Quills hatch throughout the season, providing topwater action; however, your best bet is to present flies subsurface with dry-and-dropper rigs or deep drifts along the river bottom. JAY NICHOLS

There can be some excellent midge hatches in the dead of winter below Dillon Reservoir and a red thread midge can be deadly. Because of the clear water most of the year, light tippets and fluorocarbon are essential. LANDON MAYER

scanning the river bottom for movement or the opening of the trout's mouth or other subtle clues. After you locate the trout, drift your flies (I like a Mysis shrimp pattern and a BWO or midge dropper in this stretch) two inches to the near side of the trout's mouth, and if the fish is actively feeding it will strike. This eliminates snagging, rubbing, or spooking the fish.

Urban Angling (Silverthorne)

Some of the largest trout on the Blue, known to exceed 10 pounds, are located upstream from CO 9. This stretch begins near the outlet malls on CO 9—take exit 205 and turn right onto Stephens Way. There is parking at the end of this road or by turning left onto River Road and parking there. This section runs from Iron Bridge all the way down to the forest service building, totalling approximately 2 miles of public water. Additionally, you can find a couple of small access points farther downstream on CO 9 by turning right on Rainbow Drive in Blue River Run and Cottonwood Park.

Running right through the town of Silverthorne, the Blue River can see a lot of pressure during normal business hours. Jay Nichols searches a quality run at dusk when the trout are less pressured and willing to feed heavily. You can gain access to the river below Dillon Reservoir by parking off Stephens Way or River Road. LANDON MAYER

The river below Silverthorne hosts good insect activity throughout the year, and author and guide Pat Dorsey of the Blue Quill Angler sight-fishes the Blue in town year-round with small mayflies, midges, and Mysis. "Make sure you look before every step, since trout can be hiding anywhere. Even in the dead of winter, it fishes pretty well between Town Hall and the dam."

This stretch sees larger trout that are blown downstream from the run directly below Dillon Dam, where you cannot fish, or the deep dugout holes below the dam through Silverthorne, when flows below the dam begin to exceed 500 cubic feet per second. In my opinion, anything over 600 cfs is not ideal, though you can catch fish at higher flows. According to Dorsey, "At higher flows, above 1,000 cfs, the fish are stacked along the edges; 1,200 cfs is fishable, but less than ideal." When Straight Creek, a quarter mile above the 1-70 bridge, flushes muddy water into the Blue, travel upstream of it (or farther downstream) for clearer water.

The challenge in high, fast water is getting a drift deep enough to the fish in the plunge pools where the big fish will hang at the drop-off or tailout of the run. For this reason, tight-line nymphing tactics without an indicator and with a long leader, also called Czech nymphing, are effective because they allow you to get a drift in water where you otherwise could not. Guide Jonathan Keisling turned me on to this technique. In addition to fishing around the stream improvements, also look for fish at the river's edge and in the water between these runs.

Beyond Silverthorne

Jackson Streit, owner of the Mountain Angler in Breckenridge and author of the *No Nonsense Guide to Fly Fishing in Colorado* has been fishing the Blue River since 1971 and loves fishing the lower river: "The tailwater in Silverthorne is fine in the winter, but the real gem is the lower river. In April the flows are low enough to make the canyon section near Boulder Creek and the Eagles Nest Unit a great day. Farther downriver—in the area above Green Mountain Reservoir—the river lengthens in size because of the lower level of the lake. Fish from the mouth of the lake upstream. Again, the springtime (late March to mid May) is an ideal period to work this two-mile section above Green Mountain Reservoir. There is a good run of rainbows that move into the river from the reservoir during this time. After the runoff and into the summer, flows are still good to fish the lower waters near Green Mountain, but in September and October the area around Boulder Creek fishes great again."

As the river from Silverthorne continues to Green Mountain Reservoir, the size of the trout diminishes while insect activity increases. In my opinion, this is a fair trade-off. Access, however, can be a bit tricky since there is a mix of public and private water and this stretch of the river travels through private water with regulations that do not allow you to anchor, stop, or get out of the boat.

To access the Blue past Silverthorne, continue north on CO 9 toward Green Mountain Reservoir. Access can be reached through the Blue River SWA Eagles Nest lease, Sutton Lease, Columbine Landing lease, and Palmer Gulch lease.

This angler is taking advantage of a brisk fall day on the Blue River at Palmer Gulch.
PAT DORSEY

Parking in all of these areas is well-marked. While Blue River Campground is closed until further notice due to pine beetle damage restoration work, use the trailhead nearby for the Eagles Nest Wilderness. The river at these access points is a mixture of riffles, runs, tailouts, pools, and some braided sections with islands and back channels. The Blue River SWA just before Green Mountain Reservoir offers the last good access with camping at Prairie Point, David's Springs, McDonald Flats, and Sucker Junction Campgrounds.

Streit says the pocketwater fishing is perfect for fishing a dry-and-dropper rig. "Hatches of *Baetis* can also be great on those gray days. When fishing the lower water toward Green Mountain, I like to use a nymph outfit with two flies—one must be a Golden Stone pattern. A #14-16 tan Barr's Tungstone is my favorite. Caddis is king on the Blue during the summer months, but Green Drakes and PMDs should be kept handy as well. Streamer fishing can also be very productive on the lower river when the water goes off-color during warmer spring days." Guide Pat Dorsey agrees: "I think streamer fishing is an overlooked tactic on the Blue River. It can be especially effective in the spring and fall and during the evening hours. Prime time on the Blue is between 6:00 p.m. and dark."

Most of the public water is easy to wade-fish for a healthy supply of rainbows, browns, cuttbows, cutthroats, and brookies. While there is a healthy supply of food, including good hatches of Green Drakes, PMDs, caddis, stoneflies, terrestrials, and Red Quills, the river can be on fire one day and off the next. "The Blue is known for its sporadic hatches," Dorsey says, "but the Green Drake hatch can be awesome if there are flows between 200 and 500 cfs and clear. I think the average angler overlooks the Columbine Landing access and Eagles Nest. These are two great pieces of water."

Below Green Mountain Reservoir

Past Green Mountain Reservoir, access to the Blue River can be very difficult at Green Mountain Canyon; however, if you take the road to the dam at Green Mountain Reservoir you can follow it down below the dam. From here, you can walk or wade the left side of the river half a mile upstream or a mile downstream into the Green Mountain Canyon before you get cliffed out. If you raft the canyon, there is no launch site, but boaters rappel their boats down and float 15 miles. After 3 miles of pristine public water that is the true gem of this section, the landscape opens up into private water, so you cannot touch river bottom or anything connected with the bottom—landowners will prosecute if you do not respect their land. Only an extremely experienced boater should attempt this journey as you will be navigating deep water and boulders all day.

Most of the anglers who walk and wade this water prefer Green Mountain Canyon access over the other BLM access points down stream. There are 11 miles of river between Green Mountain Reservoir and the confluence of the Colorado River along CO 9, most of which is private. Keep in mind that it is very difficult to negotiate the river when flows are below 400 cfs. Riffles, runs, pocketwater, tailouts, and pools characterize this access area. While it is

Bob Dye high sticks through prime pocketwater below Green Mountain Reservoir. In fast water, trout will concentrate where they can feed without fighting the current. PAT DORSEY

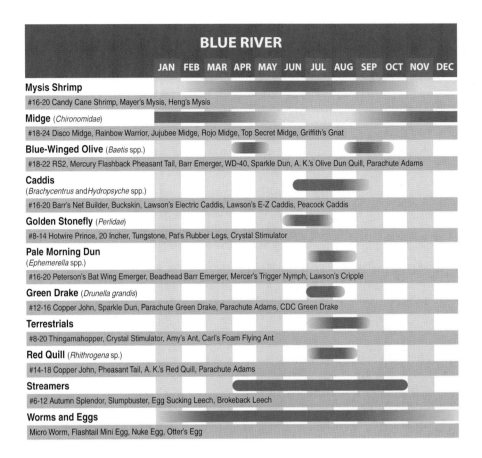

BLUE RIVER

	JAN	FEB	MAR	APR	MAY	JUN	JUL	AUG	SEP	OCT	NOV	DEC

Mysis Shrimp
#16-20 Candy Cane Shrimp, Mayer's Mysis, Heng's Mysis

Midge (*Chironomidae*)
#18-24 Disco Midge, Rainbow Warrior, Jujubee Midge, Rojo Midge, Top Secret Midge, Griffith's Gnat

Blue-Winged Olive (*Baetis* spp.)
#18-22 RS2, Mercury Flashback Pheasant Tail, Barr Emerger, WD-40, Sparkle Dun, A. K.'s Olive Dun Quill, Parachute Adams

Caddis
(*Brachycentrus* and *Hydropsyche* spp.)
#16-20 Barr's Net Builder, Buckskin, Lawson's Electric Caddis, Lawson's E-Z Caddis, Peacock Caddis

Golden Stonefly (*Perlidae*)
#8-14 Hotwire Prince, 20 Incher, Tungstone, Pat's Rubber Legs, Crystal Stimulator

Pale Morning Dun
(*Ephemerella* spp.)
#16-20 Peterson's Bat Wing Emerger, Beadhead Barr Emerger, Mercer's Trigger Nymph, Lawson's Cripple

Green Drake (*Drunella grandis*)
#12-16 Copper John, Sparkle Dun, Parachute Green Drake, Parachute Adams, CDC Green Drake

Terrestrials
#8-20 Thingamahopper, Crystal Stimulator, Amy's Ant, Carl's Foam Flying Ant

Red Quill (*Rhithrogena* sp.)
#14-18 Copper John, Pheasant Tail, A. K.'s Red Quill, Parachute Adams

Streamers
#6-12 Autumn Splendor, Slumpbuster, Egg Sucking Leech, Brokeback Leech

Worms and Eggs
Micro Worm, Flashtail Mini Egg, Nuke Egg, Otter's Egg

not always the best, or easiest water to pursue, it is worth mentioning because it is public water access supplying an escape from crowds. It also returns to a catch-and-release-only section from here to the Colorado.

Past the canyon is mostly private property until the confluence with the Colorado, which is very swampy. If you decide to pursue this area, there are two access points that offer a quarter mile of public water each. The first is accessible by taking a left on the first BLM road past the Williams Campground, and the second access is from Trough Road (approximately 8 miles farther down).

Going with the Flow

While flows are always subject to change with the demand of water in Colorado, the first step to planning your adventure on the Blue is to check water flows before you fish. You can do this through the USGS web site, waterdata.usgs.gov, or by contacting the river's local fly shop. The river is known to fluctuate dras-

An angler takes a moment to soak in the beautiful landscape a few miles upstream of the confluence with the Colorado River. Access through this stretch is dodgy, and you must respect all private property. ANGUS DRUMMOND

tically, but there is always a section of the river that will contain water levels best suited for fly fishers. If you are planning a trip in spring below Dillon, and the water levels have risen to beyond-reasonable flow (above 600 cfs), instead of calling it a day, travel above the reservoir where flows average from 100 to 200 cfs. This happens usually during runoff (from May through mid or late July).

Pat Dorsey cautions anglers that the Blue can rise several hundred cfs in a day or two: "Once the river starts to spill through the Glory Hole (the spillway or spilling basin), the river rises quickly because what enters the river via feeder creeks and the upper blue flows over the spillway." This makes your timing key to manage fishable flows beyond runoff.

If you are fishing the Blue in higher flows, use worms, stoneflies, and large beadhead imitations.

For example, the sections of the Blue around Breckenridge and below Dillon Reservoir fish best at lower flows because the water is narrower, making it almost impossible to achieve proper drift at high flows during runoff or after heavy rains. Stick to flows below 300 cfs to ensure good fishing. As you travel below Silverthorne the river gets wider, but unlike on the upper stretch there is no gauging station to let anglers know what flows are up to.

John Keefover, full-time guide with the Blue Quill Angler, shares his method for guesstimating water levels: "I typically double the flows coming out of Dillon on the lower river. During runoff, the lower river is blown out due to the feeder creeks. You can fish Eagles Nest up to 500 cfs and Blue River State Wildlife Area up to 600-800 cfs." Anything above that and the trout then have to concentrate on battling current, not feeding with lack of holding water. "High water pushes fish to the edges."

While high flows and poor visibility can be a letdown, for some anglers on the Blue above Green Mountain Reservoir it can take the action to another level. Trout feed with abandon in the dirty, high water associated with runoff. According to Dorsey: "There can be some great fishing at the inlet to Green

Mountain Reservoir during the initial phases of runoff. Don't let the off-colored water fool you—a pink San Juan Worm will hook countless fish as the water enters the reservoir. Keep in mind, this river channel is exposed in the spring due to low reservoir levels, but as the reservoir fills, this section of the Blue is buried underneath the lake." Fishing big, bright, ugly flies along the soft pockets close to the banks allows you to have the chance for a grand slam—rainbows, browns, cutthroats, cuttbows, and brook trout. Also, kokanee salmon migrate upstream from Green Mountain Reservoir starting in late August through November.

Crystal Stimulator

Hook:	#8-14 Tiemco 200R
Thread:	Orange Danville Flymaster Plus
Tail:	Elk
Abdomen:	Tying thread ribbed with brown hackle
Overwing:	Bleached elk hair/orange and pearl Krystal Flash
Thorax:	Pearl Ice Dub
Legs:	Orange Tarantula Legs
Hackle:	Grizzly

Candy Cane Shrimp

Hook:	#14-20 Tiemco 200R or bent scud hook
Thread:	White 8/0
Underbody:	White ostrich herl (three strands)
Rib:	Red Krystal Flash

Hotwire Prince Nymph

Hook:	#10-18 Tiemco 3761
Bead:	Gold tungsten
Weight:	Lead wire
Tail:	Brown goose biots
Abdomen:	Green (Brassie) and Orange (small) Ultra Wire
Thorax:	Peacock herl
Hackle:	Brown hen
Horns:	White goose biots

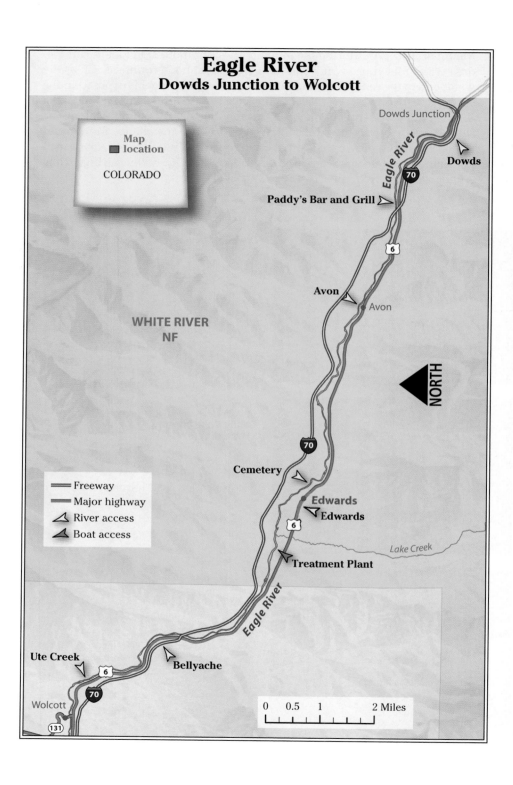

Eagle River
Dowds Junction to Wolcott

Map location

COLORADO

Dowds Junction

Eagle River

Dowds

70

6

Paddy's Bar and Grill

Avon

Avon

WHITE RIVER
NF

NORTH

70

Cemetery

Edwards

Edwards

6

Lake Creek

Treatment Plant

Eagle River

Freeway
Major highway
River access
Boat access

Ute Creek

Bellyache

6

70

Wolcott

131

0   0.5   1   2 Miles

CHAPTER 9

Eagle River

N amed by the local Ute Indians, who said the river had as many tributaries as there are feathers in an eagle's tail, the Eagle River begins in
southeastern Eagle County at the Continental Divide and flows for 70
miles to join the Colorado River at Dotsero. Unimpeded by dams, the Eagle
offers anglers a true freestone fishery for rainbows, cuttbows, and browns
ranging from 12 to 16 inches on average, with the occasional larger fish. Flows
on the river range from 220 cfs in the winter to 7,000 cfs during runoff, providing a wide range of floating and wade-fishing opportunities.

Because of the higher flows, the Eagle is one of the few in Colorado that
can be float-fished by raft and drift boat during the summer, and the water
between Edwards and Eagle will see the most fishing traffic. The upper section of river from Minturn to Dotsero can be floated, but it is a more popular
whitewater boating destination with famous Class IV runs such as Dowd
Chute. Since most of the river is off I-70, and US 6 travels parallel to the river,
it is easy to access the river by car or to run shuttles if floating.

Even though the Eagle fishes great throughout the year, it is often overlooked, and most of the time it won't be as crowded as other rivers in the
state. Fly fishers like Jeff Lyon, who guides full-time on the Eagle through
Minturn Anglers (owned by Matt Sprecher and Alex Rachowicz), says, "The
Eagle has more quality trout in size and numbers, with hatches of caddis, Yellow Sallies, Golden Stones, BWOs, PMDs, and midges all year. Other waterways in the state, such as the Arkansas, have the same hatches, but on the
Eagle you get more size and species of trout with less pressure from anglers."

The best part of the Eagle is that while it has easy access, it is not over-
fished. Many anglers pass it by, and in the height of summer, it is not uncommon to see only a handful of anglers in one day. That being said, from spring

Even though the Eagle fishes great throughout the year, it is often overlooked, and most of the time it won't be as crowded as other rivers in the state. Jeff Lyons fishes the deep water on the lower stretch of the Eagle—dark days are often best for streamer fishing.
ANGUS DRUMMOND

When the flows are dropping or low, the upper Eagle near Minturn can produce some great small-water fishing. Plunge pools supply trout with cover, oxygen, and food.
PAT DORSEY

through summer you risk blown-out water conditions. Therefore, the best times to fish the Eagle are when flows have remained steady and the caddis are in full bloom in the summer or when the trout are warming in spring and looking for midges.

The section of the river that follows I-70 from Dowds Junction (where Gore Creek and the Eagle River merge) to Dotsero typically fishes best. The Eagle can be fishable year-round if areas are free of ice, due to warmwater discharges from the water treatment plant downstream from Edwards. From March through May (pre-runoff), the river is low and the trout concentrate and feed in the warm open water. This will continue until the snow begins to melt and flows in to the Eagle, staining the river and making fishing difficult. This is when large searching imitations like 20 Inchers in sizes 12-16 can work well. After runoff, hatches turn on by July, providing superb fishing through the summer and early fall.

When the seasons are in transition on the Eagle during the fall, the trout are as well. Fishing can be very good for staging browns in September and October. JEFF LYONS

Dowds Junction to Wolcott

The Eagle begins north of Leadville and runs along US 24 where it converges with Gore Creek at Dowds Junction on I-70. This section is mostly private, but there is access just south of Minturn from a well-marked parking lot across the road from the river. The best fishing begins at Dowds Junction and runs along I-70 to the confluence with the Colorado near Gypsum. The bag and possession limit is two fish through the whole stretch.

The first access at Dowds Junction is reached by taking I-70 to US 6 West (exit 171) where you will find a series of pullouts off the highway along Dowd Chutes. This upper section has long riffled runs on bends and long straight-aways with plenty of rocks for fish to hold and feed around. The diverse structure, steep walls, and steep gradient make sight fishing difficult, but you can catch plenty of fish by targeting likely holding areas, as well as the water between the more pressured pools.

After Dowds Junction (along US 6) you can also access the river by Paddy's Sports Bar and Grill and fish 3/4 mile upstream from the bridge to 1/3 mile downstream. Access is on the north side only via a steep dirt road that goes below the I-70 bridge.

In Avon, there are two small access areas off of US 6 from Stonebridge Drive to the Arrowhead Golf Club. Avoid the well-marked private property, as well as the confluence of Beaver Creek, which is owned by Vail Resorts. Beyond the golf course, there is another well-marked pullout off US 6 that provides access downstream to Cemetery Bridge for a mile on the north side only.

Low water in the spring offers great sight-fishing opportunities on the Eagle River, like at this spot on the river near Wolcott. When wade-fishing the Eagle's slick bottom, studs on sturdy boots and a wading staff are helpful. ANGUS DRUMMOND

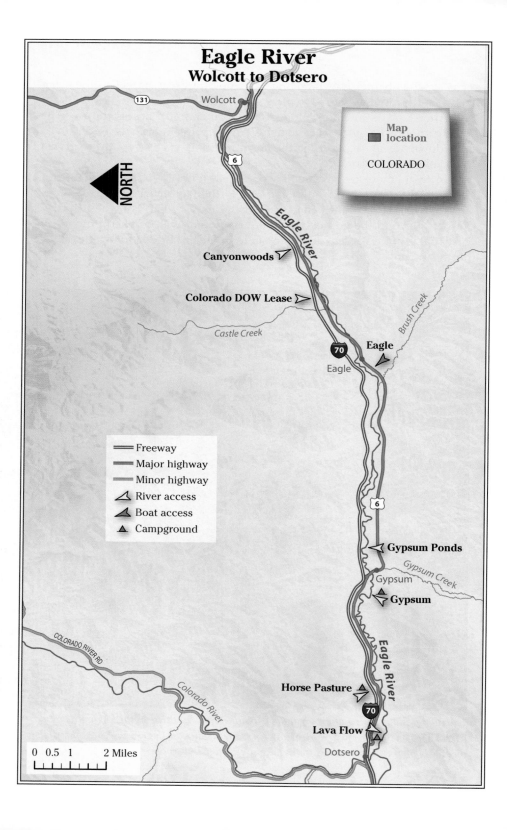

Eagle River
Wolcott to Dotsero

Map location

COLORADO

131

Wolcott

6

Eagle River

Canyonwoods

Colorado DOW Lease

Brush Creek

Castle Creek

70 Eagle

Eagle

Freeway
Major highway
Minor highway
River access
Boat access
Campground

6

Gypsum Ponds

Gypsum Creek

Gypsum

Gypsum

COLORADO RIVER RD

Colorado River

Eagle River

Horse Pasture

70

Lava Flow

Dotsero

0 0.5 1   2 Miles

NORTH

At this point US 6 passes through the town of Edwards, which has half a mile of public access on both sides of the river between the road bridge and the pedestrian bridge (which can be reached by parking at the Riverwalk Center). There is also a small boat launch at this location, but the Class IV water that lies downstream makes this a very dangerous place to put in. Instead, I recommend launching at the treatment plant just before Wilmor. This location is well-marked on the right-hand side of the road and also provides wade access on the north side for about a half mile. Bellyache and Ute Creek also provide small stretches of access before Wolcott.

Wolcott to Dotsero

In stable or lower flows, the Eagle below Wolcott can fish as well as the upper stretch. Because of numerous feeder creeks, the levels are typically higher on this stretch of the river, so avoid fishing during runoff or after heavy rains in the summer. If the water is stained, travel upstream toward Edwards and Avon.

One of my favorite flies to use when trout are looking up in the summer and fall is a low-riding foam fly like Charlie Craven's Baby Boy Hopper. LANDON MAYER

Gore Creek is a 12-mile-long tributary of the Eagle nestled in the Gore Range in White River National Forest. After descending through a rough gorge, the water will eventually be fed by Black Gore Creek. This junction is where US 6 and I-70 start traveling alongside the waterways.

Running through the Vail Valley, Gore Creek presents an intimate, small-stream setting for anglers to stalk everything from high mountain brookies to trophy-size rainbow and brown trout that see a good deal of pressure. Access points are well-marked and the area is in an urban setting with people, dogs, cyclists, and vehicles in view. You can access the river via the Vail Interfaith Chapel, the Intermountain Park Access, the Riverbend bus stop, or the area near Red Sandstone Creek.

Gore Creek caddis are the main attraction, as in the Eagle River downstream, and topwater imitations like #16-20 Garcia's Mother's Day Caddis will draw strikes. The hatch can be very exciting toward dusk as the egg-laying caddis move upstream. There is also a good population of Green Drakes during mid to late July. When these big mayflies pop the trout are looking up, because the creek is lined with willows and full of pocketwater around rocks. The best way to fish for these eager trout is with a dry fly and a tungsten-bead dropper. If the trout are suspended below the surface, a short distance of 1 to 2 feet will work; if they are hugging the bottom, extend the length. ■

The river below Wolcott isn't typically fishable until mid to late summer. Milk and Alkali creeks dump dirty, sediment-rich water into the Eagle during runoff, making late June to the beginning of December the best time to fish it. On this lower section, midges are the main game in the winter. Blue-Winged Olives hatch on cloudy days and can produce some great fishing with dry flies and a #20-22 olive Jujubee Midge or a #20-24 Jujubaetis fished on 10- to 12-foot fluorocarbon leaders. After runoff, the trout become less concentrated and spread out downstream.

The next substantial access past Wolcott is at the BLM parking area for Canyonwoods. This offers 1 1/2 miles on the north side of the river; however, there is a 50-foot easement, so be aware of private property. Farther downstream along US 6, CDOW has a fishing lease that stretches 3 miles. There are designated access points that allow for parking, although the water around Castle Creek remains private. Within the town of Eagle, pullouts along the highway from CR 307 downstream for 2 miles offer access on the north shore, and the Eagle Visitor's Center (on South Frontage Road by exit 147) offers a boat ramp as well as wading access, although the ramp at the Eagle County Fairgrounds is far less congested during tourist season. The ramp is just downstream from the pedestrian bridge.

The 4 miles of public water by the Gypsum Ponds can be reached by taking exit 140 and backtracking upriver along the dirt road heading east. From
this exit heading west on the frontage road, you can use one of the pullouts
to reach a 3-mile stretch that runs from the Gypsum BLM campground. As
with most BLM camping, the sites are primitive. Past the Gypsum campground there are two more BLM access points, Horse Pasture and Lava Flow,
although the flat, slow water here doesn't hold as many trout as the faster
runs and riffles upstream between Gypsum and Eagle.

Hatches

Like many rivers in Colorado, the Eagle followed the path of the Colorado
mining boom during the mid-1800s. Gold, silver, lead, and zinc were mined
heavily in various locations in the state. These hazardous practices began to
take their toll on the rivershed. By the 1970s, much of the river was dead and
void of fish, and it wasn't until the early 1990s that the federal government
began to take notice and intervene. With millions of dollars in cleanup efforts,
the river is beginning to return to its pristine state. It has caddis hatches from
mid to late June that, in many anglers' opinions, rival any in the state.

*Matt Miles fishes near Wolcott. Structure near the river's edge produces great holding
zones where trout feel safe in the shade.* PAT DORSEY

After runoff is the best time to pursue trout on the Eagle River. In addition to caddis, the river has year-round midge hatches and Blue-Winged Olives in the spring and early fall. Pale Morning Duns hatch in June and July, and stoneflies are another good food supply, though good dry-fly fishing can be hit-or-miss, depending on flows and the size of the hatch. ROSS PURNELL

"The best time to target the caddis hatch is after the water crests and the flows begin to drop," Kelly Bobye with Fly Fishing Outfitters says. "This typically takes place during late June through July. . . . After the river crests, you have around six weeks of higher water that allow navigation by boat. I prefer this method of covering water because you can target so many feeding lanes where trout are looking for caddis." In the fall, caddis continue to hatch and the Breadcrust work well for the larger caddis.

In addition to caddis, the river has year-round midge hatches and Blue-Winged Olives in the spring and early fall. Pale Morning Duns hatch in June and July, and stoneflies are another good food supply on the Eagle, though good dry-fly fishing can be hit-or-miss, depending on flows and the size of the hatch. In high water, I always have a stone imitation such as a #16-18 Mercer's Poxyback Yellow Sally Stone, #14-18 light or dark Befus' Wired Stonefly,

EAGLE RIVER

	JAN	FEB	MAR	APR	MAY	JUN	JUL	AUG	SEP	OCT	NOV	DEC

Midge (*Chironomidae*)
#18-24 Black Beauty, Disco Midge, Jujubee Midge, Griffith's Gnat

Blue-Winged Olive (*Baetis* spp.)
#18-22 Jujubaetis, Flashback Pheasant Tail, Barr Emerger, Mercer's Trigger Nymph, Sparkle Dun, Vis-A-Dun

Caddis
(*Brachycentrus* and *Hydropsyche* spp.)
#16-20 Larry's Better Caddis, gray Barr's Web Wing Caddis, tan Barr's Graphic Caddis, Peacock Caddis, Soft Hackle Hare's Ear, Landon's Larva

Salmonfly (*Pteronarcys californica*)
#6-10 Rogue Foam Stone, Puterbaugh's Foam Stone, 20 Incher

Golden Stonefly (*Perlidae*)
#10-14 Tungstone, black Rubber Leg Hare's Ear, Pat's Rubber Legs, 20 Incher, Crystal Stimulator, Chernobyl Ant

Red Quill (*Rhithrogena* sp.)
#14-18 Copper John, Pheasant Tail, A. K.'s Red Quill, Parachute Adams

Pale Morning Dun
(*Ephemerella* spp.)
#16-20 Peterson's Bat Wing Emerger, Beadhead Barr's Emerger, Mercer's Trigger Nymph, Lawson's Cripple Dun

Terrestrials
#8-16 black Foam Beetle, Flying Ant, Amy's Ant, Crystal Stimulator, Charlie Boy Hopper

Green Drake (*Drunella grandis*)
#12-16 Copper John, Parachute Green Drake, Parachute Adams, CDC Green Drake, Sparkle Dun

Streamers
#6-12 Egg Sucking Leech, Will's Stinging Sculpin, Slumpbuster

Worms and Eggs
Micro Worm, Flashtail Mini Egg, Nuke Egg, Yarn Egg

or #12-16 Pat's Rubber Legs as my main nymph. Though hard to time, Green Drakes hatch sporadically in good numbers June through August. Even if you do not see adults in the air, it doesn't hurt to have a topwater fly on deck.

While nymphing deep with big bugs can produce quality trout during prime hatch season, when the water is low and clear you should switch to small flies. "When flows are low on the Eagle," Jeff Lyon says, "use smaller tippets and leaders and more natural imitations instead of high-water bead-head flies. These fish are willing to feed in cold water, unlike other big waterways where other trout can become lock-jawed in the winter."

With the Colorado being fed by the Eagle throughout the year, fish will travel up the Eagle from the Colorado for holding water, food, and most importantly, to spawn in the fall. One of my favorite ways to catch these pre-spawn fish is with what I call double trouble—two streamers that are different colors, sizes, or weight. The advantage to using dual streamers is that you imitate multiple large food sources at once. Concentrating your efforts after runoff

The Eagle has caddis hatches from mid to late June that, in many anglers' opinions, rival any in the state. Starting about April, Larry's Caddis Larva imitation (above) can be very effective. LANDON MAYER

on fishing from a boat can be effective on this lower stretch, in addition to wading the lower section in September and early October when the browns begin to stage throughout the river before they spawn. I like #8-12 tan Lawson's Conehead Sculpin. Try different retrieves. Aggressive prespawn browns also take eggs such as #18-22 apricot Flashtail Mini Egg (4 mm) fished in deep runs behind or above the shallow cobblestone runs where the trout spawn. Whether fishing streamers, eggs, or nymphs, always leave spawning fish alone.

Jujubaetis

Hook:	#16-24 Tiemco 2488
Thread:	White 74-denier Lagartun and black 14/0 Gordon Griffith's
Tail:	Mottled brown India hen saddle fibers
Abdomen:	One strand black and two strands dark brown Super Hair
Flashback:	Opal Mirage Tinsel (medium)
Wing case and legs:	Gray Fluoro Fibre
Thorax:	Black 14/0 Gordon Griffith's
Coating:	5 minute epoxy

Barr's Graphic Caddis (Tan)

Hook:	#14-18 Tiemco 2499 SPBL
Thread:	Tan 6/0 Danville
Tag:	Silver Holographic Flashabou
Abdomen:	Tan Wapsi stretch tubing
Legs:	Hungarian partridge fibers
Head:	Natural gray ostrich herl

20 Incher

Hook:	#4-12 Tiemco 200R
Bead:	Brass or tungsten
Weight:	Lead wire
Thread:	Black 70-denier
Tails:	Dark brown goose biots
Rib:	Tan Rayon floss
Underbody:	Dark dubbing
Abdomen:	Peacock herl
Wing case:	Turkey tail quill slip
Legs:	Hungarian partridge
Thorax:	Natural hare's mask dubbing

Larry's Better Caddis

Hook:	#16-20 Tiemco 100
Thread:	Rusty dun
Body:	Black or olive closed-cell foam
Hackle:	Olive dyed grizzly
Wing:	Natural elk

Landon's Larva

Hook:	#16 Lighting Strike SE5
Thread:	Olive 8/0 Uni-Thread
Underbody:	Pearl Krystal Flash
Rib:	Olive Larva Lace Nymph Rib
Thorax:	Peacock Ice Dub

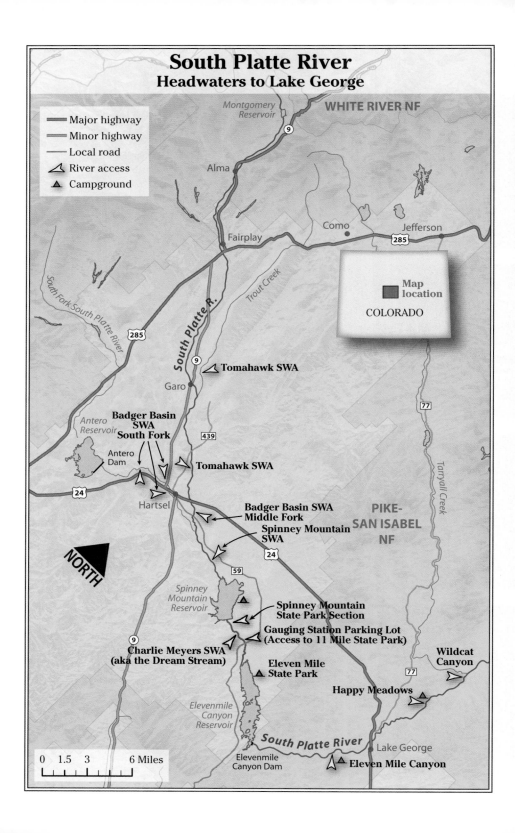

South Platte River
Headwaters to Lake George

Legend:
- Major highway
- Minor highway
- Local road
- River access
- Campground

WHITE RIVER NF

Montgomery Reservoir

Alma

Como

Jefferson

Fairplay

285

Map location

COLORADO

South Platte R.

Trout Creek

South Fork South Platte River

285

9

Tomahawk SWA

Garo

Badger Basin SWA South Fork

Antero Reservoir

439

Tomahawk SWA

77

Antero Dam

24

Hartsel

Badger Basin SWA Middle Fork

Spinney Mountain SWA

PIKE-SAN ISABEL NF

Tarryall Creek

24

NORTH

59

Spinney Mountain Reservoir

Spinney Mountain State Park Section

Gauging Station Parking Lot (Access to 11 Mile State Park)

9

Charlie Meyers SWA (aka the Dream Stream)

Eleven Mile State Park

Wildcat Canyon

Happy Meadows

77

Elevenmile Canyon Reservoir

South Platte River

Lake George

0   1.5   3   6 Miles

Elevenmile Canyon Dam

Eleven Mile Canyon

CHAPTER 10

South Platte River

I'm not just saying this because the South Platte is my home water, but I think that some of the best fly fishers in the country either guide, fish, or have spent a good deal of time on this river. Why? The South Platte River is like five rivers wrapped into one, all within a 2- to 2^1/$_2$-hour drive from metro Denver. This amazing diversity of water types and conditions, as well as different species of very selective trout, gives those who frequent it a great education and encourages versatility and the ability to adapt quickly.

From the long meadow stream at Charlie Meyers SWA (formerly called Spinney Mountain Ranch) near CO 24 to the tight quarters in the towering granite rock canyon below Cheesman Reservoir off CO 126, each section fishes differently and has its own set of challenges and rewards. Imagine every type of setting for a river from giant boulder pocketwater to riffled running water with natural and manmade structure to provide cover to slick slow-moving spring creek runs. This river has it all. Typically, well-traveled anglers do well on the South Platte because they can adjust when needed to effectively fish new water.

The other allure of the South Platte, specifically the Dream Stream, is that you can catch a trout of lifetime there. These giants—I have seen fish that I would mark in the high teens to twenty pounds—migrate up from Eleven Mile Reservoir to spawn and feed, and many of them have never seen a fly before they get to the river.

The Forks

The South Platte River starts above Spinney Mountain Reservoir where the South Fork and the Middle Fork meet 15 miles southeast of Fairplay near Hartsel. To access the South Fork of the South Platte, take US 24 East from US 285 and pass the entrances to Antero Reservoir where there are multiple pull-offs within 1 mile on the left. Continuing along US 24, take a left onto CO 9

The bruiser Gary Hort is holding moved out of cover from the rocks to begin its prowl for food on the South Platte a few hours before dark in late September. It took a #16 red Copper John. LANDON MAYER

The waters at Tomahawk on the Middle Fork of the South Platte are a great escape in the late summer and fall months. Places far up the Middle Fork such as Tomahawk State Wildlife Area, the South Fork by Buffalo Peaks, and Badger Basin are hopper-dropper country in late summer and fall, producing good numbers of fish and a nice break from crowds with action on patterns like #14-18 BC Hoppers, Fat Alberts, and Amy's Ants.
ANGUS DRUMMOND

(3 miles past the North Shore Entrance) to access a parking lot 50 yards up across the bridge. Additional parking is also located just before Hartsel in two pullouts on opposite sides. Hartsel is 1 mile from the CO 9 turnoff. This area is the Badger Basin SWA South Fork Area with special regulations of artificial flies and lures only with a possession and size limit of two fish, only one more than 20 inches, with all trout between 12 and 20 inches returned to the water immediately.

To access the Middle Fork, take CO 9 North toward Fairplay (18 miles north). While the Middle Fork begins below Montgomery Reservoir north of Alma, the highest-quality fishing begins at the Tomahawk State Wildlife Area 6 miles north of Hartsel. The CO 9 entrance is well-marked. Additionally, this area can be accessed just east of Hartsel from US 24 by turning north onto Park County Road 439, and either remaining on 439 for approximately 3 miles

Badger Basin above Spinney Mountain Reservoir is a great stop for topwater action for fish ranging from 8 to 14 inches. LANDON MAYER

and parking just before Santa Maria Ranch, or taking a right on CR 410 for access farther downstream. The Middle Fork's special regulations are artificial flies and lures only with a possession and size limit of two fish, only one more than 20 inches, with all trout between 12 and 20 inches returned to the water immediately.

For the confluence, go past Hartsel, veer right onto CO 9 South, make an immediate left onto CO 59, and go 3 miles to access the stretch above Spinney Mountain Reservoir known as Spinney Mountain SWA. This 2-mile stretch of the river is subject to rapidly-fluctuating flows throughout the year from runoff and weather, making it a prime location for migratory fish in the spring and fall when water levels rise or fall to become stable and clear water.

The best time to fish Spinney Mountain SWA is when the water levels are on the rise or stable after an increase in flow following rain or runoff. This rise in water levels will produce suitable water for the trout in Spinney Mountain Reservoir to begin the migration upriver. My favorite months are April, when Spinney Mountain Reservoir opens after the snow melts, and September, following summer's numerous storms.

When the water is low you can still have shots at trout, but a majority of the trout will return to Spinney Mountain Reservoir to consume large numbers of big insects. There is not a steady enough food supply upstream to keep resident trout fed during the summer months into early fall when flows are low. It is not uncommon for the highest water to reach 400-plus cfs and then drop to 30 cfs.

As you travel down CO 59, there are multiple access points you can reach through a gated area. Although they may appear private, they are not. The last gated parking area above Spinney Mountain Reservoir is the best access to the confluence of the South and Middle Forks, which form the South Platte. Since it is located on state land, there is a parking fee of $6 per day at the orange post next to the regulation sign where you insert an envelope with payment. From the parking lot, hike approximately a mile along the beaten path to the inlet into Spinney Mountain Reservoir. From there, you can navigate the winding deep runs on every bend—and the turbulent riffles in between—all the way upriver (approximately 2¹/₂ miles to the gauging station). Continuing above the gauging station along 1 mile of winding river,

The hunt for orange and yellow alligators is a life-changing experience in the fall between Eleven Mile and Spinney Mountain Reservoir. This section of the South Platte River has some of the largest trout in the country. Two suggestions I always give to others and follow myself are always look for the trout before you cast in suitable water, and hunt trout in the water between the runs, as the fish will move to feed and to escape any pressure supplied to the conventional deep runs. LANDON MAYER

you will meet the Middle and South Forks of the South Platte. From this confluence, the best approach is selecting the fork with the most water, which is usually the Middle Fork since its water comes from snowmelt, whereas the South Fork flows out of Antero Reservoir. The trout will simply choose the highest flow for safety.

In the spring, rainbows, cutthroats, and cuttbows between 14 and 24 inches run up from Spinney Reservoir and, at times, hold in large pods in runs and pools throughout this section of water. Concentrate on the pools, foam lines, and bends in the river where the trout concentrate in low flows (around 100 cfs or less). In the late summer and fall, as the trout run up the forks, larger prespawn browns become the main attraction. Some of these fish surpass 8 pounds and can travel 9 miles or more upriver.

Due to a lack of insect life and holding water, structure was introduced to the South Platte River from the mouth of Spinney Mountain Reservoir up 1 mile to the flow-gauging station for the Platte. With the new holding areas in place, some fish are starting to call these sections of the river home to escape the aggressive pike lurking in the shallow reservoir. The 14-inch trout that inhabit this section of water will continue to grow every year.

While there are some hatches in this short stretch of river, eggs, streamers, and attractor patterns like #16-20 red, black, green, or chartreuse Copper Johns work well. Even if the water is dirty from runoff or rain, chartreuse flies still trigger strikes. Since trout are accustomed to eating scuds in the reservoir, a #16-18 orange or olive scud works well in the river.

Lastly, if the water supports the presentation, a streamer twitched or ripped along or under these banks can be lethal. In this small water, you simply flip your fly upstream of your target and twitch it with your rod tip (6 inches or so) to imitate an injured food source while keeping a fixed amount of line and leader out of your rod tip. A #12-16 rust or black Brokeback Leech can work great, and a #8-12 rust, olive, or ginger Barr's Meat Whistle imitates the robust crayfish populations. But do not be afraid to change flies. Fish can become conditioned to fly patterns quickly and sometimes showing them something different is what it takes to catch them.

Charlie Meyers State Wildlife Area

This completely public catch-and-release tailwater is 3 linear miles long, with 5 1/2 miles of classic, winding, open-meadow river. Some of the largest trout on earth swim in these waters— rainbows, cutthroats, and cuttbows that can grow to 17 pounds (the largest I have seen), followed by browns that exceed 30 inches every year. The two main seasons for the largest trout are spring and fall, but in the summer and winter you can also catch large fish, though most are 16 to 22 inches. Having the ability to pursue trophy trout in all four seasons has now given this stretch the well-earned name of the "Dream Stream," where, on any given day, the trout you dream about can become reality.

The Charlie Meyers State Wildlife Area between Spinney and Eleven Mile Canyon Reservoirs is truly brown trout heaven. You have a better shot at a wild trophy brown here than anywhere else in Colorado. Formerly named Spinney Mountain SWA, this stretch was renamed in 2010 to honor one of fly fishing's greatest advocates, Charlie Meyers, who was the outdoor editor for the **Denver Post.** *This section was one of Charlie's favorite locations to fish.* LANDON MAYER

Once a meandering, oxbowing meadow stream in a vast, pristine valley full of wildlife, the South Platte was dammed to form two reservoirs: Spinney Reservoir, which has supplied Aurora's water since 1981, and Eleven Mile Canyon Reservoir, completed in 1932, which supplies the city of Denver with water. Along with the railroad that supplied transportation and wildflower tours, starting in the late 1800s the mining in nearby Cripple Creek brought many to strike it rich, and some of the historic ranch land, cabins, and barns are still standing to this day.

In this section of the South Platte, all water is public. Colorado State Parks and CDOW have fences running across certain zoned sections, with wooden steps for anglers' access. You can get here from the Front Range by taking US 24 West out of Colorado Springs or by following US 285 south out of Denver to US 24 East past Hartsel. By heading south on Park CR 23 for 3 miles, and then taking a left onto CR 59 for another 7 miles, you can cross the river and take your first right up to the top parking lot. This lot, located below the zoning fence, is the top parking lot of CDOW land and is known as the

Michael Heintz holds a trophy rainbow on the South Platte. With deep waters to grow in, these giants are worth the hunt above Eleven Mile Reservoir. In high flows trout cannot pass up a #12 Brokeback Leech on a dead drift.
LANDON MAYER

Upper Middle parking lot. After this is the Middle Barns parking lot, 100 yards down, with rustic old red barns in view in the distance. A mile farther south on CR 59, before you enter state land, there are two giant fence ladders that allow access to the lower and inlet portions of the river, or you can gain access from the lot by the gauging station.

The terrain, once you are parked and in place, is flat and easy to navigate and you can cover a lot of water, which is one of the things that I love about this $5^{1}/_{2}$-mile stretch. However, do not let the landscape fool you. This section of the South Platte is located at 8,700 feet, and if you are not used to the elevation, it can become a workout instead of a day of fishing. When you walk the river, the key to success is to make each section you fish a fresh start—you may have to change your depth, drift, and approach constantly.

While it wasn't always so, this area of the South Platte has become a migratory fishery and contains mostly large fish. "At Spinney, you don't tend to see a lot of smaller trout in the younger age classes nowadays, other than the young of the year's fingerlings," says Ed Engle, author of *Trout Lessons*. "That hasn't always been true, though. When the river was more of a rainbow trout fishery I think we saw a more even distribution of ages. Now it's predominantly a brown trout fishery in terms of resident trout, and we're seeing the larger fish."

With resident trout that live in the water year-round, fish also move upriver from Eleven Mile Reservoir during the summer. The Dream Stream produces, on average, larger trout than any other section of the river because they can simply escape and find refuge in Eleven Mile Reservoir. When Granite Canyon was dammed from Eleven Mile Canyon Reservoir, the water's maximum depth reached 170 feet. The fish have the luxury of feeding at numerous depths on crayfish, baitfish, insects, and more without any pressure or competition. Engle continues, "I think the most important factors that allow for the potential of the Spinney Mountain section to hold larger fish are that it's a relatively young tailwater; it's a meadow stream, which seems to provide something that larger trout like; and that Eleven Mile Canyon Reservoir is nearby. Simply put, the young tailwater provides all the nutrients necessary to support a good population of trout foods, and Eleven Mile Canyon Reservoir provides a place for the larger trout to go if the water flows get too low. Other, older tailwaters in the state do not hold the same numbers of insects or hatches, because the rivers are not as fertile as the young fisheries."

While the hunt of large trout is more than exciting, the water in the Charlie Meyers SWA also has good hatches that start with midges in the winter, followed by Blue-Winged Olives in the spring and fall, leading and following the complex, vast hatches of caddis, Pale Morning Duns, Tricos, Yellow Sallies, and midges. PMDs and Tricos are two of the largest hatches on the river and patterns like a #16-18 Barr PMD Flashback Emerger or a #18-22 black RS2 are must-haves on your rig in the heat of summer. You can also fool some of these fish with hoppers, Stimulators, and yes, even mice in high water, usually in the late hours during summer and fall days.

When you are rigging to fish the South Platte, fluorocarbon is necessary in the open, well-lit locations of the river. It is even more important in areas like South Park, where the only shade you get is sunrise, sunset, and weather.

Eleven Mile Canyon

To get to the canyon take US 24 East to the town of Lake George. The entrance to the canyon is a well-marked turn onto CR 96 in the town of Lake George, 38 miles west of Colorado Springs. The road follows the river along the entire length of Eleven Mile Canyon. Beginning upstream at the dam, which is 8 miles upstream, pullouts are obvious throughout the length of the canyon. Camping under the dam is at Spillway Campground, and most of the productive fishing is in the top 3 miles of the

Ed Engle changes patterns as he works a feeding fish in Eleven Mile Canyon. With river widths ranging from 10 to 30 feet, the South Platte is primarily a walk-and-wade river, with the exception of the Deckers area below Cheesman Canyon during high water. This river is a sight-fisherman's haven. ANGUS DRUMMOND

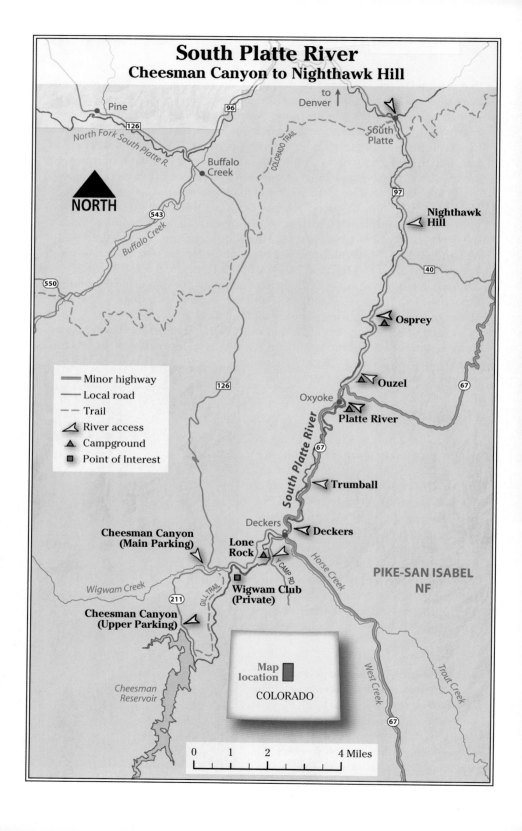

South Platte River
Cheesman Canyon to Nighthawk Hill

Pine

96

126

North Fork South Platte R.

to
Denver ↑

South
Platte

Buffalo
Creek

COLORADO TRAIL

NORTH

543

97

**Nighthawk
Hill**

Buffalo Creek

550

40

Osprey

Minor highway
Local road
Trail
River access
Campground
Point of Interest

126

Oxyoke

Ouzel

Platte River

67

South Platte River

Trumball

67

Deckers

Deckers

**Cheesman Canyon
(Main Parking)**

**Lone
Rock**

Horse Creek

**PIKE-SAN ISABEL
NF**

Wigwam Creek

Y CAMP RD

GILL TRAIL

211

**Wigwam Club
(Private)**

**Cheesman Canyon
(Upper Parking)**

Cheesman
Reservoir

Map
location

COLORADO

West Creek

Trout Creek

67

0   1   2   4 Miles

Eleven Mile Canyon is one of the most breathtaking areas to fish in the state, with pale granite walls hovering over bug-rich water. LANDON MAYER

canyon. The river is designated flies- and lures-only catch-and-release water from the dam to Wagon Tongue Road, and these regulations have really increased the size of the trout in the upper stretch. Most trout range from 12 to 16 inches, with some real bruisers thrown into the mix. Downstream 100 yards, Cove Campground is next, followed by the Twin Tunnels another mile down, which are obvious railroad tunnels carved in the days when this was a major railroad of the mining boom. Marking the end of the catch-and-release section is Springer Gulch Campground, a mile past Cove Campground.

Many anglers helped create this catch-and-release area, but no other angler was as determined and important to the cause as Dick Rock: "In 1999, we fought for a regulation change from two fish over 16 inches to catch-and-release, and we predicted that the number of fish in the top section of the canyon would increase to the point where they would begin to spill over into the standard regulation section. Because of the biomass in the river and the 2000 regulation change, that is just what has happened. More and larger fish are now found downstream in the standard regulation section. With the 2000 regulation change to C&R-only in the top section, it changed the river from mediocre to near world-class."

Unlike the meadow water of Spinney, Eleven Mile Canyon looks more like a large creek with a huge amount of structure, from natural rocks and vegetation to fallen and man-introduced trees. This creates the majority of the river's trout habitat. Steve Gossage, guide for Anglers Covey Fly Shop, has more than a decade of experience in Eleven Mile Canyon. "I think high-stick nymphing works better in Eleven Mile Canyon than the other South Platte tailwaters. You can get much closer to your targets there than Spinney Ranch or Cheesman Canyon. The Canyon is pretty user-friendly so your presentations can be a lit-

With low water in winter, Eleven Mile Canyon can be sight-fishing paradise with midging trout as long as the sun warms up the water, increasing the trout's activity. This is when a #20-24 Dorsey's Top Secret Midge is lethal for selective trout. ANGUS DRUMMOND

With the top 2 miles of Eleven Mile Canyon designated catch-and-release with flies and lures only, large trout like this rainbow can now grow to great lengths. LANDON MAYER

tle off and get away with it most of the time. It is a great place to guide beginners because of this."

Due to the amount of pressure from anglers and recreational traffic, the larger fish can be harder to catch. The best time to fish is when there is a bump in the flows, which stirs up the rich bottom, producing large amounts of food for the trout, or when insects are hatching—especially in the first few weeks of a hatch before the trout get super selective and 6X fluorocarbon leader and tippet becomes necessary, at least most of the time.

Some of the largest and longest-lasting hatches are abundant in the canyon. Dick Rock, who also holds a degree in entomology, explains. "You can just about set your watch by the hatches. From the Blue-Winged Olives in the spring and fall to the caddis, Tricos and Pale Morning Duns throughout the summer, all the hatches are very predictable. The numbers of insects is incredible and the biomass throughout the canyon is superb."

Happy Meadows

As the South Platte breaks free of the granite walls of Eleven Mile Canyon, it meanders around the town of Lake George, heads northwest beyond a private stretch for 4 miles and then flows directly into Happy Meadows. You can reach Happy Meadows by continuing west on Highway 24; take a right 1 mile west on CR 77, and then a right on CR 112. There are multiple pullouts along the road, with additional access at the Happy Meadows Campground.

Though it is a beautiful stretch, Happy Meadows is not as popular with fly fishers as other sections of the South Platte, due to its lack of catch-and-release regulations. It's frozen over during the winter and early spring, but after the thaw, from late spring through the summer and into the fall (preferably during the week to escape the camping crowds in Eleven Mile Canyon), this section of the South Platte can be a good dry-fly fishery for rainbows, browns, and cuttbows that commonly reach 16 inches or more.

Wildcat Canyon

Two miles downstream from the beginning of Happy Meadows, the river flows into Sportsman's Paradise, a private 2-mile stretch that is inaccessible for anglers. But beyond the fenced area, Wildcat Canyon is a 7-mile stretch of river that provides great fishing and fewer crowds. With the lack of angling pressure, the trout are not as selective in this area and will take some large patterns that would not be given a second look on most public sections of the South Platte. Accessible by a trail located near the Happy Meadows Campground, the 2-mile hike around the private property is worth the fly-fishing escape to a canyon that fishes best from August through October.

After the Hayman Fire in 2002, some of this pristine landscape was burned and the river was filled with silt. Because it is hard to get to, and

Connor Murphy lands a quality brown that took a PMD Cripple while feeding aggressively on Pale Morning Duns. Trout also migrate up from the reservoirs to feed in the summer, not just in spring and fall. This is a huge advantage for anglers, because you are constantly casting and hunting large trout that do not receive a lot of pressure. LANDON MAYER

For the best results fishing to selective trout in Cheesman Canyon, cast to feeding trout, and don't just search the water. LANDON MAYER

doesn't get a lot of press, this stretch has remained off anglers' radars. On the flip side, like the section at Deckers, the waters have started to rebound, and with every year the river will flush itself clean and produce better fishing. If you are looking for a getaway for the weekend or want to test the small-creek rod you have sitting in its case, this is a great spot.

Cheesman Canyon

Nine miles after flowing through Wildcat Canyon, the South Platte enters Cheesman Lake. Below the lake, the river begins its 5-mile journey through Cheesman Canyon. This section of river was designated catch-and-release in 1972, and for decades some of the sport's top anglers have battled trout within these walls, making the history of the canyon part of every adventure you partake of when you hike in. As Pat Dorsey, well-known angler, author, and part owner of the Blue Quill Angler put it, "Fishing the canyon is like hitting from the blue tees at Augusta—it is the most technically challenging fishing in the West."

The Gill Trail runs the entire length of the canyon and offers two points of access, both marked with signs that direct you down to the river. One is at the bottom of the canyon, and another at the top below Cheesman Dam. The top trail is demanding but the rewards from unpressured water are great. Trail restoration has been a big issue here, so please use the marked trails to gain access, as off-trail hiking increases erosion.

To access the trail from Cheesman Lake, take US 285 South from Denver to Pine Junction. Continue on CO 126 South to Forest Road 211 toward the lake. From Colorado Springs, take US 24 West to Woodland Park and CO 67 North to Deckers. At Deckers, veer left onto CO 126 to Forest Road 211. The lake entrance is clearly marked. The trailhead is on your left with its own parking lot before the lake.

Pat Dorsey high-sticks the pocketwater upstream from Trumbell. Out of all the tailwaters of the South Platte, Deckers runs the farthest below a dam, making the terrain of the river resemble a freestone fishery instead of tailwater. LANDON MAYER

To access the Gill Trail from below, follow the same directions as above but turn into the paved parking off CO 126, 4 miles north of Deckers. The lower parking is also clearly marked. Trail access from the lower lot is easier to navigate than that of the upper trail, and contains a display that maps the entire trail, marking such famous spots as the Family Pool and Icebox. Don't spend all of your time on these famous holes, but explore the waters between these runs.

Because Cheesman Canyon trout see so many anglers each day, they can be tough to catch. Some of the best opportunities for fishing Cheesman are during cloud cover, when *Beatis* mayflies are more abundant. Never leave home without a #20-22 Stalcup's Baetis nymph, #18-22 Sparkle Wing RS2, and #18-22 Barr BWO Flashback Emerger ready to present to actively feeding trout. The cloud cover makes the anglers less detectable and allows the fish to feed longer throughout the course of a day. Also, Cheesman trout are easier to catch whenever there is an increase in flow, which causes the water to become stained and pushes more food to the trout. Best flows are 100 to 400 cfs, with 250 being ideal. This is low enough for most anglers to cross the river in certain sections, allowing access from low and high bank sides.

Lastly, a big key to success is searching for the right targets. Pat Dorsey says, "Anglers who sight fish will catch considerably more trout than those who flog the water and blind fish. A 6X tippet is mandatory. Finding a feeding fish is your best bet—ignore the non-feeders and target a feeding fish."

On your next trip to Cheesman, follow these three rules and you will find yourself fooling some of the most wary fish in the United States: Time your trip for sustainable flows and weather conditions; find feeding trout willing to eat the fly instead of hacking water; and use a 6X fluorocarbon leader and tippet, and downsize all of your imitations.

Deckers

As the Platte continues its journey below Cheesman, it passes through private water on CO 126 before flowing next to and past the town of Deckers, which gives this section of the South Platte River its name.

From Denver or Colorado Springs you can be on the water within an hour and a half, making this section of the South Platte a favorite for anglers who want a getaway without the extended drive. Deckers is one of the oldest named trout fisheries in the state of Colorado, with anglers pursuing fish here since before the 1950s. This watershed has gone through many trials and tribulations caused by man and Mother Nature, which forever changed the hatches, number of fish, and techniques used to catch them. The most well-known drastic turn of events happened in the summer of 2002, when the Hayman Fire swept through 150,000 acres of Colorado landscape, surrounding and meandering through many sections of the South Platte—but none closer than at Deckers. For years following the blaze, snowmelt, rain, and runoff washed several thousand tons of sediment into the rocky terrain of the Deck-

ocated in the giant valley of South Park, surrounded by what seems to be an endless sky, the reservoirs of Antero, Spinney Mountain, and Eleven Mile are all within a 20-minute drive of one another and have large trout eager to take the fly.

Antero Reservoir is located west of Hartsel on US 24. There are two pull-ins for the reservoir that are clearly marked with signs for the north and south shore access. East of Hartsel, US 24 will continue to the small Wilkerson Pass. Before you reach the pass, CR 29 is the main road that will lead you to Spinney Mountain Reservoir and Eleven Mile Canyon Reservoir. Turn at the sign for Chaparral Park General Store, owned by Rob Robinson. If you get lost, Rob's store is bright red, and in the middle of this flat valley, it cannot be missed. He or his staff can always help lead you in the correct direction.

Antero

Known as one of Colorado's fastest trout-growing reservoirs, Antero is considered one of the best fly-fishing stillwaters in the United States. With depths only reaching about 20 feet at its deepest point, it offers ideal conditions for anglers to get their flies to the trout from almost anywhere on the water. While it has constantly produced a wealth of quality fish, this came to a halt in 2002 when it was drained after the Hayman Fire to reduce the amount of water that had evaporated from the rivers.

This came as a blow to all anglers, who grew to love this paradise and the trout it produced day in and day out. The question then became: Will this amazing fishery ever return to its full potential? When it reopened in July 2007, the answer was clearly yes. Numerous trout over 7 pounds were caught. Our wonderland had returned. Nevertheless, with this new success came a new challenge for Antero: The slot limit put in place when it reopened.

The new regulations allowed four trout to be kept, with only one exceeding 20 inches in length. While these regulations seemed realistic at first, they soon caused more harm than good since bait-hooked fish were being released to die as anglers "upgraded" their catch. What do you think happens when an angler catches his limit of fish (all under 20 inches), keeps fishing, and then hooks a 20-incher?

Now the limit is two trout over 20 inches, allowing the smaller trout a chance to grow to their full potential. Despite not being artificials-only, this fishery is strong, with an above-average food supply and natural springs.

Spinney Mountain Reservoir

What sets Spinney Mountain Reservoir apart from others in the state are the regulations to help ensure the safety of the fishery. Like Antero, in the first five years of Spinney's opening, it was an unbelievable trophy trout reservoir. This was caused by the overabundance of high-protein scuds that inhabit the reservoir. However, with a big bag limit and heavy angling pressure, it did

Using the buddy system at ice-off is a great way to sight fish for cruising trout. One angler stands high on the red rocks of Antero Reservoir directing the casting angler below on where to present the fly. LANDON MAYER

not take long for the state to realize they had to enforce strict regulations to save it.

Like Antero, this large body of water is approximately 35 feet at its deepest point, making it an ideal depth for fly anglers to reach the trout. You can only use flies and lures, with a bag limit of one trout over 20 inches. There is no ice fishing or night fishing, so the reservoir is closed from when it freezes until ice-out. Over the last five years, the number and size of the trout has increased and should continue to do so for years to come. The key to this is managing the pike population to keep it to a minimum, allowing the trout to reproduce and grow to their full potential. One clear advantage to these shallow bodies of water is accessibility by boat, as well as the shore being so close to the trout, vegetation, and food supply.

Eleven Mile Reservoir

Eleven Mile Reservoir is a trophy trout factory known to grow large numbers of fish that have the potential to reach 20 pounds, with water depths reaching 100-plus feet. Some of these fish feel no angling pressure for a majority of their lives, which is responsible for supplying the astonishing giants entering the South Platte River.

With a number of drop-offs and a variety of bays to pursue, it can be challenging to find the trout in this reservoir. One key is to concentrate on the shallow waters from the beginning of ice-melt on the reservoir's edge until mid-May. This is the time when these monsters will cruise the warm shallows in search of food without fear of getting eaten by pike. Once the trout disperse, look for warm, windswept bays that keep you protected and food-filled breaks around this body of water. These areas will supply warmth from the blown-in surface heat and a large supply of food. ■

Rubber Leg Hare's Ear

Hook:	#16-18 Tiemco 5262
Bead:	Gold
Thread:	Tan 8/0 Uni-Thread
Tail:	Hare's mask guard hairs
Body:	Hare's ear dubbing
Rib:	Oval gold tinsel (medium)
Thorax:	Hare's ear dubbing
Wing case:	Turkey tail fibers
Legs:	Black rubber (small)

Rojo Grande (Red)

Hook:	#12-16 Tiemco 2302
Beads:	Black tungsten (3/32) and red silver-lined glass (small)
Gills:	Ultra Floss
Thread:	Red 140-denier Ultra Thread
Rib:	Silver Lagartun (fine)
Collar:	Peacock herl dyed bright green

Hunchback Scud (Orange)

Hook:	#14-20 Tiemco2487
Thread:	Orange 8/0 Uni-Thread
Abdomen:	Orange Antron dubbing with underbelly fibers picked out
Back:	Clear plastic
Rib:	Monofilament

ers fishery, suffocating the river bottom. However, with change, new growth, and the demand that the high water fluctuating in the South Platte supply Denver's water, the river has begun its transformation back to life. Starting in 2008, the month of May brought an incredible surprise to many anglers and hungry trout: an enormous caddis hatch lasting through June.

Well-known angler and fly tier Stan Benton describes how the river has changed over the years: "After the high-water year [of 1995], the entire bottom structure of the river around Deckers changed. Many of the holes were filled in, and new channels had been formed. Before the high-water year the highest flows I witnessed were around 650 cfs. At the peak of the high water, flows reached 3,200 cfs, and the water was about 4 inches below the bridge at Trumbull. That year you could literally fish in the parking lots. When customers would ask me where to fish, I would reply 'Pennsylvania or New York, because the entire West is blown out.'

"The year after, fishing had significantly declined and the fish populations were greatly reduced. That was about the time that whirling disease was identified in the system and the DOW ascribed the decline in the South Platte fishery to it.

"As far as larger fish were concerned, before 1995 I would normally catch between seven and ten fish a year over 20 inches at Deckers (excluding Cheesman Canyon). The interesting thing is that I would catch all of the larger fish in January, February, and March. Then in 2002 the Hayman Fire had the greatest negative impact on the Deckers area. The fishery was just beginning to show some real sign of recovery when the fire occurred. The subsequent silting of the river has impacted bug populations and, as a result, fish populations. Many sections of the river at Deckers were silted to the point that they could not hold fish. What we need is another high-water year to blow some of the silt downstream and re-channelize the river.

"Since the fire, the river is showing better signs of life with caddis in major populations consisting of *Brachycentrus* and *Hydropsyche*. Blanket hatches have been a rarity, but from mid-April through July over the past few years, it is now the main source of food—the insects can cling to structure and not rely on the silted river bottom, resulting in big hatches. The good news now is trout are relocating to new water and have a heavy food supply to sustain growth."

Because of the supply of extraordinarily large trout from the private clubs, the lower section of Cheesman Canyon and the upper section of Deckers are often supplied with escaping trout that are flushed downstream or migrate upstream in high flows and in the spring and fall. This plays an important role on the public-water stretches of the South Platte, because the unpressured fish newly introduced into Deckers are willing to take imitations such as a #10 Amy's Ant that would be passed up by an educated trout. Special regulations from the Wigwam Club to the Scraggy View Picnic Ground are artificial flies and lures only with a possession and size limit of two fish 16 inches.

If you used to fish Deckers before the Hayman Fire, understand that it has changed completely since then. According to Dorsey, "the river has become a caddis and stonefly river, and tactics and patterns have changed dramatically. We now fish larger bugs—for example, Amy's Ants and Pat's Rubber Legs—compared to 15 years ago. The caddis hatch occurs in June, later than a freestone river, because the water is cooler for a longer period of time. The Golden Stonefly hatch occurs in July and August."

Danny Brennan, owner of Flies and Lies, believes that the water from Deckers downstream is one of the hardest areas to sight-fish, with the addition of Horseshoe Creek providing sediment and dirty water with rain and snowmelt. "Reading water, spotting risers, and drifting through soft seams are critical for success in this section," he says.

From Deckers, Y Camp Road leads upstream and dead-ends at private land. There are several pullouts and parking areas along this section clearly marked with parking signs. Half a mile downstream from the private water at the end of Y Camp Road, the river leaves the road briefly and access is via an unmarked, ungroomed trail for a quarter of a mile. The river comes back to the road across the stream from Lone Rock Campground, which can be reached off of CO 126 just north of Deckers.

At Deckers, you can take CO 67 North downstream to find parking behind the stores, as well as restrooms and cabin accommodations. Another 50 yards

Some of the best fly fishing on the South Platte is during or just after a large storm when dark skies supply trout with cover from above. ANGUS DRUMMOND

downstream from the turnoff, there are additional parking areas on the left and 50 yards farther down on the right, just before and after the bridge.

One mile downstream at Trumbull, you can access the river via a parking lot immediately after the town on the left or via additional pullouts half a mile farther down. There is a private stretch after these pullouts and the river veers away from the road. After you enter Pike National Forest, public water picks back up, with the Platte River Campground providing facilities. Continuing down, there are multiple pull-offs clearly marked.

At this point, the paved road becomes Douglas CR 97 just after Pine Creek Road turns toward Sedalia. Ouzel Campground and Scraggy View Picnic Ground, both just past the turnoff, also provide access between pullouts. Osprey camping area, a mile down, is the last camping before the road turns to dirt, with Nighthawk Hill providing some access a mile past this. After this is the Colorado Trailhead, and eventually the South Platte will fork off near the old South Platte Hotel, a thriving landmark until it was burned down in 1912. At the confluence of the North Fork, the road turns back to the west and becomes CR 96, following the North Fork for 10 miles back to Foxton and Buffalo Creek.

At the old town of South Platte, the river travels north toward Denver and the Chatfield Reservoir. One of the last ventures for many anglers who pursue trout in the South Platte River is Waterton Canyon where the river flows into Chatfield Reservoir.

Waterton Canyon

Waterton Canyon is not as well known as the rest of the South Platte, at least to out-of-town anglers, but it can provide good dry-fly fishing for 6- to 12-inch trout close to Denver. "Waterton Canyon offers anglers a year-round trout fishery," Tad Howard from Colorado Trout Hunters explains. "Techniques and tactics change through the seasons depending on stream flow and weather, but there is exciting action to be had all year. Summer and fall offer anglers who do not mind a bit of a hike—or like to pack a rod on their bicycle—a good chance to catch many trout on attractor dry flies, alone or with droppers, such as Humpies, Elk-Hair Caddis, Stimulators, and Parachute Adams."

The best fishing is generally between March and October, with good midge hatches starting as early as mid-February, and Blue-Winged Olives beginning in March. Summer brings caddis and stoneflies. With larger Golden Stoneflies crawling about the water, #10-14 Pat's Rubber Legs can produce good numbers of trout in the high-water seasons of June and July.

According to the Denver Water Board, Waterton Canyon is scheduled to be closed from January 31, 2011, through December 31, 2011, to remove 625,000 cubic yards of sediment from the reservoir. (The reservoir currently has more than 1 million cubic yards of sediment.) If the project proceeds ahead of schedule, Denver Water may extend the work into 2012 to remove as much of the sediment as possible. Any schedule changes will be posted at denverwater .org/Recreation/WatertonCanyon/FAQs/.

CLEAR CREEK

Kerry Caraghar

Clear Creek is one of the most overlooked trout fisheries on the Front Range of the Rocky Mountains, offering fishing access points from mountain elevations on down to the Mile-High City. These access points offer anglers the option of fishing before, after, or even during the workday. The headwaters of Clear Creek chart a course for the South Platte River starting near Loveland Ski Area and ending near Denver. Clear Creek parallels US 6 west of Golden where this majestic creek enters Clear Creek Canyon. One's imagination can easily revert to a time when narrow gauge trains, bellowing smoke, traveled this route, delivering supplies to the mining communities.

For many decades this watershed fell victim to near devastation caused by mining for gold and other heavy metals. The legacy of Colorado's colorful mining history left a scar on Clear Creek. Thankfully, all four forks of Clear Creek either have been restored or are in the process of being returned to their natural state by Federal Superfund cleanup efforts, and Clear Creek has become one of the healthiest wild trout fisheries on the Front Range. This little river is a shining example of how conservation and restoration efforts by groups such as Trout Unlimited can protect our coldwater fisheries for generations to come. Clear Creek now supports a very healthy and diverse population of both stocked and wild trout ranging in size from 6 to 16 inches and even an occasional 20-incher. I have landed brown trout, rainbows, cuttbows, brookies, and cutthroats throughout the public water open to fly anglers.

The insect population is also very healthy, not unlike any other freestone river. Mayflies, stoneflies, caddisflies, and midges sustain this healthy fish population. I can assure you that anyone lucky enough to catch the Green Drake hatch in August will be completely oblivious to any background noise from I-70. I start fishing Clear Creek in late March and continue through mid-May. After the June runoff slows down, you'll find the fishing great from about July until the ice comes back in late October. Look for over 18 miles of public access from downtown Golden to the Bakerville exit 221 off I-70.

One of my favorite spots is the Mayhem Gulch Open Space in Clear Creek canyon off US 6. I'm also likely to be found at the Philadelphia mill site 2 miles west of Idaho Springs on the Stanley Road. This park offers anglers ample space for day-use picnicking and fishing. My very favorite spot can be found by hiking upstream from the Bakerville exit toward Loveland Ski Area. ∎

While the beginning of the canyon starts near the town of South Platte, Denver is a better access portal. To get to the canyon, follow Wadsworth Boulevard (CO 121) south of CO 470 past Chatfield Reservoir to the Kassler Center, where you will find public parking. This canyon offers over 6 miles of water up to Strontia Springs Dam. As the South Platte continues north into Denver, the opportunities for quality trout fishing drop. Anglers have found productive fishing for carp around and in the downtown areas of Denver, however. For those wanting a change of pace, these wary fish can put up a good fight.

Urban Carp

Barry Reynolds

I first began plying the waters of the South Platte River as it meanders through the Denver metropolitan area many years ago. My discoveries both then and now keep me returning to this hidden gem that sits in plain view of millions of people but until recently received very little attention.

I fish the Platte several days a week throughout most of the year and only the coldest of weather will keep me from it even during the winter months. I fish the whole river, starting at the spillway area below Chatfield Reservoir and continuing on out past 160th Avenue, which basically covers the entire Denver metro complex and outlying cities. There is a lot of water to fish and most of it receives little pressure.

Just below the dam the spillway kicks out large brown trout, some to 12 pounds or more, but as you move closer to the downtown area the water loses some of its ability to support coldwater species and warmwater fish such as large- and smallmouth bass, channel catfish, and walleye have become more abundant over recent years, offering willing anglers a virtual potluck of warmwater fly-fishing opportunities.

My main quarry and point of interest is the carp. Carp provide all that I seek out in my fly fishing: They get big (up to 40 pounds). They spend a great deal of time rooting and tailing for food in shallow water—sight fishing at its best. They make strong powerful runs and are one of the few fish in freshwater that will show you your backing. They are highly intelligent and selective and will make you a better angler by challenging your presentations, fly selection, and approach.

My favorite time of year to pursue carp on the South Platte is May through September. The water is warm and generally very low and gin-clear, creating great opportunities to sight-fish for tailing carp in super skinny water on the numerous sand and mud flats. Carp are very active during this period, and only the occasional release of water from Chatfield Reservoir above can spoil the fishing with high water. I look for flow rates somewhere between 100 cfs and 160 cfs for the best fishing conditions.

Fly selection and presentation are an ever-changing game, and you must be prepared to switch flies constantly but also present the fly multiple times. One of the most prevalent food sources on the Platte is crayfish, and my most successful carp flies are those that mimic crayfish—espeically in the summer. My two favorite go-to patterns include the Clouser Swimming Nymph and the Barry's Carp Fly. Both imitate small crayfish well, and carp usually respond to them. During the cooler months, I usually switch to small nymphs. But carp are omnivores and can be selective at times, feeding on a wide variety of things such as aquatic nymphs, leeches, aquatic worms, snails, and clams as well as aquatic and terrestrial vegetation including weeds, cottonwood seeds, and grass.

Maybe even more important than fly selection, your presentation will likely determine your success. When presenting carp with a fly I like to cast past the carp and then strip the fly back to intercept the carp as it lazily roots along the bottom. Never cast directly on top of the carp unless it's your only option or all other options have failed. Your retrieve should be slow and steady so as to not spook them. Once I locate feeding fish, I cast beyond the lead fish, strip the fly back to the fish's feeding lane, and then allow the fly to sink to the bottom. Many times the carp will move to the fly as it sees it falling, but if the carp does not react, then try a small, 1-inch strip and pause again. Remember, your first cast and presentation will be your best chance for a hookup.

My tackle for carp includes a 6-weight rod with a floating weight-for-ward fly line and a 9-foot, 8-pound fluorocarbon leader. A fluorocarbon leader is a bit tougher and stands up better to the nicks and abrasions you're likely to encounter while fishing the urban waterways. Many anglers use heavier gear—rods up to 8-weight—but I have a good 6-weight, which is all the rod I have needed to take many carp over 35 pounds.

Stillwater Carp

Brad Befus

Carp share similar feeding characteristics with redfish and bonefish, making them easy to find in shallow water where you can sight-fish to them. Choosing a specific fish to cast to will provide the best results, but it can be challenging to choose the right fish and present the correct fly at the proper position in the water column. Watch the fish closely and determine if it is feeding. Tailing or nose-down rooting on the bottom, cruising slowly in shallow water or open water, sipping off the surface, and chasing prey are all signs of feeding carp.

Being opportunistic feeders, carp will eat about anything, and many standard trout patterns will work fine. They feed on all the same aquatic invertebrates, crustaceans, mollusks, leeches, and baitfish that trout, panfish, and bass feed on, as well as terrestrial insects when available. Aquatic vegetation, terrestrial vegetation, seeds, and berries should not be overlooked. Good general-purpose patterns that imitate a variety of aquatic life forms include Befus' Swimming Carp nymphs (#8-12), Barry's Carp Fly (#8-12), Egan's Headstand (#10-12), Befus' Wiggle Bug (#6-14), and Zimmerman's Backstabber Carp Fly (#4-6). Every carp addict's fly box should include crayfish, leeches, and baitfish imitations. Subdued, earthy colors and patterns with natural movement seem to be preferred. Use unweighted flies that exhibit neutral buoyancy to fish carp that are suspended at a specific depth. This allows for the fly to remain at the fish's depth and in its sight window for a longer period of time while being retrieved.

Dry flies should consist of mayflies, midges, plant seeds, berry imitations, and even floating vegetation. Matching the hatch when fishing for carp includes food items you may not have thought of before! All carp patterns should be dressed on stout heavy wire hooks, especially dry flies. Even modest-sized carp will work over fine wire hooks.

SOUTH PLATTE RIVER

	JAN	FEB	MAR	APR	MAY	JUN	JUL	AUG	SEP	OCT	NOV	DEC

Midge (*Chironomidae*)
#16-24 Purple Thing, Rojo Midge, Mercury Black Beauty, Jujubee Midge, Top Secret Midge, Griffith's Gnat, Brooks' Sprout Midge

Blue-Winged Olive (*Baetis* spp.)
#18-22 Flashback Pheasant Tail, CDC Loop Wing Emerger, Johnny Flash, Flashback Barr Emerger, Mercury RS2, Parachute Adams, Vis-A-Dun

Caddis
(*Brachycentrus* and *Hydropsyche* spp.)
#16-20 Barr's Net Builder, Buckskin, Pettis' Pulsating Caddis, Peacock Caddis, black Puterbaugh's Foam Caddis

Pale Morning Dun
(*Ephemerella* spp.)
#16-20 Flashback Barr Emerger, Burke's Hunchback Two-Tone, Sloan's Mighty May, Dorsey's Mercury PMD, Peterson's Bat Wing Emerger, Sparkle Dun, Vis-A-Dun

Golden Stonefly (*Perlidae*)
#8-14 Hotwire Prince Nymph, 20 Incher, Tungstone, Pat's Rubber Legs, Stimulator

Little Yellow Sally (*Isoperla* sp.)
#14-18 yellow Copper John, Mercer's Poxyback Little Yellow Stone, Tungsten Prince, Befus's Slow Water Sally, yellow Puterbaugh's Foam Stone, Stimulator

Trico (*Tricorythodes* sp.)
#18-24 black RS2, Barr's Drowned Trico, A. K.'s Quill Body Trico Dun, Trico Spinner

Red Quill (*Rhithrogena* sp.)
#14-18 Copper John, Pheasant Tail, A. K.'s Red Quill, Parachute Adams

Terrestrials
#8-12 Charlie Boy Hopper, Stimulator, Kingfisher's Red Legged Hopper, Amy's Ant, black Foam Beetle, BC Hopper

Streamers
#6-10 Lawson's Conehead Sculpin, Slumpbuster, ginger Meat Whistle, Circus Peanut, Brokeback Leech

Sow Bugs, Scuds, Worms, Crane Flies, and Eggs
#12-16 Pat's UV Scud, McLean's Hunchback Scud, Flashback Scud, Dubbed Body Sowbug, Micro Worm, red San Juan Worm, Barr's Cranefly Larva, Otter's Egg, Nuke Egg

Nine- to twelve-foot, 1X to 4X leaders with fluorocarbon tippet and a floating line will cover most situations. A clear intermediate fly line works well when there is wind or for fish that are hyper-sensitive to the shadow of the fly line. Silicone fly floatant can be applied to the line to help it float if necessary. Rod size will be determined by the size of the fish and the size of the lake or pond. Five- to eight-weight rods are the norm. Reels should have a good drag and be able to hold at least 100 yards of backing. Generally, most trout anglers already have the equipment to become a carp chaser.

Each stillwater carp fishery will have its own character and challenges. If you approach these fish cautiously, make accurate casts to present the fly into the fish's sight window, and fish the fly to mimic the food item that is being imitated, the carp will do the rest. Just hold on and enjoy the ride.

Amy's Ant

Hook:	#6-12 Tiemco 5262 or 5263
Thread:	Tan or brown 6/0 Uni-Thread
Body:	Brown over tan Fly Foam (2 mm)
Legs:	Brown rubber (medium)
Hackle:	Brown rooster neck or saddle, trimmed
Body:	Olive Krystal Chenille
Underwing:	Rainbow Krystal Flash
Overwing:	Cow or yearling elk hair
Thorax:	Bronze Arizona Synthetic Peacock Dubbing

Red Tube Midge

Hook:	#18-22 TMC 2488H
Thread:	Black 8/0 Uni-Thread
Body:	Red UTC wire (small) and Hareline Clear Micro Tubing
Tuft:	Hareline Egg Veil

Top Secret Midge

Hook:	#18-24 Tiemco 2488
Body:	Brown 8/0 Uni-Thread
Wing:	White Fluoro Fibre
Rib:	White 6/0 Flymaster Plus (do not reverse rib)
Thorax:	Rust brown Fine and Dry dubbing

Barr Crane Fly Larva

Hook:	#6-8 Tiemco 200R
Weight:	.020-inch-diameter lead wire
Thread:	Olive 70-denier Ultra Thread
Tail:	Pale olive gray marabou
Rib:	3X tippet
Shellback:	Olive Flyspecks Thin Skin
Body:	Gray-olive or tan Arizona Synthetic Dubbing

COLORADO'S
BEST FLY FISHING

NORTHWESTERN

During the summer, Colorado's rivers have hatches of numerous insects. When presenting multiple adults on the surface to selective trout, think small or in numbers. Trout feed on several insects at once, rather than selecting a single adult, when a film of food is on the surface.
LANDON MAYER

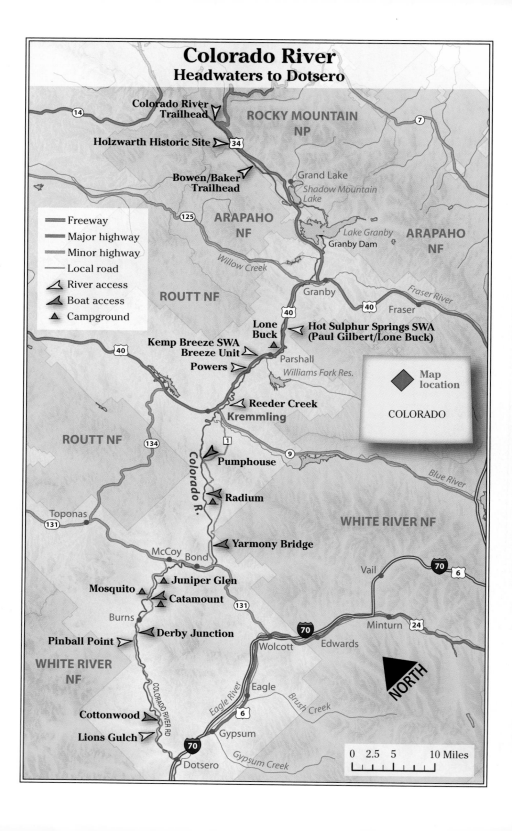

Colorado River
Headwaters to Dotsero

Colorado River Trailhead

ROCKY MOUNTAIN NP

14

7

Holzwarth Historic Site

34

Bowen/Baker Trailhead

Grand Lake

Shadow Mountain Lake

125

ARAPAHO NF

Lake Granby

ARAPAHO NF

Granby Dam

Willow Creek

ROUTT NF

Granby

Fraser River

40

40

Fraser

Legend
- ══════ Freeway
- ══════ Major highway
- ══════ Minor highway
- ──── Local road
- River access
- Boat access
- Campground

Lone Buck

Hot Sulphur Springs SWA (Paul Gilbert/Lone Buck)

Kemp Breeze SWA Breeze Unit

Powers

40

Parshall

Williams Fork Res.

Map location

COLORADO

Reeder Creek

Kremmling

ROUTT NF

134

1

9

Pumphouse

Blue River

Radium

Toponas

131

WHITE RIVER NF

Colorado R.

Yarmony Bridge

McCoy

Bond

Vail

70

6

Juniper Glen

Mosquito

Catamount

131

Burns

70

Minturn

24

Derby Junction

Pinball Point

Wolcott

Edwards

WHITE RIVER NF

COLORADO RIVER RD

Eagle River

Eagle

Brush Creek

NORTH

Cottonwood

Lions Gulch

6

Gypsum

70

Dotsero

Gypsum Creek

0   2.5   5   10 Miles

CHAPTER 11

Colorado River

The Colorado River flows over 1,400 miles from its origins in Rocky Mountain National Park through Utah and Arizona before ending at the Gulf of California in Mexico. While this river's water is heavily diverted for human use, it still offers excellent opportunities for trout for over 160 miles in Colorado as well as in Lee's Ferry, Arizona. From attractor fishing for brookies in small, alpine meadow headwaters to deep nymphing for broad-shouldered brown trout in the powerful flows near Glenwood Springs, the Colorado River offers something for every fly fisher.

As the Colorado cuts through the state, it grows with multiple key tributaries such as the Blue, Eagle, and Roaring Fork. These tributaries supply the Colorado River with cool water, creating prime locations for large trout. In return, these tributaries receive runs of fish that grow large in the main river. For this reason, targeting tributary inlets in the spring, summer, and fall can produce some of the biggest trout in the state.

One of the benefits of this enormous piece of water is that you can find solitude. I remember floating the Colorado in early fall with guides Bob Dye and Pat Dorsey and taking numerous 'bows and browns all day on small midge patterns with few other anglers in sight. If you ever need a pick-me-up from the crowds that are on many waters in the height of summer, and want stunning scenery with willing fish, float the Colorado River in the fall.

RMNP to Kremmling

The Colorado starts humbly as a high mountain creek, descending south parallel to the highway into a flat, grassy landscape where it is surrounded by tall pines and brush that run along the river's edge for approximately 10 miles through Rocky Mountain National Park. This section of the Colorado River has a healthy supply of brook trout and browns eager to take a fly in an intimate setting that provides a great escape for anglers from the hustle

Bob Dye releases a reel-screaming rainbow that he caught on a Strawberry Jam Midge, a pattern of his own design. Fish this size are not uncommon on the Colorado. LANDON MAYER

The headwaters of the Colorado River during runoff. This spot is on the west side of RMNP, accessible via the Colorado River Trail on the west side of US 34. In addition to the headwaters of the Colorado, anglers should also explore the headwaters of the Cache la Poudre and Big Thompson in the park. LANDON MAYER

and bustle of the regular world—or even from some of the more pressured waters in the state.

The headwaters can be accessed through RMNP (see directions in the RMNP chapter) or more directly by taking I-70 to US 40 West toward Granby. At Granby, US 34 East heads into the western side of RMNP, but in the winter, there is no access through the park from Estes Park, as US 34, or Trail Ridge Road, is not maintained in the winter.

Moving downstream along US 34, you can reach the first fishing access point in the park by taking the Colorado River Trail. The well-marked trailhead has parking and facilities but no camping. The trail runs north along the Colorado and provides sporadic access to the river. As the water levels drop from runoff, you can expect some insect activity from caddis and PMDs or BWOs, but with the cold waters you will do better using attractors and terrestrials, especially ants.

Approximately 2 miles down on US 34, still in RMNP, there is a picnic area before Timber Creek that also provides access (as does the Holzwarth Historic Site, another 1/2 mile down US 34). The Holzwarth access is where the hiking trail intersects the water. From here, the last good access in RMNP is another 2 miles down US 34 at the Bowen-Baker Trailhead, which also has a picnic area with facilities.

The upper Colorado River has some of the best float fishing in the state. During the fall when the water is low the trout will concentrate in deep runs. ROSS PURNELL

At this point, the Colorado leaves RMNP and flows through Shadow Mountain Lake and Lake Granby, with a mile of tailwater to access in between these two lakes from Green Ridge Campground below Shadow Mountain Dam. Fishing is closed from Shadow Mountain Dam down to Twin Creeks October 1 until December 31; on January 1, fishing is allowed for 500 yards from the dam downstream until March 15 when fishing restrictions end. Water here can fluctuate from 40 to 2000 cfs, so make sure to time your trip for dropping or low flows.

While it may be tempting to try to access the area below Granby Dam via CO 627, a landowner has put up a "No Trespassing" sign on the road and is blocking access to the tailout below the dam. Private property dominates the Colorado from here to Granby.

The water remains 15 to 30 feet across with the addition of the Fraser River at Granby. Flowing through ranch land, the river meets numerous tributaries and continues to pick up speed. Continuing through Granby and along US 40 to Kremmling, the Colorado runs parallel to the highway. While there is no fishing in the Windy Gap Reservoir, CDOW has designated the sections from Fraser River to Troublesome Creek as Gold Medal water with catch-and-release regulations to Troublesome Creek.

The first access along this stretch is on both sides of the river from from Hot Sulphur Springs State Wildlife Area, which includes Paul Gilbert Day Use Area and Lone Buck Campground, approximately 4 miles downstream from Windy Gap Reservoir, with parking well-marked. Be careful, though, as the 50-foot hike down to Byers Canyon is extremely steep with loose rocks. If you choose to spend the night, Lone Buck Campground is located on the western edge of this access area with primitive camping in designated areas only.

Approximately 2 miles downstream from Lone Buck is access from CO 3 (see the Williams Fork chapter), with three more parking areas located before Sunset Bridge, a mile past Parshall in the Kemp/Breeze SWA's Breeze Unit. There is handicap access in the second lot. The Colorado in Middle Park is still good wade-fishing, as it parallels US 40 and receives the confluence of the Williams Fork. Fishing is public here on both sides of the river. From this point it is around 6 miles to Kremmling, with the Powers access providing a small stretch on the north side that fishes well during high flows, although it

The Colorado above the confluence of the Williams Fork River near Parshall. This is one of the Colorado River's best wade access areas after runoff. LANDON MAYER

is nestled in between private property signs that need to be obeyed. Regulations from Troublesome Creek to Rifle change to a bag-and-possession limit of two trout, with the exceptions listed in the Dotsero to Rifle section below. Pat Dorsey warns anglers that mosquitoes can be bad in this area through the third week of August: "Wear long-sleeved shirts and Buffs, and bring plenty of repellent!" he says.

After Kremmling, as you turn onto CO 9 to continue your journey along the Colorado, you can take a left onto CR 33 and double back a little over 4 miles to hit Reeder Creek. This offers half a mile on both side of the river. The public water here is full of large riffles, heavy seams, deep soft pools, and foamy side channels. With the largest insect population on any section of the Colorado River, it is a must for the serious dry-fly angler. In this section, stoneflies begin their migration toward the banks, where the nymphs break out of their shells on the river's edge, in May. When the ungodly-big, orange-bellied bugs take flight, you would swear you are looking at an insect that has flown in from the movie *Jurassic Park*.

Bob Dye rerigs to fish a deep seam. It is true that the difference between a good angler and a great angler is one split shot. Taking the time to adjust your depth gives you control of your flies as they drift. LANDON MAYER

Starting in late May in Little Gore Canyon (just upstream of Radium), the stoneflies work upriver to Hot Sulphur Springs by late June. The clearer the water, the better the fishing. "The Salmonfly in this stretch is one of the most overlooked hatches in Colorado," says local guide Bob Dye. "Since the bugs hatch during peak runoff, the water levels can be challenging because the visibility is gone and the trout have to concentrate on battling the current, not feeding in it. This is why you do not see a lot of anglers pursuing these big bugs. When you do hit it right, it can seem endless with action." When the nymphs are on the move, the trick to angling success is to bounce the bottom by concentrating your depth on the bottom of the river. "I probably change weight and depth more than most," Dye says, "and am not afraid to consistently move. As a guide on crowded waters, you learn to fish the non-obvious."

Kremmling to Dotsero

As US 40 turns away from the Colorado River near Kremmling, take CO 1 (Trough Road and Pumphouse Road) from CO 9 south out of Kremmling. This road will follow the river from Kremmling to State Bridge, but it will not follow the whole length of the river and travels a fair distance away from it at times. Gore Canyon, a couple of miles west of Kremmling, can fish well, but is often difficult to access for a 4- to 5-mile stretch where expert rafters and kayakers attempt the Class V run in the canyon.

After Kremmling, the Blue River adds cool water to the Colorado as it races through Gore Canyon. Because of this increase in flow, these sections are best fished in the lower water of spring and fall, which coincides with the migration of rainbows, cuttbows, and brown trout. At the bottom of the canyon, the river heads south to Dotsero and fishes well both from boat and by foot. This is one of the most remote locations on the Colorado, with sagebrush scattered in the distant landscape and cottonwood trees along the river's edge.

For a half-day float, Pumphouse to Radium is a nice 4-mile stretch with south-side wading access between the Cottonwood camping site and the Radium Recreation Site. If you wish to wade at Pumphouse, take the trail on the south side of the river that leads up from the parking lot and runs along the river for a little over a mile. If you wish to wade below Pumphouse, there is access for a quarter mile below the parking lot with no trail. For a full-day float take out at Yarmony Bridge; this will supply you with over 6 miles of floatable water. You can also float from Yarmony Bridge to State Bridge.

To get to Pumphouse, take CO 9 South and CO 1 West (Trough Road) to gain access below the confluence of the Blue, which begins the lower section. This road ends at CO 131 with fee access at State Bridge.

When floating, Dye likes to use flies that differ from the norm, such as the leech, which is a prominent but overlooked food item (at least by anglers). "I use a pine squirrel leech with a midge (#18-22 Flashback Black Beauty) or a *Baetis* dropper (#18-24 olive or gray RS2, #18-22 Flashback RS2, #18-20 Befus'

Bad Boy Baetis, or #18-22 Barr Flashback BWO Emerger.)" Hit the banks and edges of structure, and use tungsten cones to get your leech down in deeper water. There is a healthy supply of caddis and mayflies in this section of the Colorado River and a Stimulator with a #14-16 Breadcrust Nymph or #14-18 Buckskin trailing off the bend is deadly.

From Yarmony Bridge to State Bridge (at the intersection of CR 1 and CO 131), you will encounter 1 1/2 miles of river suitable for wading in low flows. You can continue down CO 1, or you can access State Bridge upstream by traveling 15 miles north from I-70 at the Wolcott exit off of CO 131. "State Bridge to Catamount (14 miles) is another one of my favorite stretches, and I spend most of my time in the spring and fall here," says Dye. "It has braids, riffles, and deep runs—classic Western river water. Some of the bigger browns live here too. On a recent shocking of the river, some fish in the 10- and 12-pound range were noted. Typical nymph rigs under an indicator are best, but on the right day tandem streamer rigs can be deadly, like a #6-12 natural

The Colorado River near Pumphouse. Don't let the crowds of summer keep you away all year—the low flows of fall offer great concentrations of trout in deep pools. LANDON MAYER

In the low water of late fall, Bob Dye nymphs deep holding water downstream from Pumphouse. LANDON MAYER

Barr's Slumpbuster with a slim body since there are a lot of dace minnows in this part of the river."

If you take CO 131 north past McCoy, you can continue to follow the Colorado River by taking a left onto Colorado River Road. Good floats along this area include Yarmony Bridge to Catamount, Catamount to Derby Junction, Derby Junction to Cottonwood, and Cottonwood to Dotsero. All access areas are clearly marked.

Yarmony Bridge to Dotsero is long for a full-day float, so camping is recommended at Windy Gap, Double Pine, Sagebrush, Cottonwood, Juniper Glen, Mosquito, and Lyons Gulch. All sites are primitive with no facilities. You can also access this location by road for numerous wading opportunities. Take CO 131 to CR 301 seven miles to many wading access points. Be aware, however, that it is technically illegal to cross the railroad tracks that sit between the road and the access points.

Continuing to Dotsero along CO 301, you will encounter numerous take-outs. While Derby Junction has a takeout that charges a small fee, Pinball Point, a mile past Derby Junction, has a primitive ramp. Cottonwood Island, another 4 miles downstream, offers the next takeout, with Lions Gulch another mile down, and then you reach Dotsero where the Eagle River joins the Colorado.

Dotsero to Rifle

West of Dotsero the river plunges between the steep walls of Glenwood Canyon. Floating is a great way to navigate this section, but wading anglers can also do well at pull-offs like No Name Rest Area and Grizzly Creek with big

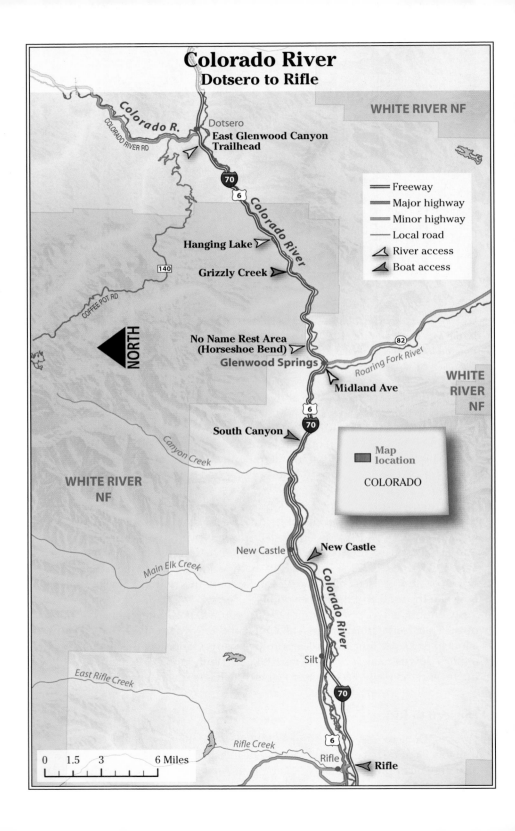

Colorado River
Dotsero to Rifle

WHITE RIVER NF

Colorado R.

COLORADO RIVER RD

Dotsero

**East Glenwood Canyon
Trailhead**

70

6

Colorado River

Hanging Lake

Grizzly Creek

140

COFFEE POT RD

NORTH

**No Name Rest Area
(Horseshoe Bend)**

Glenwood Springs

82

Roaring Fork River

Midland Ave

WHITE
RIVER
NF

6

70

South Canyon

Canyon Creek

WHITE RIVER
NF

	Freeway
	Major highway
	Minor highway
	Local road
	River access
	Boat access

Map
location

COLORADO

New Castle

New Castle

Main Elk Creek

Colorado River

Silt

70

East Rifle Creek

0   1.5   3   6 Miles

Rifle Creek

6

Rifle

Rifle

During spring and fall lots of trout congregate in the deep runs below shallow water and eggs work extremely well. My favorite egg patterns for all rivers in the state are #18-20 Flashtail Mini Egg, #18-22 Nuke Egg, and #18-20 Otter's Egg. LANDON MAYER

stonefly imitations (try a #16-12 black Pat's Rubber Legs). Below the Roaring Fork confluence, the water cuts through a vast valley before crossing state lines.

In this section of the river, you have a chance at a real trophy—a trout over 8 pounds is not out of the question. One of the reasons this water is so productive is that the Eagle and Roaring Fork rivers help reduce the silt that can form above Dotsero. Veteran guide Kyle Holt also says that the tributaries also help in other ways: "The Roaring Fork supplies cool temperatures and increased volume to the lower Colorado (Glenwood Springs to Rifle). The insect hatches are much more prolific. The diverse size of the fish is also amazing; you see tiny ones all over and every age class up the ladder. Who knows what lurks in this water? We all have stories of hooking violent creatures we never saw. I have seen browns over 30 inches in this section. A brown was caught in the late '80s that weighed 16$1/2$ pounds." Holt continues, "The Colorado fishes the best every time there is a biological change in the river, usually due to a change in season."

Big attractor dry flies and Prince Nymphs and Copper Johns tied with tungsten beads are effective during the summer. With browns on the prowl, you can also do well skating a Morrish Mouse through the glare on the water's surface at dusk. With any of these imitations, concentrate on the river's edge in deep pockets, structure, or descending gravel bars. The middle of the river is often too swift for trout to hold.

The first access from I-70/CO 6 is at the east Glenwood Canyon trailhead 2 miles past Dotsero, which provides parking, and, with the exception of the private property at the No Name exit, most of the river access until the town of Glenwood Springs (approximately 2 miles). Additional access to the trail can be reached through Hanging Lake. All of these points are very well-marked exits. Bob Dye says that one of the most overlooked section of the Colorado River is the lower stretch from Dotsero to New Castle. "Because the

COLORADO RIVER

	JAN	FEB	MAR	APR	MAY	JUN	JUL	AUG	SEP	OCT	NOV	DEC

Midge (*Chironomidae*)
#18-24 Black Beauty, Rojo Midge, Griffith's Gnat, Jujubee Midge, Brooks' Sprout Midge

Blue-Winged Olive (*Baetis* spp.)
#16-22 Mercury Flashback Pheasant Tail, Copper John, Flashback Barr's Emerger, RS2, Jujubaetis, Bad Boy Baetis, Sparkle Dun, Vis-A-Dun

Caddis
(*Brachycentrus* and *Hydropsyche* spp.)
#16-20 Larry's Larva, Graphic Caddis, Buckskin, Beadhead Breadcrust, black Puterbaugh's Caddis, Hill's Devil Bug, Peacock Caddis

Salmonfly (*Pteronarcys californica*)
#4-8 Pat's Rubber Legs, 20 Incher, Barr's Tung Teaser, Befus' Wired Stone, Bitch Creek Nymph, Puterbaugh's Salmonfly, Rogue Foam Stone

Golden Stonefly (*Perlidae*)
#6-12 Barr's Tungstone, Pat's Rubber Legs, Hare's Ear, Crystal Stimulator, Amy's Ant, Madam X

Yellow Sally (*Isoperla* sp.)
#14-16 yellow Copper John, Mercer's Poxyback Little Yellow Stone, Tungsten Prince Nymph, Stimulator

Pale Morning Dun
(*Ephemerella* spp.)
#16-20 Barr's Emerger, Dorsey's Mercury PMD, Pheasant Tail, Vis-A-Dun, Sparkle Dun, Cannon's Snowshoe Dun

Trico (*Tricorythodes* sp.)
#18-26 black RS2, Barr's Drowned Trico, A. K.'s Quill Body Trico Dun, Trico Spinner

Red Quill (*Rhithrogena* sp.)
#14-18 Copper John, Pheasant Tail, A. K.'s Red Quill, Parachute Adams

Blue Quill (*Paraleptophlebia* sp.)
#14-18 Copper John, Pheasant Tail, Parachute Adams, Sparkle Dun

Terrestrials
#8-16 Thingamahopper, Charlie Boy Hopper, BC Hopper, Black Ant, Foam Beetle, Baby Boy Cricket

Sow Bugs, Scuds, Worms
#14-20 orange Pat's UV Scud, McLean's Hunchback Scud, Flashback Scud, Dubbed Body Sowbug, Micro Worm, Flashtail Mini Egg, Otter's Egg

Streamers
#6-10 Egg Sucking Leech, Autumn Splendor, Slumpbuster, Circus Peanut, Lawson's Conehead Sculpin, Sex Dungeon

lower river is big water, I use heavy flies and long leaders (up to 15 feet long) to reach the river bottom where a lot of the trout will hold."

Two miles downriver from Hanging Lake is the Shoshone Power Plant, so making a drift to Grizzly Creek not recommended—wading is the best option. Grizzly Creek is at exit 121; parking is on the north side of the interstate with Grizzly Creek Trail running along the river in Glenwood Canyon, a beautiful and productive 10-mile stretch of river that is easily accessed and provides great bank fishing. The mouths of No Name and Grizzly Creeks are off-limits to fishing from March 15 to May 15 and October 1 to November 30 for 50 feet on each side of the river mouth to protect spawning trout.

Bob Dye spots a pod of feeding trout for Pat Dorsey. Using the buddy system always helps, especially from a high vantage point. LANDON MAYER

Once you reach Glenwood Springs, there is public access on the south side downstream from the confluence of the Roaring Fork and along Midland Avenue. You can reach this by taking CO 82 South and going right on 7th Street. Midland Avenue is on the right. Two Rivers boat launch is across from here.

The Colorado travels 8 miles to New Castle from Glenwood Springs, then another 8 miles to Rifle with a stretch of north-bank wading access for 2 miles at the South Canyon boat launch just past West Glenwood. New Castle also has Tibbett's pullout located off exit 105, where you can make a U-turn and head upstream for 2 miles to a large dirt pullout. Rifle also has access for a mile with parking at the tourist center.

In the fall, once the water levels on the river are running low again, brown trout start to migrate up the Roaring Fork, Eagle, and Colorado to spawn. Eggs, streamers, midges, and *Baetis* imitations can attract numerous strikes on low-water fall days. Holt explains that streamer fishing is your best shot at a trophy: "Not only getting the bite, but being prepared with the right gear to actually catch it. Six- or seven-weight setups with sink-tip lines or heavy tungsten conehead streamers will get the flies to the trout's depth. Finding where they are in the water column and delivering the fly or flies to that zone is the ticket."

The White River

Flowing out of the Flat Tops Wilderness area, the White River is perhaps one of the most overlooked and underrated rivers in the state. Because it is off the beaten path, it has healthy populations of larger trout.

There is public access along the forks as well as the main stem downstream to Meeker. Special regulations for most of the river (including North and South Forks) are a bag and possession limit of two fish from headwaters to the CO 13 bridge in Meeker with the exception of the Nelson-Prather, Wakara, and Sleepy Cat easements, where it is catch-and-release, artificials only.

To reach the North Fork, take I-70 to Rifle and then CO 13 north through Meeker to CR 8 (Trapper's Lake Road). The North Fork begins below the lake with the confluence of the South Fork at Buford. Access along the North Fork starts at the Flat Tops Wilderness area just below the lake. Additional access is at White River National Forest, Snell Creek, Lost Creek, and the Rio Blanco County Campground. This winding section of water has a good supply of cut banks that give the trout, including high numbers of cutthroats, areas to hide and feed without the stress of predators.

The South Fork access starts at the South Fork Campground, with another downstream at the Oak Ridge SWA Bel Aire access off of CR 17. This area is a bit of a bushwhack, but a trail runs along the river. This stretch of water also has lots of cutthroats in the 12- to 14-inch range.

After Buford, the first access is Lake Avery with the fish getting larger as you get closer to Meeker. Sleepy Cat is next and less than a mile from Lake Avery. You may fish downstream for almost 2 miles, with another access point around the ponds for another mile. This is an easement on private property, so respect the land and landowners.

Wakara access is next. It's a very small stretch with the Nelson-Prather Trout Unlimited Access an additional 3 miles down. The Nelson-Prather TU access runs down to the green cabins on the left. Fish only on the side of the river closest to the road. Do not cross the bridge or fish from the bridge.

Perhaps one of the most productive places for large trout lies in the Meeker City Park, where the river is open to the public from the Circle Park bridge, at 4th and Water streets, downstream to the 10th Street Bridge. The fish here are known to exceed 20 inches, so you will truly have a good chance to battle large trout on a daily basis.

Beadhead Breadcrust

Hook:	#12-18 Tiemco 5262
Bead:	1/8- or 3/32-inch brass
Thread:	Brown Uni-Thread
Abdomen:	Red phase ruffed grouse quill over yarn underbody
Collar:	Grizzly hen

Garcia's Rojo Midge (Purple)

Hook:	#18-22 Tiemco 200R
Bead:	Red silver-lined (extra small)
Gills:	Ultra Floss
Thread:	Purple 70-denier UTC
Rib:	Fine blue Lagartun
Collar:	Peacock herl dyed bright green

Mercury RS2

Hook:	#18-24 Tiemco 101
Thread:	Gray 8/0 Uni-Thread
Tail:	Gray hackle fibers
Abdomen:	Adams gray Superfine
Wing:	White Z-lon
Thorax:	Adams gray Superfine
Bead:	Silver-lined glass (extra small)

Bad Boy Baetis

Hook:	#20 Tiemco 3761 or 2488
Thread:	Beige and olive 6/0 Danville
Tail:	Mottled partridge fibers
Abdomen:	Beige 6/0 thread
Thorax:	Olive squirrel/Antron Dubbing
Rib:	Olive 6/0 thread
Wing case:	Medallion Sheeting
Legs:	Mottled partridge fibers

Flashback Barr Emerger (PMD)

Hook:	#16-22 Tiemco 2487
Thread:	Light cahill 8/0 Uni-Thread
Abdomen:	Blended olive and brown dubbing
Thorax:	PMD Superfine dubbing
Tail:	Brown spade hackle fibers
Wing case:	Pale olive or cream hackle
Flash:	Mirage Tinsel (medium)
Note:	For the BWO, substitute iron-gray thread, blue dun hackle fibers for the wing case, and Adams gray Superfine dubbing.

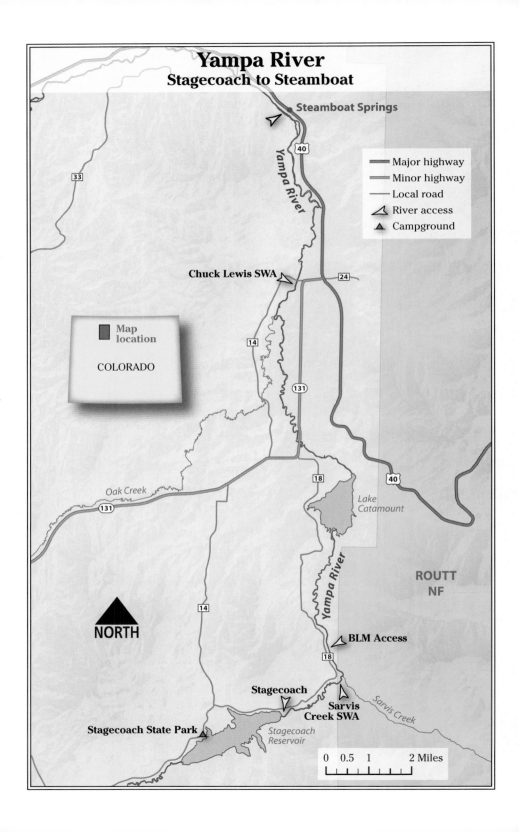

Yampa River
Stagecoach to Steamboat

Steamboat Springs

40

Yampa River

33

| Major highway |
| Minor highway |
| Local road |
| River access |
| Campground |

Chuck Lewis SWA

24

14

Map
location

COLORADO

131

18

40

Oak Creek

131

Lake
Catamount

14

NORTH

Yampa River

ROUTT
NF

BLM Access

18

Stagecoach

Sarvis
Creek SWA

Sarvis Creek

Stagecoach State Park

Stagecoach
Reservoir

0   0.5   1   2 Miles

Yampa River

N amed after the Yampatika Ute Indians that used to inhabit the area, the Yampa is the second-largest river in the state, rising in the Flat Tops Wilderness on the northwestern side of the state and flowing 250 miles before it meets the Green River. The rainbows in this fishery were decimated in the mid-2000s by whirling disease, and a hybrid Hofer strain was introduced. With no competition, this whirling-disease-resistant strain has reproduced wonderfully in the wild. When you hook into one of the Yampa's wild rainbows, you're reminded of how strong wild trout are during the fight. There is nothing like the adrenaline rush you feel with a fish on the end of your line that is head shaking so hard it will pull your arm straight down with every movement, or the humbling feeling of staring at a hook that once looked destructive only to be straightened out from this power of the fish. "The Yampa River is the best wild-trout river in the state," says John Barr. "I would even say it is in the top 10 for productive fisheries in the nation." One of my other favorite features of the Yampa River is the potential for large trout, courtesy of the good food supply and the many miles of water that allow fish to adjust and find feeding locations when flows fluctuate.

The only catch is that it is remote—the Yampa is four hours from the two main cities of Denver and Colorado Springs. But that generally means crowds are light, and even the fishing in town is good. (Steamboat supplies some of the best fishing on the river, located just off Main Street.) It is also a great four-season destination and one of my personal favorite mountain towns, with skiing, snowshoeing, fishing, and good hospitality always available. Most of the trout are found from the headwaters above Stagecoach Reservoir downstream to Hayden.

Kirk Deeter, coauthor of *The Little Red Book of Fly Fishing*, shares his views on this river: "The Yampa is one of the most technically alluring rivers in the state because its character changes dramatically, from a classic tailwater below Stagecoach Reservoir, to a warmwater pike fishery well downstream of Steamboat Springs. So anglers can try all techniques and flies, from tiny midge emergers to gaudy streamers, depending on where they go. It's also an all-season fishery . . . I think it's the best autumn trout river in Colorado."

John Barr holds a great Yampa Brown that slammed a caddis just before dark. As we were walking to the water all you could hear was fish exploding on egg-laying caddis.
LANDON MAYER

The September skies on the Yampa River bathe the river in warm light. With the sun ready to set, these conditions are prime time for streamers and large browns. JAY NICHOLS

Upper Yampa

From the headwaters of the Yampa River, also known as Bear River, the water is narrow and shallow before reaching Stagecoach Reservoir, where it then flows through three bodies of water. This section of the Yampa River is not as familiar to many anglers as the lower, wider stretches of the waterway, but it has a lot of smaller fish (6 to 12 inches) that are willing to crush dry flies.

To reach Bear River and the Stillwater, Bear, and Yamcola Reservoirs, turn onto CO 131 before Steamboat and follow it to the town of Yampa. Turn right onto CR 7, and after about 6 miles you will enter the Routt National Forest. Access to the river and reservoirs is through obvious pullouts, as any parking lots are for trailheads not near the river. As you start below Stillwater Reservoir and head downstream, the Bear River is visible to your right, varying from 50 to 200 yards away from the road. This section is approximately 3 miles in length and has both slow, meandering meadow sections and steeper pocketwater.

Above Yamcola Reservoir and below Bear Reservoir is a small half-mile section of stream. The river is more easily accessed from either the inlet of

Ross Purnell, editor of **Fly Fisherman** *maga-zine, holds a nice rainbow from the public water downstream of Stagecoach Reservoir.*
LANDON MAYER

Yamcola or below the dam at Bear Reservoir, as the road is not near the river here. The river through this portion is steep, with pocketwater and small pools.

Farther downstream on CR 7 is Yamcola Reservoir. The fishing from the Forest Service boundary to the dam at Yamcola is characterized as pocketwater intermixed with beaver dams and logjams. There are approximately 4 1/2 miles of stream in this section. It is primarily a rainbow trout fishery, but browns, brook, and cutthroat trout are also present.

The three reservoirs, Yamcola, Bear, and Stillwater, are all fishable from float tubes or canoes. There are no boat ramps, so portable boats are the only means of floating. Not built for recreation, these reservoirs have no official parking. For anglers who are sick of the smell, noise, and turbulence caused by motorboats on many public stillwaters, these large bodies of water are a great escape.

Stagecoach State Park

There is no public access from the town of Yampa downstream until you reach Stagecoach State Park. From Steamboat Springs you reach Stagecoach by heading east on US 40 and then south on CO 131. Stay on CO 131 for approximately 6 miles and then turn left on CR 14. (There is a brown Stagecoach State Park sign at the turn.) After approximately 6 more miles on CR 14, you will reach Stagecoach Reservoir. To get below the reservoir and fish the tailwater portion, turn left into the first State Park entrance off CR 14. Another immediate left will get you onto a dirt road that parallels the lake's shoreline toward and below the dam. This road is closed yearly from January 1 through April 1. The river section is open year-round, and you can walk, bike, or snowshoe into the tailwater section when the access road is closed to vehicle traffic. The public access from the dam downstream is about .6 mile in length and is catch-and-release, with artificial flies and lures only.

Steve Henderson, owner of Henderson Fly Fishing, gives some good tips on timing a trip for productive fishing with less pressure: "Targeting the water during the best hatches, like the *Baetis* in spring and fall on cloudy days, when the trout have cover from weather and are not wary with the clouds above. Another one of my favorite times is winter or early spring, when you have to snowshoe or ski to the river. Because it is tough to reach, the trout during this time of year do not see pressure and will not shy away from the fly."

Once the headwaters flow into the pike- and trout-filled reservoir of Stagecoach, the river receives a makeover as it begins to tail below. The river directly below the dam takes on a classic tailwater look, with good width and depth accommodating the ideal coldwater temperatures most trout find refuge in year-round. There is about a half mile of fishable water on the inlet side of the reservoir. The reservoir itself offers good float tubing on the west side of the lake and in the shallow bays.

Sarvis Creek has great dry-fly action on the slick water edges. JAY NICHOLS

One of my favorite stretches of public water is located past the private water below Stagecoach Reservoir. While some think the parking lot below the dam is the length of the river the public road leads you to more open water. ROSS PURNELL

For those anglers with patience and dedication for other species, Stage-coach Reservoir can produce some very large pike in the few fingers and round bays on its edges. In May and June, the pike cruise the shoreline for 2-3 weeks while performing the rituals of their spawn. Additionally, the lesser-fished season for these large predators is late September and October. When in the area at these times, don't forget the 8-weight rod. The results can be large, scary, and rewarding.

Sarvis Creek State Wildlife Area and BLM section

Continue past the parking area at Stagecoach along a narrow dirt road for an additional 1½ miles until you reach the SWA. There is a parking area at a bridge crossing. Upstream from the bridge, there are almost three-quarters of a mile of public water and about 150 yards of access downstream of the bridge. There is a short private section approximately 300 yards long beginning on the downstream border of the SWA. After this private section, there is another public BLM section that is about half a mile in length. Brown BLM signs tell you when you are entering and leaving public lands along this section. These sections are fishable year-round, with vehicle access from the end of June until mid-November (depending on road conditions). Foot or snowshoe access is the alternative method when the road is closed. Special regulations call for artificial flies and lures only, with a possession and size limit of two fish until Walton Creek, where it becomes catch-and-release only until the James Brown Bridge in Steamboat Springs.

With Steamboat Springs becoming a popular destination for hitting the slopes within a small-town atmosphere, hitting the river in the winter season can be a great adventure. Below Stagecoach Reservoir the river will remain open year-round. In addition to snowshoes, you can travel by snowmobile to reach this open water. To snowshoe or cross-country ski in, there are two access points. CR 18 is maintained in the winter and you can use the Sarvis Creek SWA; a better and less-crowded alternative is to park at the first entrance to Stagecoach Reservoir off CR 14. To snowmobile in, it is better to hire a guide or go through an outfitter to avoid the restrictions for motorized vehicles, and gain access to private water as well.

While traveling through the open landscape before Steamboat Springs, the river again tails below Catamount Reservoir. The water entering this large body is mainly private, with some access from guide trips through some great shops located in town, like Steamboat Flyfisher on Trout Street. Below Catamount Reservoir, the river travels through many ranches, mostly private. This section of the river is also accessible through local shops and members of the Rocky Mountain Angling Club.

Chuck Lewis State Wildlife Area

The Chuck Lewis SWA is farther downstream, located just south of Steamboat Springs. Access is from US 40 east and then right onto CO 131. Stay on CO 131 for .4 mile and then turn right onto CR 14. There is a parking lot on the right before a bridge, with a total of 2 miles of water to fish in this SWA and a parking area located in the middle. There are two other parking areas, both accessed from CR 14 on the west side of the river. Extensive river restoration has been done in this SWA, spearheaded by a local fly-fishing club, the Yampa Valley Fly Fishers, and the Yampa Valley Stream Improvement Charitable Trust. There are small riffles with longer runs dominating this section of the Yampa. "The unique thing about the Yampa River is how much private land is accessible to anglers. Even if you have to pay a guide fee, there are other rivers throughout this state that allow no traffic at all. We are lucky to have good relationships with many landowners that own great sections of the river," Henderson explains.

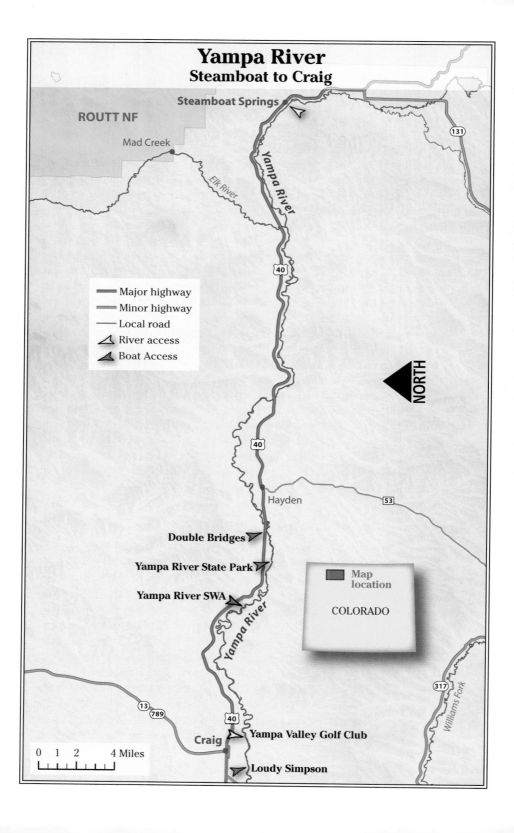

Yampa River
Steamboat to Craig

ROUTT NF

Mad Creek

Steamboat Springs

Elk River

Yampa River

40

Major highway
Minor highway
Local road
River access
Boat Access

NORTH

40

Hayden

53

Double Bridges

Yampa River State Park

Yampa River SWA

Yampa River

131

Map location

COLORADO

317

Williams Fork

13
789

40

Craig

Yampa Valley Golf Club

Loudy Simpson

0 1 2   4 Miles

The Yampa in town provides terrific fishing. There are almost 6 miles of water to explore through Steamboat Springs. JAY NICHOLS

Downtown Steamboat Springs

The town section of the Yampa River is an incredible urban trout fishery with multiple access points. From US 40, 5th Street runs along the river, and access can be found at the many bridges this town has to offer. It is designated as a catch-and-release fishery from the confluence of Walton Creek downstream to the bridge on Shield Drive (James Brown Bridge). There are almost 6 miles of water to explore through Steamboat Springs. Access to the river is also available from US 40 on the east side of the river or CR 14 (River Road) from the west side.

The Steamboat Springs Core Trail is a bike and pedestrian path that parallels most of the river along the publicly-accessible sections. Heading west on US 40 there are a few good parking areas: Rotary Park off Mt. Werner Road, Fletcher Park off Pine Grove Road, and Trafalgar Park off Pamela Lane. Parking spots in the downtown portion of Steamboat Springs are numerous but limited to 2-hour parking. A good way to experience the Yampa River

Some of the largest Trico hatches I have seen in the state occur below Steamboat from July through September. When the adults die, they often sink, and a Barr's Drowned Trico Spinner can be the ticket for success. LANDON MAYER

through town is by car, hopping from spot to spot and utilizing the core trail to move up- and downriver. From the James Brown bridge to the CO 394 Bridge near Craig regulations are artificial flies and lures only, with a possession limit of two fish.

Paul Russell, owner of Yampa River Outfitters, gives great advice for sight-fishing in town: "Use the elevation of the footpath and bridges for sighting trout in the water. This is a great way to prevent spooking trout by staying below the fish at a good distance, in addition to having an aerial view to determine what side of the river to approach the fish from and where to cast from."

West of Steamboat Springs

As you continue on US 40 past Steamboat, the Elk River flows into the Yampa, providing a push of cool water as well as another great fishing spot. A majority of the Elk remains private until you travel closer to the headwaters, approximately 30 miles upstream, where the river splits into three waterways. Continuing past Steamboat west on US 40, the Yampa can be accessed 2 miles west of Hayden at Double Bridges. Yampa River State Park and Yampa River SWA can be accessed another 2 and 4 miles, respectively, from the Bridges.

The Yampa can also be fished in the town of Craig. Craig lies west of Hayden along US 40, and fishing can be accessed at the Yampa Valley Golf Course and Loudy Simpson Park. Both the park and the golf course are located south of town. The golf course can be reached by turning south onto Ranney Street and going over the Yampa River bridge. Then turn left on CO 394, go half a mile, and turn left into the golf course entrance. Loudy Simpson is located another 2 miles down CO 394 on the right.

To float this section of the Yampa, the first access for boat put-ins is at Pumphouse, at mile marker 56, although many people prefer to put in at

Steve Hoffman landed this 8-pounder on a Morrish Mouse waked across the surface under moonlit skies. Hearing the toilet-flush rise was a heart-pumping event for all.
LANDON MAYER

Eric Pettine

The North Platte River is often overlooked by Colorado anglers, which is the reason it is hard to tempt me away from this fine fishery most summer days. I love fishing a river in solitude. If you do too, the place to be is on the Colorado portion of the North Platte—the Gold Medal section from the forest access at Windy Hole to the Colorado-Wyoming state line. You will catch wild fish, fish seldom or never caught before. It's more than likely the fish you land will never be caught again.

You will need to do some hiking, perhaps more than a little. If you don't have good legs, don't walk into the Northgate Canyon. Instead, drive into the forest access and fish the big pool at the boat launch. The next 7-mile stretch is public-access fishing, except for a quarter-mile of private water at the Ginger Quill Ranch. There's another access to the river at the Colorado state line, but you'll need a good map to figure out how to get in there.

Originally, there were no trout native to the North Platte drainage, but the fish in the river now were born and grew up in the river. They are truly wild fish. The population of rainbow and brown trout does not approach that of a tailwater fishery in numbers, but the fish are beautifully colored and feisty, as wild fish often are.

One of the best times to fish this section of river is during June, when the river is high with runoff flow and there's a fine stonefly hatch. You'll need to float the river to fish it. However—and this is important—do *not* attempt to float this section unless you are an experienced oarsman. There are some serious rapids in this area, including the Class V OFR, noted on the float maps. OFR is short for "Outrageous F——g Rapid." From the perspective of my personal (and painful) experience, I can tell you that there are at least five fly rods and reels somewhere in the deep pool below OFR.

Double Bridges, just past the town of Hayden. If you float this section, start early, because this is a long, slow float. A takeout at Loudy Simpson Park provides a 10-mile or so journey. Yampa River SWA, located 2 miles past the state park, can also be used as a put-in or takeout, with an additional boat ramp at Loudy Simpson in Craig. Keep in mind that Juniper Canyon (downstream from the park) is Class III and should only be attempted by very experienced boaters.

When fishing these sections, expect few numbers of fish, but they will be of respectable size—in the upper teens and lower 20s. Pike and some smallmouth bass can also be targeted, but currently in low numbers. Because the water widens and slows, there is not as much habitat for the trout to thrive in past the town of Craig.

Despite runoff in June, the elevation of over 8,000 feet slows the melt at night. The water clears a bit and then tends to color as the day goes on. The rest of the time, use streamers such as #8-12 Autumn Splendor and black Slumpbusters.

Nevertheless, the real star of the fishing show are the incredible Trico spinners that start falling in early August and continue well into September. The fly can be measured by the metric ton. There are times when you literally cannot see the willows on the opposite bank for the cloud of Tricos over the water. Fishing during the height of the spinnerfall is hopeless. The times to catch fish during the Trico season are at the very beginning and toward the end of the event.

Guides often don't bother to put their anglers on the hatch, because fishing the Trico spinnerfall is technically challenging. With patience and practice, however, you can master the technique. Remember that when the fish are holding high in the water column, their cone of vision above the water is very limited. With care, you can approach them for a short cast. For such a small reward, the fish do not move out of their feeding lane very far. Accurate casting is imperative, and a soft cast will be necessary to avoid spooking the fish. Practice short, accurate casting at home on the lawn. At my home shop, St. Peter's Fly Shop in Fort Collins, I often see rod shoppers trying to cast a whole line when trying out a trout rod. The issue should be whether the rod will cast 30 feet of line accurately and set the line down softly. Think about it: How often do you cast 90 feet of line to fish for trout in a river? Once you have a good trout rod and a good deal of short casting practice, you're ready to fish the North Platte River Trico spinnerfall. Remember that it takes an entire morning, patience, and a good angler to catch four or five fish on tiny Trico spinner flies. ▪

Seasons

The Yampa River can jump from 200 cfs in late spring (March/April) to 20,000 cfs through early summer (July), and the only stretch of water remaining fishable is below Stagecoach Reservoir, directly below the dam, where there is clearer water and less flow. In the spring, the ideal time to hit the river is the warming transition that starts runoff. If you are on the water in the three-week stretch prior to melt before water clarity is ruined, large numbers of big trout will pod up in the newly melted pools, drop-offs, and warming riffled runs. This is also a great time to fish below Catamount and Stagecoach Reservoir, where the water is ice-free all year.

The river will still fish in high water, and when the flows are up, it is a good time to float the river on the lower stretches outside of Steamboat

Steve Henderson searches some water upriver from Steamboat, Colorado. In the winter, skis and snowmobiles become the most efficient way to get to some stretches. LANDON MAYER

Springs. As water levels begin to drop steadily, usually by the end of June or beginning of July, the river turns on with hatches, with fish spread out from high water.

The Yampa's fish feed on the standard fare—caddis, Pale Morning Duns, stoneflies, Tricos, Blue-Winged Olives, and hoppers—but also on viral crayfish and mice, making for some interesting tactics. For instance, before, during, or after a full moon phase on the lower wide sections of the river, swinging a #8-12 Morrish Mouse imitation on the water's surface in the first two hours after sunset can trigger some of the most intense-sounding riseforms from some very large browns. There is nothing like setting the hook to the sound of what seems like a toilet flushing in the middle of the river and then watching a prehistoric-looking predatory brown trout on the river's edge by headlamp.

YAMPA RIVER

	JAN	FEB	MAR	APR	MAY	JUN	JUL	AUG	SEP	OCT	NOV	DEC
Midge (*Chironomidae*)												

#18-24 Purple Thing, Rojo Midge, Mercury Black Beauty, Jujubee Midge, Griffith's Gnat, Brooks' Sprout Midge, Top Secret Midge

Blue-Winged Olive (*Baetis* spp.)

#18-22 Pablo's Cripple Baetis, CDC Loop Wing Emerger, Mercury RS2, Johnny Flash, Flashback Barr's Emerger, Parachute Adams

Caddis
(*Brachycentrus* and *Hydropsyche* spp.)

#16-20 Larry's High-Vis Caddis, black Puterbaugh's Foam Caddis, Graphic Caddis, Lawson's E-Z Caddis

Golden Stonefly (*Perlidae*)

#6-12 Barr's Tungstone, Pat's Rubber Legs, Hare's Ear, Madam X, Crystal Stimulator, Amy's Ant

Pale Morning Dun
(*Ephemerella* spp.)

#16-20 Flashback Barr Emerger, Burke's Hunchback Two-Tone, Sloan's Mighty May, Dorsey's Mercury PMD, Peterson's Bat Wing Emerger, Sparkle Dun, Vis-A-Dun

Yellow Sally (*Isoperla* sp.)

#14-16 yellow Copper John, Mercer's Poxyback Little Yellow Stone, Tungsten Prince, Stimulator

Terrestrials

#8-18 black Foam Beetle, Flying Ant, Amy's Ant, Crystal Stimulator, Charlie Boy Hopper

Red Quill (*Rhithrogena* sp.)

#14-18 Copper John, Pheasant Tail, A. K.'s Red Quill, Parachute Adams

Trico (*Tricorythodes* sp.)

#18-24 black RS2, Barr's Drowned Trico, A. K.'s Quill Body Trico Dun, Trico Spinner

Streamers

#6-10 Whitlock's Double Bunny, white Articulated Leech, Slumpbuster, Meat Whistle, Circus Peanut

Worms and Eggs

Micro Worm, Flashtail Mini Egg, Nuke Egg, Otter's Egg, red Wire Worm

For the more traditional hatch matcher, Steve Henderson recommends fishing a dropper: "The Yampa River has some of the largest hatches you may ever see on a river. At the same time, it can be temperamental as a dry-fly fishery, with a majority of the trout concentrating below the water's surface during a blanket hatch because there is as much (if not more) food below. This is why fishing a dropper imitation is a must for year-round success."

With an overwhelming supply of crayfish and sculpins, the water can turn into a streamer-feeding frenzy at the right time and flow. If you imitate these food sources and concentrate on either high water when the trout spread out in the river or in low-light situations when they are not as noticeable from predators above, you will understand why they say "the tug is the drug." John Barr showed how effective the #8-14 ginger Barr's Meat Whistle (crayfish imitation) is on this section of water in Colorado and abroad. As he puts it, "Throughout the United States, crayfish are one of the most abundant

Steve Henderson, co-owner of Steamboat Fly Fisher in Steamboat, Colorado, shows off a large buck in full color on the Yampa River. If you time it right just before runoff, when the snow is melting but the water is clear, here are the rewards. STEVE HENDERSON

This Yampa brown took a Copper John, which is an incredibly effective fly not only for all waters in the state, but around the world. LANDON MAYER

North, East, and South Delaney Buttes lakes provide great stillwater fishing near the Yampa River. Two miles past Granby on US 40, take CO 125 north, and just before Walden, head west on CR 12 and continue west as the road turns into CR 18. North Delaney, the most popular and the one designated Gold Medal, has browns ranging from 14 to 22 inches (some much larger) that feed on Chironomids, scuds, Callibaetis, and damsels throughout the year. LANDON MAYER

and overlooked food sources. In the Yampa especially, you can have over 100 crayfish within a section of water that is 40 feet in length. With that much protein darting around, the trout cannot ignore a properly presented crayfish." Unlike the mature crayfish, juveniles are often olive and half the size, so it is important to have rust and olive imitations in your box when you are on the streamer hunt for large trout, pike, and carp.

Once you travel past Craig to the lower section of the Yampa, it continues toward the Green River. You still have some opportunities at smallmouth, pike, and catfish in this section. While they are not as plentiful as they were before the killing began in 1999, it is a nice change of pace to target these aggressive warmwater-dwelling species. Long casts with sink-tip lines or a slow retrieve can be productive. Imitations like #8-12 brown or gray Clouser Minnow can work well.

Elk River

A tributary of the Yampa, the Elk River starts in Routt National Forest where the Middle, South, and North Forks of the Elk converge, high above the Steamboat Valley. To access these headwaters go north on CR 129 (Elk River Road) from US 40 toward Steamboat Lake State Park. Shortly past Glen Eden, turn right on CR 64 (Seedhouse Road). Upon entering Routt National Forest, CR 64 turns into FR 400, leading you to the forks. The first public water is where the forks converge along CR 64, approximately 9 miles upstream from Glen Eden and at the point where CR 64 crosses the North Fork. While most of the river is private below Glen Eden, you can also access it at the Christiana SWA, located approximately 8 miles north of the turn onto CR 129 from US 40. The forks are fishable from about mid-July through late September before the first frost.

As the river descends 40-plus miles toward the large valley where it will eventually enter the Yampa River, the Elk slows in terrain and begins to widen, taking on the appearance of a larger waterway. With a majority of the water on Elk River remaining private, a 1 1/2-mile stretch of public water in the Christiana State Wildlife Area is often overlooked as anglers pursue the Yampa River. Many of the private sections can still be accessed through local guide services such as Yampa River Outfitters (owned by Paul Russell), giving you the opportunity to fish to lightly-pressured trout.

The Elk runs four degrees cooler than the Yampa River year-round, supplying cooler water temps during the peak heat of the summer. This can trigger some of the large fish from the Yampa to find refuge in the cooler water of the Elk while temps on the Yampa remain high.

Parachute Adams

Hook:	#12-22 Tiemco 100
Thread:	Iron gray 8/0
Tail:	Brown and grizzly spade hackle fibers
Wing:	White calf body hair
Hackle:	Brown and grizzly
Body:	Gray Superfine

Double Bunny

Hook:	#2-6 Tiemco 5263
Thread:	Black 3/0
Body:	Olive over white rabbit strips
Eyes:	Lead eyes
Gills:	Red hackle with rubber legs
Fins:	Red hackle with rubber legs

Barr's Drowned Trico

Hook:	#14-22 Tiemco 2488H
Thread:	Black 6/0 Danville
Tail:	Pale watery dun hackle
Abdomen:	Black tying thread coated with Hard as Nails
Wings:	White Antron
Thorax:	Black Quick Descent Dubbing

Poxyback Little Yellow Stone

Hook:	#14-16 Tiemco 200R
Thread:	Yellow 6/0 Danville
Antennae/ tail:	Pheasant tail fibers
Abdomen:	Pale yellow Haretron
Rib:	Copper wire
Shellback:	Mottled turkey tail
Wing case:	Mottled turkey tail, epoxied
Thorax:	Pale yellow Haretron
Legs:	Partridge or Grouse
Collar:	Creamy gray Haretron

Pablo's Baetis Cripple

Hook:	#18-20 Tiemco 200R
Tail:	Rust Z-lon
Body:	Olive brown Superfine
Hackle:	Gray dun hackle
Thorax:	Olive Superfine
Post:	Gray Z-lon

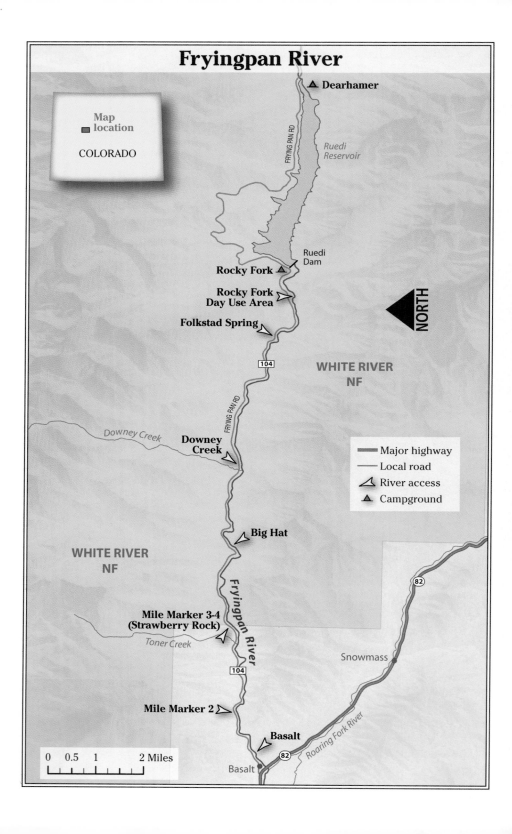

Fryingpan River

Map location

COLORADO

FRYING PAN RD

Ruedi Reservoir

▲ Dearhamer

NORTH

Ruedi Dam

Rocky Fork ⊿

Rocky Fork
Day Use Area ⊿

Folkstad Spring ⊿

104

WHITE RIVER
NF

FRYING PAN RD

Downey Creek

Downey
Creek ⊿

Major highway
Local road
⊿ River access
▲ Campground

WHITE RIVER
NF

⊿ Big Hat

Fryingpan River

Mile Marker 3-4
(Strawberry Rock) ⊿

Toner Creek

82

104

Snowmass

Mile Marker 2 ⊿

⊿ Basalt

82

Roaring Fork River

Basalt

0   0.5   1   2 Miles

NORTHWESTERN

CHAPTER 13

Fryingpan River

hile the origin of the name "Fryingpan" remains unclear, one story
involves a mountain man fleeing Ute Indians only to run into another
tribe farther down the pass and uttering the complaint that he had
"gone from the frying pan into the fire." William Bright, in his book *Colorado
Place Names*, recounts another story: "Some trappers were attacked by the
Utes, and all but two were killed. One went for help—leaving the other, who
was seriously wounded, in a cave. He marked the spot with a frying pan in
the fork of a tree. When he returned with soldiers, the wounded one was
dead, but the frying pan helped them to locate the body."

In any case, the actual town, once called Fryingpan Junction, was incorporated as Basalt in 1901, and the mountain town filled with immigrants who
came from Switzerland and Northern Italy to work for the railroad mines and
coal smelters. With the closing of the mines, the railroad closed and the few
remaining folks took up ranching. Today, the Fryingpan (also spelled "Frying
Pan") is one of the most popular areas to fish in the state, and one of the most
famous in the country for large trout, great hatches, and beautiful scenery.

Forming near the Continental Divide just northwest of towering Mount
Elbert, which stands at 14,433 feet, the Fryingpan flows northwest toward the
town of Meredith. From Meredith the Pan heads nearly due west through
Ruedi Reservoir and travels along CR 104 for 14 miles before the town of
Basalt, where it meets the Roaring Fork River. Camping is at Little Maude,
Little Mattie, and the Molly B just above the dam at the Ruedi Reservoir.
Above the reservoir, camping is available at Deer Hammer (along the inlet
of the Upper Fryingpan), Rocky Fork, and then Chapman Gulch Camp-
ground beyond.

One of three tailwaters in the state that has Mysis—and that means
trout that weigh in the double-digits—the Fryingpan is the only one that
allows access to the release section below the dam. You can literally nymph
the outflow from the reservoir, called the Toilet Bowl because of its swirling

currents at high flows. Every species of trout in Colorado, with the exception of greenbacks, can be caught in it. The entire river is artificial flies and lures only, and all trout (except browns) must be returned to the water. Since populations are so high, brown trout have a possession and size limit of two fish, 14 inches.

The one downside to this river is the pressure during prime time, which comes with the territory on famous tailwaters throughout the state. To avoid crowded conditions, time your trip around the people. One way Will Sands (guide and manager for Taylor Creek Fly Shop) has done this is fishing the low-light hours before nightfall. "Many anglers hit the daytime hatches when the bugs and trout are easy to see. While this is productive, after a big day on the water in the sun, I like to go out three hours before dark when fish feed heavily on Rusty Spinners. There are truly some magic hours of solitude on this river." Another way to find solitude is to fish the runs in between the famous holes.

There are three ways to reach the Fryingpan River from various locations in the state. The most common way is to take I-70 from either direction to Glenwood Springs and then head south to Basalt on CO 82. In summer and fall, you can take in the breathtaking views of Independence Pass. To access the pass, take US 24 from Buena Vista (see the Arkansas River map) to Twin Lakes. Then take CO 82 West over the pass, through Aspen toward Basalt. From Basalt, take Fryingpan Road (CR 104) and head toward Ruedi Reservoir. Lastly, if you are doing the Mysis shrimp circuit and trying to fish all three tailwaters in one trip, you can get to the Fryingpan from Gunnison by traveling west on US 50 to CO 133 North, ending at Carbondale on CO 82 just west of Basalt.

Flowing northwest toward the town of Meredith, the headwaters of the Fryingpan River can be accessed from CR 104 or Fryingpan Road heading off

CO 82. This often-overlooked water is filled with pocketwater runs, supplying good fishing in summer and fall. The most productive water for large trout begins at Rocky Fork Day Use Area, which extends down to about mile marker 10. At the Rocky Fork Day Use Area turnoff, a dirt road leads to the famous Toilet Bowl. Continuing down-

Will Sands lifts a tank brown above the Bend Hole. The unique coloration of the trout is due to their high-protein Mysis shrimp diet. Winter's cold keeps many anglers off the water, allowing big trout to feed stress free.
NICK WILLIAMS

Numerous anglers hunt for trout near the Bend Hole. JAY NICHOLS

stream, the Flats flows even and wide for 100 yards or more before the Bend Hole, a deep, slow-moving abyss home to many large, deep-dwelling trout. A trail on river left follows the river downstream. On river right, the high dirt road is good for spotting trout, and it is common to see anglers walking up- and downstream hoping to see a giant. This section continues downstream all the way to mile marker 10.

From Baetis Bridge near mile marker 13 you can look upstream and see in the distance a series of large rocks scattered in the middle of the river. These lead into a long, deep-riffled run that extends downstream to the bridge, with some large rocks submerged in the slick water flowing to the bridge and beyond. This stretch of water is classic dry-fly water. The extended riffles are not so powerful that they will sink a small dry, yet there is enough disturbance

Sands' Epoxy Mysis Shrimp (above) is effective when trout are concentrating on live shrimp, which have translucent bodies. From Baetis Bridge upstream to the Toilet Bowl you will have the highest concentration of Mysis, especially when flows peak in May or June. JAY NICHOLS

to supply cover for the many trout that hold there to feed. Parking is available on both sides of Baetis Bridge.

Below Baetis Bridge, a long stretch of water supplies calm edges and long, even runs with submerged structure throughout. This is an ideal area for trout to hug the river's edge or hold in the structure between each meal. This water travels down to the Slide Pool where you can encounter some of the larger trout that are swept downstream in higher flows. The last stretch of water in the Rocky Flats Day Use Area is the Bridge Pool, located a quarter mile downstream from the Bend Hole. This section offers great holding water for quality trout and some of my favorite water to fish dry flies.

The section from mile marker 12 downstream to marker 11 features Slide Pool, Picnic Pool, Mean Joe Green Pool, and 22-Inch Pool. This section of the river can be easily overlooked by anglers as they travel upriver to the Toilet Bowl, Bend Hole, and Baetis Bridge. With faster water around structure and deep pools, many large trout find refuge here, and the warmer water farther from the dam creates prolonged hatches and good dry-fly activity. Private water begins just upstream from Pruessing's Bridge, above mile marker 11. While there is a 0.7-mile stretch of access between mile markers 11 and 10 at Folkstad Spring, the river above mile marker 10 through mile marker 9 remains private.

Farther downstream the river changes from small pockets to long, deep runs that can be good for topwater activity. The Downey Creek access stretches a mile from the Cap K Ranch (just above mile marker 9) past mile marker 8 to just above the Peachblow Bridge. The water surrounding the bridge is also private, but a forest service pullout approximately 20 yards downstream from the bridge provides a quarter mile of access. From the forest service pullout past mile marker 7 until Big Hat Bridge is private, with a small (.3 mile) section of public water just past Big Hat Bridge. From mile marker 6 to just upstream from Larson's Bridge is a private lease for Frying Pan Anglers, with the next public water at mile marker 4.

Between mile markers 4 and 3 and at mile marker 2, there are pullouts with good river access. The water between mile markers 4 and 3 is all public, with a private stretch between mile markers 3 and 2. The public water between mile markers 4 and 3 is filled with classic runs and pools that are spaced out. This leaves a lot of water in between for exploring. From mile marker 2 to the regulations displayed at the Fryingpan River sign pullout just before Basalt, the gradient of the river becomes very steep and access is difficult, although there is a trail to the river near the display. This lower stretch of the river provides less pressure and is away from the road, giving you some solitude. The water runs fast, with nice pockets around rocks and good riffles around bends and the river's edge.

Seasons on the Pan

Because of the solitude, winter is my favorite time on the Pan. The flows are often low and steady, ranging from 70 to 100 cfs. This depth—with clear water—makes sight-fishing the way to go, even in some of the deepest runs like the Toilet Bowl below the dam or the Bend Hole. The prime areas for looking for trout in open water are from mile marker 10 upstream. The trout, some very large, are not as pressured, and often are easier to creep up on and more willing to take the fly. Mysis shrimp, midges, and *Baetis* are the main menu. There are some good midge and BWO hatches in late and early winter, when insulated cloud-filled days provide a little extra warmth.

Amazingly, browns in the Fryingpan spawn until February and this phenomenon captures the attention of rainbows, cuttbows, and cutthroats up to 10 pounds, enticing them to leave the safety of their deep water or hiding spots and concentrate on the shallow flats between deep runs. Fishing an egg imitation such as an apricot or Oregon cheese Flashtail Egg (4 mm) works well; just don't walk on the spawning beds, and leave the spawning fish alone.

Because Ruedi Dam is not very tall, the release from the gauging station is turbulent but not enough to kill all the shrimp that make their way into the river. In fact, a good majority of the shrimp are alive until they meet a hungry trout downstream or get caught in vegetation or structure and then die. This plays a huge role in how you present Mysis to these trout and which fly to use.

If a Mysis is alive, it looks transparent as it moves through the water. A dead Mysis is a creamy opaque white. On the Blue and Taylor most of the shrimp are dead by the time they reach public access on the river because you cannot fish below the dam for 100 yards. By the time those shrimp drift downstream, the water shooting out of the dam has killed them. The exception is the Fryingpan.

At times, the trout look like they are rising, but in fact they are consuming Mysis in the surface film. To overcome this hurdle, Will Sands fishes a variation of the dry-and-dropper rig to imitate both live and dead shrimp: "I use a #14-18 Tim Heng's Mysis as my main fly. The pattern is made of material that can absorb fly floatant to keep it riding in the film. Then, 16 to 18 inches below that, I drop my #14-18 Epoxy Shrimp that, with its subtle weight, rides below the surface. The main Mysis is cream in color. This lets you keep a visual of the fly or flies as they drift downstream. The fly becomes the indicator until you see the trout consume it. Having the ability to adjust length and depth by watching your shrimp drift to the trout is the best way to sight-fish using Mysis shrimp." This dual-shrimp setup is a productive way to fish in shallow or deep water.

Along with the shrimp, the Pan also has healthy hatches of Blue-Winged Olives, Pale Morning Duns, midges, caddis, and stoneflies, but the big hit is the Green Drake hatch. As the hatch progresses upstream from Basalt, the trout in between—including the largest—will gorge themselves on this awesome food supply. When anglers are so pumped up about a certain hatch, some of the other important food sources can be overlooked. "When the Green Drakes are at their peak, PMDs are coming off just as thick," Sands says. "A lot of anglers will solely rely on the Drakes for takes. I recommend trailing a second dry fly, such as a #16-18 Mathews' PMD Sparkle Dun, or, if the trout are wary from pressure above, an emerger like a #16-18 PMD Flashback Barr Emerger."

Fishing emergers in the film works for every hatch on the Pan. When the Blue-Winged Olives are thick, trailing a #20-22 STD, #18-20 BLM, #18-20 Beadhead Pheasant Tail, or #16-20 black or green Copper John works well. The key, no matter what food source you are imitating, is to make sure it is easy for the trout to consume the fly. Even though trout—especially big ones—have to eat to survive and maintain size, pressure and cold-water conditions during some of the best seasons make the trout less active on the take. You literally have to put it right in front of their noses sometimes. ∎

Higher flows (sometimes rising above 600 cfs) of spring urge the trout out of the once-calm deep water and into shallower water where they are visible. When targeting these large fish, hit the water early in the spring when the trout are in prespawn mode and try to fish a few days after high water. From mid to late spring, intense BWO hatches get these now shallow-holding trout looking up and taking food off the surface. Some of the largest trout I have ever seen eating dry flies were concentrating on the topwater spring hatches. "Prerunoff can be some of the best Blue-Winged Olive activity on the Pan," says Art Rowell, manager of Frying Pan Anglers. "With flows remaining steady at this time, the water temperatures are more consistent, without the release of cold water that occurs during runoff. Knowing that the weather can change daily, paying attention to cloud cover, and moving around the river from mile markers 12 to 8 will give you plenty of river to explore."

Angus Drummond searches the upper stretch of the Fryingpan for midge-eating trout. Art Rowell, manager of Frying Pan Anglers, says that "you literally can have topwater activity in all twelve months of the year on this river." LANDON MAYER

FRYINGPAN RIVER

	JAN	FEB	MAR	APR	MAY	JUN	JUL	AUG	SEP	OCT	NOV	DEC

Mysis Shrimp
#14-20 Tim's Mysis Shrimp, Will's Epoxy Mysis, Candy Cane Shrimp, Mayer's Mysis

Midge (*Chironomidae*)
#18-24 Black Beauty, Jujubee Midge, Disco Midge, Barr's Pure Midge Larva, Thread Midge, Griffith's Gnat, Sprout Midge

Blue-Winged Olive (*Baetis* spp.)
#18-22 Will's STD, Heng's BLM, Flashback Barr Emerger, RS2, Sparkle Dun, Vis-A-Dun

Caddis
(*Brachycentrus* and *Hydropsyche* spp.)
#16-20 olive Rick's Transparent Pupa, Graphic Caddis, Lawson's E-Z Caddis, Larry's High-Vis Caddis

Pale Morning Dun
(*Ephemerella* spp.)
#16-18 Flashback Beadhead Barr's Emerger, Pheasant Tail, Bat Wing Emerger, Furimsky's BDE, Vis-A-Dun, Sparkle Dun

Green Drake (*Drunella grandis*)
#12-16 Tungstone, Pheasant Tail, Lawson's Cripple, Furimsky's Foam Drake, Sparkle Dun, Parachute Drake

Red Quill (*Rhithrogena* sp.)
#14-18 Copper John, Pheasant Tail, A. K.'s Red Quill, Parachute Adams

Golden Stonefly (*Perlidae*)
#8-14 Tungstone, Pat's Rubber Legs, black Rubber Leg Hare's Ear, Stimulator, Chernobyl Ant

Terrestrials
#8-16 Crystal Stimulator, H & L Variant, Flying Ant, Foam Beetle, BC Hopper, Dave's Hopper

Streamers
#6-10 Will's Stinging Sculpin, Conehead Autumn Splendor, Slumpbuster, Lawson's Conehead Sculpin

Worms and Eggs
Micro Worm, Flashtail Mini Egg, Nuke Egg, Otter's Egg

With snowpack at its prime and high white banks covering the river's edge, glare can make it hard to see trout. I like to use a Buff and good polarized glasses to spot fish. Once the trout is in front of you, watch its behavior before you cast. This will tell you right away if the fish is feeding on top, in the film, or subsurface, or simply holding on the bottom. Remember, you want your flies to drift directly to the trout to prevent the fish from having to expend energy to feed.

May and June is another rewarding time in the spring, with large rainbows, browns, and cutthroats replenishing the nutrients lost during the spawn. The growing vegetation, melting snow, and blue skies look beautiful, and with the addition of caddis to their diet, the fish have plenty to feed on.

In summer, *Baetis*, PMDs (their bodies are salmon-colored), and caddis provide good dry-fly fishing, but the main event is the Green Drakes. Crowds are the biggest challenge at this time of year, but Will Sands explains how to get around that: "A majority of anglers that visit the Fryingpan fish from the dam to around the middle of the river, leaving the whole lower stretch untouched. I will cover the whole river in one day of guiding, hitting each location—upper, middle, and lower—on the river. For those who have not experienced the lower stretch, the hopper-dropper action is awesome." Imitations like a #14-16 Charlie Boy Hopper with a #16-20 BLM, #16-22 Beadhead Pheasant Tail, #18-20 Pheasant STD, or #16-20 green Copper John trailing below is a winning combination on the lower stretch of the Fryingpan.

Similar to the spring, fall begins to produce cooler water as winter nears and the brown and brook trout begin to become more aggressive as they prepare to spawn. I like to concentrate from the middle of the river all the way to the dam. The crowds start to die down at this time, and some of the trout that were in hiding are willing to come out and play.

Some *Baetis* hatches in the fall will last for hours. In addition, the same stormy days that are perfect for *Baetis* are also good for streamers, especially fished in deep runs like the Bend Hole and the gauging station run upstream. On the Pan, color is important. Imitations like #10-12 Will's Stinging Sculpin, #6-12 black/olive/tan Lawson's Conehead Sculpin, #6-14 natural/rust Barr's Slumpbuster, and #10-14 Autumn Splendor will work well.

Will Sands battles with a quality brown on the lower Fryingpan. LANDON MAYER

One of my favorite times of the year to fish the Pan is the fall. Fishing streamers such as Tim Heng's Autumn Splendor (above) is a welcome change of pace and very effective.
LANDON MAYER

John Gierach, Colorado fishing icon and author of numerous books including *No Shortage of Good Days,* prefers the fall over the spring BWO hatches. "I like this season over the spring with the hatches extending longer due to weather. Cloudy conditions provide perfect temperatures with multiple sizes of adults on the surface at the same time. This creates a challenge of matching the hatch I have found fun for many years. The Fryingpan can get crowded during the fall, but it has every water condition you can think of in an intimate setting. You will have no shortage of water to cast dries."

"When I am fishing dries I prefer a hand-tied leader system I learned from A. K. Best. The first two-thirds is stiff with the business-end third supple, allowing the fly to turn over well on the surface. For length I like fishing the shortest leader I can get away with to help with accuracy and casting on the water—on the Fryingpan this is usually around 9 to 10 feet. My favorite fly for BWOs is A. K.'s Parachute Quill. I will tie it standard and then with some of my ties I will use a clear plastic wing. This can make a difference at times for very selective trout."

"I usually fish a dry-dropper unless I am catching a lot of fish on the dry; then I will cut the dropper off to prevent tangles. For the second fly I like to use an olive RS2 or Roy Palm's BWO emerger. I prefer fishing simple patterns because they are easier to tie, and I hate fishing a fly I am worried about losing."

Sands' STD (Pheasant)

Hook: #18-20 Tiemco 100 SP-BL
Bead: Black 1/16" tungsten
Thread: Black 14/0 Gordon Griffith's
Tail: Lemon wood duck flank
Abdomen: Pheasant tail and cream micro
           dubbing
Thorax: Peacock herl
Wing case: Black Thin Skin and one strand of
           pearl Flashabou coated with epoxy
Legs: Lemon wood duck flank

Sparkle Dun (Green Drake)

Hook: #10-12 Tiemco 100
Thread: Olive 8/0 Uni-Thread
Tail: Olive Z-lon
Abdomen: Olive Superfine
Rib: Olive Z-lon
Wing: Deer hair
Thorax: Olive Superfine

Sands' Epoxy Mysis Shrimp

Hook: #16-20 Tiemco 200R BL
Thread: Beige or white 8/0 Uni-Thread
Body: 5 Minute epoxy
Eyes: 16- to 20-pound fluorocarbon
Antennae: White CDC with wood duck flank
Feelers: White Z-lon

Heng's Mysis Shrimp

Hook: #16-18 Tiemco 200R (barbless)
Thread: White 8/0 Uni-Thread
Antennae: White Angora goat dubbing
           (10-12 fibers)
Thorax/
head: White Angora goat dubbing
Shellback: Ziploc Baggie strip or 1/8" Scud
           Back (clear)
Abdomen: Pearl tinsel

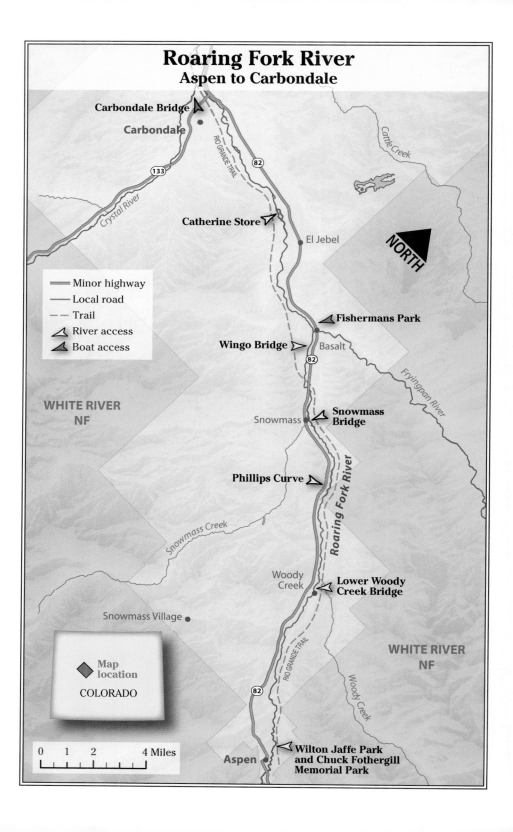

Roaring Fork River
Aspen to Carbondale

Carbondale Bridge

Carbondale

RIO GRANDE TRAIL

82

Crystal River

133

Catherine Store

El Jebel

Cattle Creek

NORTH

Fishermans Park

Wingo Bridge

Basalt

82

Fryingpan River

WHITE RIVER
NF

Minor highway
Local road
Trail
River access
Boat access

Snowmass Bridge

Snowmass

Phillips Curve

Roaring Fork River

Snowmass Creek

Woody Creek

Lower Woody Creek Bridge

Snowmass Village

WHITE RIVER
NF

Map location

COLORADO

RIO GRANDE TRAIL

82

Woody Creek

0   1   2   4 Miles

Aspen

Wilton Jaffe Park and Chuck Fothergill Memorial Park

CHAPTER 14

Roaring Fork River

Once known to the Utes as "Thunder River," the Roaring Fork is a Gold Medal freestone that begins below breathtaking Independence Pass and drops fast in elevation before receiving tributaries like the Fryingpan and Crystal River, which are fly-fishing destinations in their own right. With ample public water on its journey to the Colorado River, there is plenty of great water on this river for fly fishers to pursue large rainbows, brown, and cuttbow trout (known to grow larger than 20 inches), both by boat and by boot. No doubt, the main attraction on the river is the Green Drake hatch, but it also has great caddis and PMD hatches, as well as fantastic fishing for bruisers migrating from the Colorado River. Since CO 82 runs parallel to the water, anglers can find launching areas and pull-offs easily during their travels. In addition to wading access points, there are numerous put-in and takeout points for floating the river either by raft or drift boat. Local shops can help you decide where to put in and take out, depending on water and fishing conditions.

Although there is a significant amount of public access on the Roaring Fork, it is not as easily located as the access points along the Fryingpan. Local shops can assist anglers in determining access points. The water above Basalt is often overlooked because the river is not as easily noticeable as the lower stretch. With less pressure from boats than in the water downstream, I think the fish here are easier to catch.

From the Front Range, take I-70 to Glenwood Springs and then CO 82 South to Basalt. During the summer and fall, you can also take Independence Pass. Take CO 24 from Buena Vista (see Arkansas River Map) to Twin Lakes. Then take CO 82 over the pass, through Aspen, and toward Basalt.

The Upper Roaring Fork (Aspen to Basalt)

The headwater flows through the White River National Forest from the confluence of Difficult and McFarlane creeks. Stop and take an hour or so to explore these creeks and beaver ponds above Aspen. The selective cruising

Will Sands holds a nice Roaring Fork rainbow that could not resist a Beadhead Prince Nymph. Sands loves this pattern because it works year-round. LANDON MAYER

brook and brown trout can test the cast of any angler presenting an attractor dry fly.

This stretch of river fishes best for brookies and rainbows from mid-June through October. These willing fish take big attractor dry flies and nymphs fished in the deep plunge pools. This entire section to Lower Woody Creek Bridge is catch-and-release only. Below Aspen, the wild trout water along the Rio Grande Trail is some of the most popular fishing in the area, with quality catch-and-release water from Slaughterhouse Bridge to Wilton Jaffe and Chuck Fothergill Parks. It is accessible from the north side of the river for around 5 miles, with parking well-marked at all three locations. Trout become larger as you travel downstream, with rainbows and browns becoming the dominant species. Access at this point is the Lower Woody Creek

Will Sands fishes the smaller water above Lower Woody Creek Bridge. While its tributaries make the Roaring Fork valley a fly-fishing mecca, they can affect the water clarity on the lower Roaring Fork, so make sure you time your trip to hit low or clear water. If you have already made the trip, and the water is reddish brown, continue upriver toward the headwaters. Water that is off-color with a hint of green or tea color is actually very good and with 1 to 2 feet of visibility you can have good fishing. LANDON MAYER

The upper Roaring Fork River near Snowmass Ski Area does not hold the largest trout on the river, but it makes up for it with numbers of 10- to 12-inch trout. This can be some of the best all-day action with drys. ROSS PURNELL

Bridge, with 2 miles of public water on the south bank as well as two stretches at mile markers 30 and 29 known as Phillips Curve. Parking is well-marked. When wading this stretch be sure to have studs and a staff to help navigate the slick river bottom.

The river near Lower Woody Creek Bridge is some of my favorite water to wade-fish and has more holding water than the upper river, allowing large trout to find refuge while feeding on hatches of stoneflies, caddis, and mayflies. There can be excellent fishing on top as well as year-round sub-surface action. Will Sands, from Taylor Creek Fly Shop, says the best fly for the river is a #12-16 Prince Nymph. "I will catch more trout with this fly than any other imitation on a regular basis. Even on the coldest days in late season, the fish seem to key in on stoneflies."

From Woody Creek down to the Colorado River regulations change to artificial flies and lures only, with a possession and size limit of two fish, 16 inches (except for Three and Four Mile creeks' confluences, which are off-limits

The Roaring Fork near Lower Woody Creek Bridge is a narrow setting that can hold trout in the 20-inch class. Don't pass up the chance to fish large stone imitations in these tight quarters. ROSS PURNELL

during the spring and fall spawn). Additional access before Basalt includes the Old Snowmass Bridge just past mile marker 27.

Head north over the Old Snowmass Bridge and take your first left to a parking lot approximately half a mile downstream. From the bridge, access is on the north bank only. Wingo and Trestle Bridges also provide short stretches just before you hit Basalt, where the water widens as it meets the Fryingpan River.

Middle Roaring Fork (Basalt to Carbondale)

Access in the town of Basalt is on the north side only for 3 miles between the upper and lower bypass bridges off CO 82. Parking for this section is located off Two Rivers Road and is well-marked. Farther downstream, Hooks Bridge

Anglers float the section near Catherine's Store. From Green Drakes to gold aspen trees, the Roaring Fork River can supply you memorable days of watching a quality brown smash Green Drakes on the surface, or feeling the tug of a 23-inch rainbow taking your streamer. LANDON MAYER

Kim Dorsey begins a battle on the Roaring Fork downstream from Basalt, Colorado. Targeting dark-colored water is key to finding the drop-off points trout need for cover. PAT DORSEY

provides a short stretch with parking off Willits Lane, as well as a 1½-mile stretch off Valley Road. Both areas are north-shore-access only. Blue Creek Ranch access and Catherine Bridge access are reached by turning left at Catherine's Store Road, and parking is in the north shore parking lot just past the bridge. The trail is paved and provides easy access to the river on the north side.

While most maps show put-ins for boats at Upper and Lower Basalt (bypass), Hooks Bridge, and Catherine's Store, the ramps are very bad with treacherous water between. These Class III rapids have unsafe launching sites, making them risky to navigate. Most fly fishers put in at Carbondale Bridge, or upstream at Hooks Bridge, and take out in Glenwood Springs for a full-day float; for a half day, take out at Westbank Bridge near Cattle Creek. You can fish out of hard boats or rafts, though rafts make it easier to get into some of the access areas. All of these access areas provide quality wade-fishing as well.

With various access points available throughout Carbondale, be sure to stop in one of the fly shops to get accurate directions and advice. The Gianinetti

Anglers search the slack water edges near Carbondale for the big bugs. Green Drakes hatching in the afternoon are one of the river's main attractions. LANDON MAYER

access, just upstream of the bridge on CO 133, is accessible only from the east-bound lane on a rough dirt road, and fishing is only allowed on the north side of the river. Access for Carbondale Bridge is after CO 133 before the Sutank Bridge and can be reached by taking a left at the Roaring Fork Marina, then taking the right at the first fork and the left at the second fork before back-tracking a couple of miles to the parking lot (there are small signs that can be easily missed, but the private property is well-marked). These waters are angler-friendly for navigation, with good put-ins and takeouts and some awesome trout holding water.

The biggest draw to the river is by far the annual Green Drake hatch, which starts around the first week of July and provides some of the year's best fishing. If possible, the best way to fish this hatch is by boat. You can cover more water, present to more trout, and access water that is private by way of foot. If you do have to wade the river, be ready to drive up and down to hit the prime runs that can be spread out a bit.

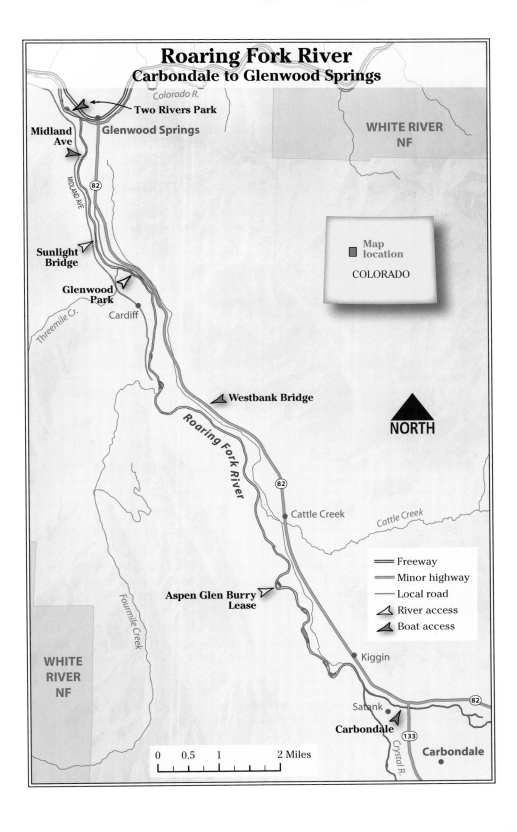

Roaring Fork River
Carbondale to Glenwood Springs

Colorado R.

Two Rivers Park

WHITE RIVER NF

Midland Ave

Glenwood Springs

MIDLAND AVE

82

Map location

COLORADO

Sunlight Bridge

Glenwood Park

Threemile Cr.

Cardiff

Westbank Bridge

Roaring Fork River

NORTH

82

Cattle Creek

Cattle Creek

Freeway
Minor highway
Local road
River access
Boat access

Aspen Glen Burry Lease

Fourmile Creek

WHITE RIVER NF

Kiggin

Satank

82

Carbondale

133

Crystal R.

Carbondale

0   0.5   1   2 Miles

ROARING FORK

	JAN	FEB	MAR	APR	MAY	JUN	JUL	AUG	SEP	OCT	NOV	DEC

Midge (*Chironomidae*)
#18-24 Black Beauty, Rojo Midge, Griffith's Gnat, Jujubee Midge

Blue-Winged Olive (*Baetis* spp.)
#18-22 CDC Loop Wing Emerger, Johnny Flash, Flashback Pheasant Tail, Heng's BLM, Furimsky's BDE, Parachute Adams

Caddis
(*Brachycentrus* and *Hydropsyche* spp.)
#16-20 Lawson's Electric Caddis, Deep Sparkle Pupa, Barr's Graphic Caddis, Garcia's Mother's Day Caddis

Pale Morning Dun
(*Ephemerella* spp.)
#16-20 Barr Emerger, Dorsey's Mercury PMD, Pheasant Tail, Vis-A-Dun, Sparkle Dun, Cannon's Snowshoe Dun

Red Quill (*Rhithrogena* sp.)
#14-18 Copper John, Pheasant Tail, A. K.'s Red Quill, Adams

Golden Stonefly (*Perlidae*)
#10-14 Prince Nymph, 20 Incher, Pat's Rubber Legs, Crystal Stimulator

Terrestrials
#8-16 Thingamahoppers, Charlie Boy Hopper, BC Hopper, Black Ant, Baby Boy Cricket

Green Drake (*Drunella grandis*)
#12-16 Tungstone, Pheasant Tail, olive/black Rubber Leg Copper John, 20 Incher, Lawson's Cripple, Furimsky's Foam Drake, Stalcup's Drake, Sparkle Dun, Parachute Drake

Streamers
#6-12 Will's Stinging Sculpin, Slumpbuster, Egg Sucking Leech, Lawson's Conehead Sculpin

Worms and Eggs
Micro Worm, Flashtail Mini Egg, Nuke Egg, Otter's Egg

Lower Roaring Fork (Carbondale to Glenwood Springs)

Tim Heng of Taylor Creek Fly Shop likes the lower river from Carbondale to Glenwood Springs because it's easy to float and offers the best chance at larger fish. "One of my favorite times of the year to fish the Fork is when the water is high and even a bit discolored. The fish are all stacked up right next to the bank and are more concentrated than at most any other time of the year. I certainly don't land a lot of these fish because they get out in the current and head downstream in a hurry, but I sure love to fish for them when most other anglers think the water is way too high to be fishable. My two favorite techniques are dry-and-dropper or short nymph rig." Tim's #16-20 Baetis BLM is a great addition to any nymph rig on the Fork.

Keep in mind that when you are deep nymphing on the Roaring Fork, you will catch some monster whitefish. While some anglers turn up their noses at them, the Roaring Fork has some world-class specimens—big, eager, feeding machines that in heavy flow can put up a great fight. If you are in prime trout holding water with great cover, oxygen, and food supply but hooking whitefish after whitefish—and you don't want to—lighten your rig to drift in the middle or subsurface columns. Whiteys are notorious for holding deep on the bottom in huge numbers.

Continuing on CO 82 past Carbondale, a pullout at mile marker 9 provides access to both the Burry Lease and the Aspen Glen easement, although you must stay off the Aspen Glen property. From here downstream to Glenwood Springs, access comes in 1/4- to 1/2-mile stretches at the Westbank Bridge (2 miles past Cattle Creek) and Sunlight Bridge (the Sunlight Ski Area turn) off CO 82, and there is also access in Glenwood Springs at Glenwood Park along Midland Avenue, which runs parallel to the south shore.

Finally, the confluence with the Colorado can be reached in town by taking a left on the 7th Street Bridge and parking at Veltus Park. This area is also

Good communication between anglers is the key to float fishing. Angus Drummond and Will Sands work as a team while floating near Glenwood. As my good friend and experienced guide Eric Mondragon says, "If you need to be closer, let me know. If you need a better angle, I will tell you. The result is developing the right drift where the boat and flies are moving at the same speed." LANDON MAYER

With a healthy population of sculpin in the river, #6-12 Will's Stinging Sculpins, olive/tan Lawson's Conehead Sculpins, and ginger Meat Whistles all work well for the river's browns (and other trout). Try using a double streamer or sculpin rig with a 20- to 24-inch piece of OX tippet connecting the two flies. LANDON MAYER

wheelchair-accessible and allows public access to both sides of the river. In the spring and fall, it is not uncommon to catch large migratory fish here. Whenever you are trying to time these runs, think early—April and October. Most migratory fish will move one to two months before the spawn to find quality staging water to feed and find cover in. Bright imitations like orange Flashtail Mini Eggs (4 mm and 6 mm) or large streamers like #6-10 Slumpbusters and #8-12 Autumn Splendors will often trigger aggressive takes.

The lower stretch of the river is a bug factory. In addition to the Drakes, late April caddis hatches near Glenwood Springs are so thick you will get a mouthful of bugs just walking in town. Before the hatch has a chance to migrate upriver, runoff usually begins blowing the river out. Try to stay ahead of the hatch if you can at this time or come back in the evening to hit the egg-laying caddis before dark. Edges, calm water, and ideal seams are great areas to concentrate when imitating these flies. In addition to the caddis, Yellow Sally stones are an overlooked hatch. My favorite Yellow Sally imitation of all time is a #14-16 Mercer's Poxyback Little Yellow Stone. Trail this behind an adult Green Drake, and the trout on the edges will not stand a chance.

Stinging Sculpin

Hook:	#8 TMC 2499BL
Cone:	Gold tungsten
Thread:	Brown 210-denier Danville
Tail:	Tan Grizzly Mini Marabou
Body:	Metz Glimmer
Chenille:	Variegated Brown Metallic
Head and collar:	Deer hair

Rubber Leg Copper John (Olive/Black)

Hook:	#10-18 Tiemco 2499SP-BL
Bead:	Gold tungsten
Weight:	Lead wire
Thread:	Black 70-denier Ultra Thread
Tail:	Brown goose biots
Abdomen:	Olive and black Ultra Wire (Brassie)
Wing case:	Black Thin Skin and holographic silver Flashabou, coated with epoxy
Thorax:	Bronze Arizona synthetic peacock dubbing
Legs:	Black round rubber (extra small)

Prince Nymph

Hook:	#4-18 Tiemco 5262
Bead:	Gold or copper
Thread:	Black and red 8/0
Body:	Peacock herl
Tail:	Brown goose biots
Hackle:	Mottled brown hen
Rib:	Silver or gold tinsel
Back:	White goose biots

Web Wing Caddis (Dun)

Hook:	#12-18 Tiemco 100
Thread:	Iron gray 8/0 Uni-Thread
Hackle:	Grizzly
Body:	Dun Superfine
Wing:	Mottled gray Web Wing

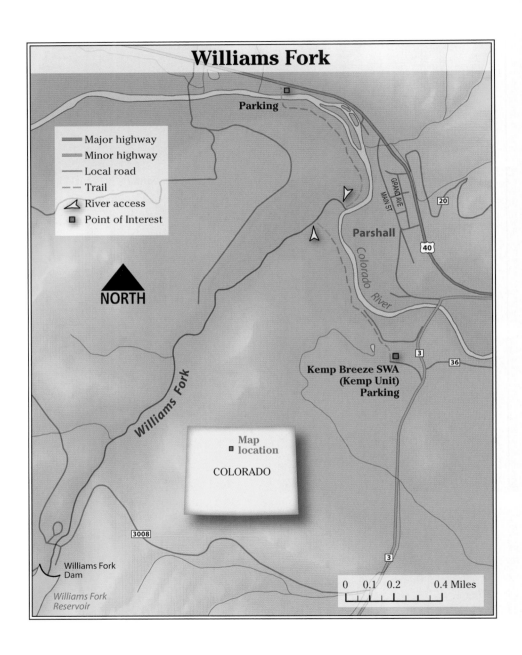

Williams Fork

Parking

Major highway
Minor highway
Local road
Trail
River access
Point of Interest

NORTH

GRAND AVE
MAIN ST

20

Parshall

Colorado River

40

3

36

Kemp Breeze SWA
(Kemp Unit)
Parking

Map
location

COLORADO

Williams Fork

3008

3

Williams Fork
Dam

Williams Fork
Reservoir

0   0.1   0.2   0.4 Miles

CHAPTER 15

Williams Fork River

Beginning at Grand County in Arapaho National Forest on the Continental Divide, the Williams Fork River travels 30 miles before reaching the Colorado River. The best fishing is in the 2-mile tailwater between the dam and the confluence with the Colorado River, which can often provide solitude because of the limited access and trails along the river that allow you to hike upstream or down. Though it is a small stretch of water, it provides more walking opportunities than many other tailwaters in the state, and you can cover lots of ground to both find fish and escape other anglers. Tucked well away from the road, this stretch of water fishes well in the spring, summer, and fall when large rainbows, browns, and cuttbows migrate from the Colorado River.

In the summer you can take a shortcut to get to the river by turning right onto Ute Pass Road 10 miles north of CO 9 /I-70 junction and coming in from directly south of the Williams Fork. Otherwise, take US 40 through Parshall. Camping is located at the South Fork Campground, which has no amenities but can be enjoyed in a small RV or tent. The entire river from the dam to the confluence with the Colorado is catch-and-release, flies and lures only.

To get to the river, you can either park on the north bank of the Colorado along US 40 in the pullout for the Breeze Unit and cross the Colorado through the Parshall Hole, or turn onto CR 3, park at the Kemp Unit, and take the trail along the south side of the Colorado to the confluence. If you choose the first option I recommend only taking this route after mid-July when the water is 600 cfs or lower. Pat Dorsey says: "Part of the Colorado is private . . . do not tresspass here. There is a small section of private water between the Parshall Hole and the confluence of the Williams Fork. Both ends of the property are roped off with a yellow rope and clearly marked with no trespassing signs. there is a small easement on river right to walk past this private section. Do not stray out into the hayfield, but stay on the marked trail."

The lower Williams Fork just above the confluence with the Colorado River has nice some pools and runs. LANDON MAYER

To hike in from the Kemp Unit, turn right onto CR 3 as you head out of Parshall. The parking lot is well-marked, and the trail from the lot will lead you along the south side of the Colorado River to the confluence of the Williams Fork. Visible from the parking lot, there is an old, broken-down barn located to the left of the trail as it descends downhill. For those new to this access, the route can be confusing, because it appears like you are traveling through a ranch. After you pass the barn, you will pass through two gates that have signs posted reminding you to close the gate behind you; these gates are perhaps 100 yards apart at opposite ends of the property. After the last gate, the trail cuts through a meadow and then parallels the Colorado. When you are following the Colorado, the trail can appear private but remains in clear view. You can cut your travel time down with a mountain bike.

Once you reach the Williams Fork and begin to head upstream, you will have to navigate on both sides of the water. There is a fence lining both sides of the river that at times will be so close to the river's edge you cannot move farther upstream. This makes crossing the best way to reach new water. Look before you step into the water, both for safety and to prevent spooking edge-dwelling trout. I prefer to approach likely water from downstream when possible.

When you first reach the river from the trail, there is a great long riffled run upstream, and below is the confluence with the Colorado River. If you reach the water by crossing the Colorado, the first section you will reach is the confluence—head upstream to hit this run. Moving upriver from the first run above the confluence, you will encounter a series of deep pools with nice rif-fled seams meeting slick edgewater. Upstream from there are a few braids in the river, with narrow water on both sides providing great edgewater (espe-cially for dry flies). After you pass the braids, the river will continue to flow in a consistent manner with long riffled runs that provide deep water and undercuts on either side. Leading into these runs is fast riffled water that you should fish.

These riffles and runs continue for a mile or so upriver, with structure like fallen timber and large boulders in various spots. The structure water will usually hold quality trout looking for cover. The water moving around the fallen trees is fast and often challenging to land fish from, so be sure you steer

In the fall, substantial browns migrate up the Williams Fork from the Colorado River and will take a wide range of patterns. Sight-fishing in a small setting is exciting. LANDON MAYER

It's important to keep a low profile, especially when the sun is out and the water is clear.
LANDON MAYER

the fish away from the wood. The rocks will provide breaks in the water, supplying great viewing windows to see to the bottom of the pool where many larger trout will hold. Always look for deep locations in the river—the trout will use all the cover they can get, even a depression in a shallow run. The second mile is predominantly pocketwater.

Moving up toward the dam, the waters will narrow and provide more rocks, braids, and steep banks. This water is harder to see fish in unless the flows are 100 cfs or lower, though the river fishes well between 100 and 200 cfs. I often look for large migratory browns in the seams, runs, pools, and eddies in this section.

Approach

Even though the relatively easy walk often deters crowds, it is always best to fish this river during the week and be prepared to move up the 2 miles to find water that is open and has seen less pressure. This river is no wider than 20 feet in most parts, so you can sight fish it effectively. Because the trail is so close to the river and you have the cross-section of water as you move upstream, the trout are pressured from movement above. To overcome this obstacle, take the time to look before you cast, especially on the edges of the banks and runs. Lastly, before casting, take the time to watch the trout's behavior to see if it is feeding.

Remember that you want to cross to walk on the low side of the river, not the high bank. Fish from the low-bank side of each run, using the high banks to sight and a low body position to remain undetected. This is a great way to see what is in the run. Then present from a lower location, keeping any movement from above out of the equation. You will land more trout on the river every time.

If you cannot spot a target or the sighting conditions are tough, cover every inch of a run to present the imitations to the trout. Most of the runs are narrow and have visible seams and turbulent water that trout would call

Ryan Lark concentrates on the edge seams of the Williams Fork River halfway between the dam and the Colorado River confluence. When fishing rivers with slick bottoms, it's wise to stay on the banks so you can safely move upstream or down when playing a fish.
PAT DORSEY

Williams Fork Reservoir is one of the most productive pike fisheries in the state, with a great midge hatch in late May and early June. The west side of the lake is an ideal location for pike to hold, in addition to the inlet. There are two main bays, Johnson Gulch and McQueary Gulch, that remain shallow for a fair distance before dropping off to 8-plus feet. This is prime water for pike to travel through during the spring or cruise around before ice-over in the fall. In addition to the Williams Fork Reservoir, the following bodies of water and rivers are prime locations for pike, using the same timing and techniques that apply to this reservoir: Eleven Mile, Spinney, Stagecoach, Sanchez, and Tarryall Reservoirs, the Yampa River below the town of Craig, and the Rio Grande near Alamosa.

When gearing up for pike, many say that 8- to 10-weights are ideal for throwing big wet flies. I find that an 8-weight is often undergunned in heavy wind. Ten-weights have the power to punch through winds known to exceed 30 miles an hour. The two main lines you want to have are floating and sinking lines. Multi-tips can work well, as long as the loop-to-loop connection is coated with UV knot sealer or the loops are small enough to run through the guides. For the leader setup I like to use 0X 9-foot leaders with an 18-inch bite section of 25- to 35-pound hard Mason mono. While some situations will call for wire, the mono prevents the dreaded hinge or bend in the wire after a strike. This can cause the fly to move unnaturally in the water, decreasing takes.

For most anglers, the most common season to pursue pike on the fly is in the late spring and early summer when the pike are pre- or postspawn and cruising the shallow bays, fingers, and inlets in pursuit of prime water or food. The second season, which often goes unnoticed, is the fall. Like the warming spring, in the fall (late September/October) the pike will cruise the

home. According to Dorsey, "This river has good numbers of fish, and they are not easy to see. Methodically cover the water, especially toward the head end of the runs when a midge hatch is evident or a strong *Baetis* hatch is in progress. Anglers will need lots of weight in their nymphing rig, the water moves with a purpose, and you need to get your flies down quickly."

Timing

Like most waters in Colorado, the river flows will fluctuate year-round, causing the fish to adjust to the rise and fall of the water. Before going to the Williams Fork, check the stream flows. Pat Dorsey, who guides on the river, gives the most concise breakdown that I have ever heard.

reservoir again in search of food before ice-over begins. The difference at this time is the depth at which they feed. Beyond most of the water you fish in the spring is a drop-off (second shelf), a prime area for trout or other food sources to cruise, making it an ambush spot for the pike or tiger muskie. The drop-off points can vary from 8-12 feet in most situations. To obtain the proper depth, count as you let your fly sink before you retrieve. Once you get a strike, follow, or hit at a certain depth, count that long for every cast to ensure your fly is at the same depth as the hunting pike.

When you are retrieving the fly, try different speeds, lengths, and pauses on each presentation. In addition, throw mends in your line to slightly change the direction of the darting fly, triggering a strike from a following fish. Most importantly, do a figure-eight with your rod tip while the leader and fly are in the water after a retrieve. Pike, tiger muskie, and muskie are notorious for following the fly or prey until the last minute in shallow water. When you are selecting a fly, think dark in clear water (black/rust/purple) and bright in cloudy water or mud lines (yellow/chartreuse/white). The following is a list of preferred patterns for success: # 2-8 rust/black Barr's Meat Whistle, #2-10 blue/white Lefty's Deceiver, #2-6 black Bunny Leech.

Like most gamefish pursued on the fly, pike can become conditioned quickly. They also have to adapt to water levels and food supplies. When you are working the shallows, fan the water systematically, concentrating toward the shoreline as well. Try new areas or locations that look like prime ambushing spots. The rewards are fast, powerful strikes from a truly unique predator.

To access the Williams Fork Reservoir from US 40, take CR 3 and follow the signs to the reservoir. CR 3 will connect with CR 33, which will lead you around to the opposite shore of the reservoir. ■

"As a whole, Denver Water holds water back when the Colorado is running off, storing water in Williams Fork Reservoir to be used later in the summer season. When Williams Fork Reservoir fills, it spills, and flows can reach 1,200 cfs. After 500 cfs, the river is really unfishable. I typically do not like to fish it over 300 cfs. Post runoff, Denver Water generally holds on to the water until the Colorado River gets a little on the low side, 200 cfs, and then they release water from the Williams Fork for downstream irrigation needs on the Western Slope." I prefer flows from 150 to 200 cfs. This seems to be enough water to supply the trout with cover while making it manageable to wade across. Higher and lower flows will still produce good results but might create the challenge of wary fish in low water or tough wading in high flows.

WILLIAMS FORK

	JAN	FEB	MAR	APR	MAY	JUN	JUL	AUG	SEP	OCT	NOV	DEC

Midge (*Chironomidae*)
#18-24 Mercury Flashback Black Beauty, Rojo Midge, Jujubee Midge, Griffith's Gnat

Blue-Winged Olive (*Baetis* spp.)
#16-22 Stalcup's Baetis Nymph, Mercury Flashback Pheasant Tail, Copper John, Barr Emerger, RS2, Jujubaetis, Sparkle Dun, Vis-A-Dun

Caddis
(*Brachycentrus* and *Hydropsyche* spp.)
#16-20 Larry's Larva, green Graphic Caddis, Buckskin, Beadhead Breadcrust, black Puterbaugh's Foam Caddis, Hill's Devil Bug, Peacock Caddis

Golden Stonefly (*Perlidae*)
#6-12 Barr's Tungstone, Pat's Rubber Legs, Hare's Ear, Crystal Stimulator, Amy's Ant, Madam X

Yellow Sally (*Isoperla* sp.)
#14-16 yellow Copper John, Mercer's Poxyback Little Yellow Stone, Tungsten Prince, Stimulator

Pale Morning Dun
(*Ephemerella* spp.)
#16-20 Barr's Emerger, Dorsey's Mercury PMD, Pheasant Tail, Vis-A-Dun, Sparkle Dun, Cannon's Snowshoe Dun

Trico (*Tricorythodes* sp.)
#18-24 black RS2, Barr's Drowned Trico, A. K.'s Quill Body Trico Dun, Trico Spinner

Red Quill (*Rhithrogena* sp.)
#14-18 Copper John, Pheasant Tail, A. K.'s Red Quill, Parachute Adams

Terrestrials
#8-16 Thingamahopper, Charlie Boy Hopper, BC Hopper, black ant patterns, Foam Beetle, Baby Boy Cricket

Sow Bugs, Scuds, Worms, Eggs
#12-16 Pat's UV Scud, McLean's Hunchback Scud, Flashback Scud, Dubbed Body Sowbug, Micro Worm, Flashtail Mini Egg

Streamers
#2-10 Egg Sucking Leech, Autumn Splendor, Slumpbuster, Circus Peanut, Lawson's Conehead Sculpin

Browns (some in the 8-pound range) can start swimming up from the Colorado as early as August or as late as the second week of November. I think the best time frame is mid-September through November. This will allow you target the trout in the pre- and post-spawn state. Concentrate on deep runs and the drop-off points, where the staging fish will readily take flies. Spawning trout aren't eaters, so if you see trout in the act, move on to feeding fish. Always watch for and avoid redds at this time of the year.

Hatches

The Williams Fork River has one of the best Red Quill hatches I have ever seen. Late summer and fall are good time frames on this river because the water levels have dropped, allowing the trout opportunities to feed without battling the current.

Fellow angler and friend Pat Dorsey informed me of this hatch, and he told me that it was trout nirvana. He explained, "I was on a trip with a client a few days ago when a storm rolled in. The clouds started gathering, producing a great Blue-Winged Olive hatch. Then, to my surprise, Red Quills by the truckload were floating downstream, causing a feeding frenzy. Put on a #16 A. K. Red Quill and the trout cannot refuse." To match both insects at the same time, I like to trail a #18 BWO Mathews's Sparkle Dun 18 inches behind a #16 A. K.'s Red Quill.

With midges available from late fall through spring, you can do well with small imitations like a #18-22 Mercury Flashback Black Beauty. The midges in the spring months can be as large as a size 18. Following the midges and BWOs are a wealth of caddis, stoneflies, PMDs, and Tricos.

During the fall, large brown trout move up the Williams Fork River from the Colorado River. Targeting deep water with disturbance on the surface is a good bet for staging trout. LANDON MAYER

Pat Dorsey lands an average-size brown that was feeding during a heavy BWO and Red Quill hatch. As Pat put it, "Fishing this hatch late when the weather moves in is like trout nirvana with 12- to 16-inch eager trout looking up. All of a sudden the surface erupts with rising trout making the next hour stories to be told for a lifetime." LANDON MAYER

Two sets of eyes are always better than one. Pat Dorsey and I team up to fool a feeding trout. JAY NICHOLS

When matching the predominant foods, try using a heavily-weighted fly like a Copper John, a worm imitation, or a weighted caddis larva such as a #16 Beadhead Breadcrust as the bottom fly, with a #18-20 Mercury Pheasant Tail, Sparkle Wing RS2, Rainbow Warrior, or Barr Emerger above. A heavy fly on the bottom eliminates the need for split shot, making your rig appear as natural as possible as it plunges to the depths of these deep trout waters.

A. K.'s Red Quill

Hook:	#14-18 Dai-Riki 305
Thread:	Rust 6/0
Tail:	Medium dun hackle fibers
Body:	Quill stem from reddish brown hackle
Thorax:	Tan dry-fly dubbing
Post:	White turkey flat
Hackle:	Medium brown

Stalcup's Baetis

Hook: #18-22 Dai-Riki 270
Thread: Olive 8/0 Uni-Thread
Tail: Partridge
Abdomen: Olive brown D-rib
Thorax: Olive Superfine dubbing
Legs: Partridge
Wing case: Brown Medallion Sheeting

Graphic Caddis (Green)

Hook: #14-18 Tiemco 2499 SP-BL
Thread: Olive 6/0 Danville
Tag: Silver Holographic Flashabou
Abdomen: Olive Wapsi Stretch Tubing
Legs: Hungarian partridge fibers
Head: Natural gray ostrich herl

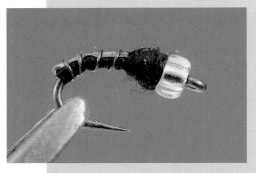

Mercury Flashback Black Beauty

Hook: #16-24 Tiemco 2487 or 2488
Thread: Black 70-denier Ultra Thread
Body: Tying thread
Rib: Copper wire
Head: Black beaver or rabbit dubbing
Flash: Mylar tinsel

Lawsons's Conehead Sculpin (Tan)

Hook: #4-10 Tiemco 5263
Cone: Gold tungsten
Thread: Light tan or color to match
Head: Light tan wool, spun and clipped
         to shape
Pectoral
fins: Hen saddle hackle
Gills: Red wool
Tail: Straight-cut rabbit fur strip over
         a few fibers of yellow Flashabou

COLORADO'S
BEST FLY FISHING
SOUTHWESTERN

*Unlike the Front Range, southwestern Colorado is arid
and desert-like. During hot weather, fish early and late.*
ANGUS DRUMMOND

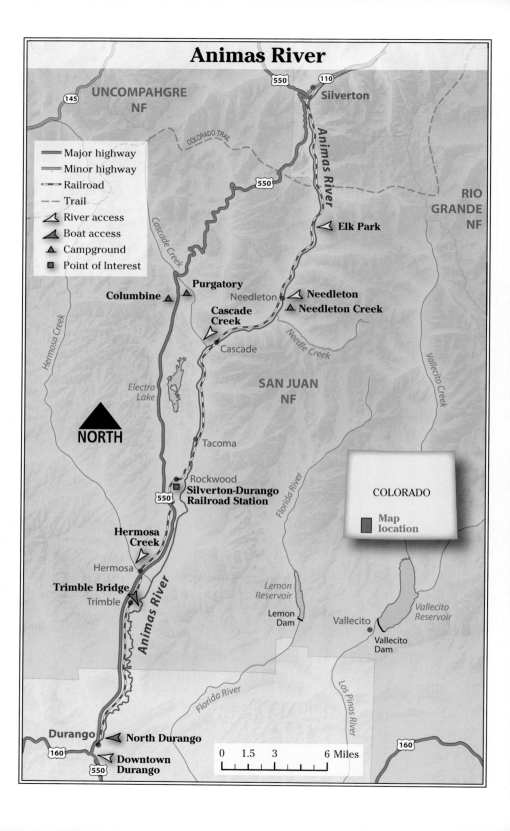

Animas River

UNCOMPAHGRE NF

145

550 110 Silverton

COLORADO TRAIL

Major highway
Minor highway
Railroad
Trail
River access
Boat access
Campground
Point of Interest

550

Animas River

Elk Park

RIO GRANDE NF

Cascade Creek

Columbine ▲ ▲ Purgatory

Needleton ◁ Needleton

Cascade Creek

▲ Needleton Creek

◁ Cascade

Needle Creek

SAN JUAN NF

Electra Lake

Vallecito Creek

NORTH

Tacoma

Rockwood

Silverton-Durango Railroad Station

550

Hermosa Creek

Florida River

Hermosa Creek

◁ Hermosa

Trimble Bridge

◁ Trimble

Animas River

Lemon Reservoir

Lemon Dam

Vallecito

Vallecito Reservoir

Vallecito Dam

COLORADO

■ Map location

Los Pinos River

Florida River

Durango ◁ North Durango

160

◁ Downtown Durango

550

0 1.5 3 6 Miles

160

CHAPTER 16

Animas River

N amed by the Spanish as *El Rio de las Animas Perdidas*, or River of Lost Souls, the Animas is the last undammed river in Colorado. It begins high in the San Juan Mountains at the confluence of the West and North Forks near the ghost town of Animas Forks, and eventually flows into Animas Canyon before joining the San Juan River, 110 miles from its head-waters. Though once devastated by mining, the Animas has rebounded in the last 15 years. Now it has Gold Medal status (average trout size is 14 to 15 inches) and provides many opportunities for anglers to enjoy quality fish-ing, especially from July through October, in one of the most pristine areas of the state.

Though Durango is isolated in the southwest corner of the state, the town has great accommodations in a beautiful downtown with lots of local flavor— and some of the best fishing is right in town. Moderate weather during the winter allows anglers to fish the Animas year-round. "Although prime fish-ing on the Animas is from mid-June through October, we get some wonder-ful Indian summer days here in the Southwest in the dead of winter," John Flick, co-owner of Duranglers in Durango, explains. "Fishing on the Animas can be incredible right here in town in January or February. People can come skiing at Purgatory and go fly fishing on the same trip."

While this river can produce some of the best fishing in the southwest side of the state, it can also be one of the most challenging rivers. One day it is on, and the very next day its selective trout can humble you in a minute. For those who reside in the town of Durango or surrounding areas, it is con-venient to hit the river when it is fishing well. If you are traveling to fish the river, timing is key, and you should look to July and August for the best flows and hatches. Call one of the local shops to make sure you come when

The best time to fish the water upstream of Durango is after runoff, which is generally from late June through September. As the water drops, the trout will have the opportunity to find holding water to feed on caddis and mayflies such as PMDs and BWOs without battling the current. WILL BLANCHARD

the water is on the drop, or holding steady. To get to the Animas from the Front Range, take I-25 South to Walsenburg and then US 160 West to Durango. From the Western Slope, take US 50 East to Montrose and then US 550 to Durango.

Upper Animas

North of Silverton, the Animas starts as a small stream before gathering volume from the North Fork, West Fork, and Cinnamon Creek (collectively known as the Animas Forks) as it flows through a steep canyon to Hermosa.

This area is extremely rugged, and you are sure to find solitude fishing the many headwater pools. The water here is clear and green with a mix of pockets and deep pools and is full of hungry rainbow, cutthroat, brook, and brown trout from 8 to 16 inches that will take a hopper/dropper rig.

To fish the river upstream of Hermosa, catch a morning train ride on the Silverton Narrow Gauge Railroad from Durango or Rockwood (for more information, visit durangotrain.com). Starting from Durango takes longer and eats away at your fishing time, so many drive to Rockwood, a small town approximately 15 miles north of Durango along US 550. This is one of the great backcountry trips in the United States that not only takes you back in time but also provides access to miles of wilderness water. In addition to the main river, plenty of feeder creeks provide good fishing. Remember to prepare for any unforeseen weather or emergencies, including an unexpected overnight stay.

The train runs from the first week of May to the end of October (call for exact schedule) and charges adults (age 12 and over) $86.36 plus a freight fee of $10 per backpack. Call (970) 247-2733 for reservations and to get the list of flag stops and the timetable for each. The best time to fish via the train is from July to October. From Rockwood, there are two main stops for the train that

According to CDOW, 70 percent of the Animas' trout population are rainbow trout, 25 percent brown trout, and 5 percent cutthroat trout. In addition to great hatches, don't overlook fishing streamers. There is a good population of sculpins in the river. WILL BLANCHARD

interest fly fishers—Needleton and Elk Park—and both are only accessible from the train. Needleton, approximately 12 miles upstream from Rockwood, accesses Forest Trail 575, which runs along the river on its eastern side. You can fish and camp at Needleton Creek campground if you want to make this a multiday adventure. Elk Park, which is an access point to the Colorado Trail for hikers, is another 4 miles upstream and also has river access both up- and downstream. Cascade Creek, where it merges with the Animas, can also be worth a stop—ask the conductor to drop you off at the bridge near the confluence and use Purgatory Trail (Forest Trail 511) to access. Not every train stops at these points, so make sure that you speak with the conductors and

To catch one of the large trout in town, you must keep a low profile and hunt for them. Slow down, scan all good-looking water, and fish it thoroughly. "On the Animas, don't overlook the 'pillow' of those big boulders in the current," John Flick says. ANGUS DRUMMOND

On the Animas, and many other rivers in the state, a lot of fish hug tight to the banks. Drift a large attractor like this Crystal Stimulator to search for aggressive trout. Other good attractors include a #8-14 Charlie Boy Hopper, #14-16 Renegade, #14-16 Trude, and a #14-16 Humpy. LANDON MAYER

let them know of your plans. Additionally, ask them to explain the signal for flagging down the train.

Downstream from Rockwood, Hermosa Creek, another good trout stream, can be reached by taking US 550 six miles south from Rockwood to Hermosa Village. Just north of the bridge over Hermosa Creek, turn and follow CR 203 until it meets a north-south road that parallels the highway. Turn right at CR 202, and follow this road uphill to the end. Hermosa Creek Trail follows the creek.

From Silverton to the Tacoma Power Plant upstream from Durango, the Animas is a Class IV to V run for experienced kayakers only, and there is no point in trying to float-fish this section of the river. It has several falls and drops over 2,000 feet in only 24 miles. As you continue downstream from Hermosa on US 550, the Animas widens to over 100 feet, providing long riffles, runs, and deep pools that hold lots of trout. Look for pull-offs along the

With some of the largest wilderness areas in Colorado near the Animas, there is more water than you could cover in a lifetime. Streams like Hermosa Creek, the Florida and Piedra rivers, and the East and West Fork of the San Juan offer anglers plentiful opportunities to break away from crowds and explore new water and scenery.

In addition to public land, you can fish miles of water on the Ute Reservation with a permit. "I think the most overlooked fishing access in our region is the Southern Ute Indian Reservation," says Duranglers' John Flick. "The Southern Utes own most of the water south of US 160 to the New Mexico border on the Animas, Los Pinos, Piedra, and San Juan rivers. With their permit, which we sell, you can access most of this water. The Utes have done a good job with stream rehab and management. These are all great fisheries and don't get a lot of pressure. In general, all these rivers fish from April to November, except for spring runoff."

According to the Southern Ute Department of Natural Resources' web site (southern-ute.nsn.us/WRMWeb/fishing_permits.html) permitted Non-Tribal Members can fish on the Animas, Los Pinos, Piedra, and San Juan rivers through designated access points. "Fishermen must use the access points identified on the maps to enter and exit stream corridors, which are located only on tribal trust lands. Fishermen may move up or down the stream corridors without securing additional permission, but may not continue on to allotted or private lands unless authorized by the landowner. The stream corridor is bound by a 5-foot distance from the edge of the water on both sides of the stream, provided, however, fishermen may depart from this corridor only to the extent necessary to avoid a barrier located within the corridor. Use of designated access points and stream corridors is allowed for fishing only."

With a wilderness that seems never-ending, the rivers, creeks, and streams are best researched by atlas. These waters would make a perfect extended trip. "The Weminuche Wilderness is the largest wilderness in the state and is in the middle of the second-largest national forest in the state. There are more streams, creeks, and lakes than an angler could fish in a lifetime," says John Flick. "My partner, Tom Knopick, and I have fished and guided all the waters in southwest Colorado for over 26 years. We have yet

highway to mark access. Private land is also well-marked. You can put in at Trimble Bridge for an 11-mile, Class I float to the North Durango takeout. John Flick tells anglers to take their time and search the water carefully for the best results: "Find a feeding fish first, then fish to that fish. They feed very subtly. They are up for a few seconds, then down, and you don't see them. Most anglers pass up water too fast. You need to take your time and scan good-looking water for 15 to 20 minutes before moving on."

The Piedra "is a great fishery from April to November that does not get a lot of pressure," says John Flick. When targeting trout in narrow waterways such as the Piedra River, look for deep plunge pools and shade. LANDON MAYER

to find a piece of water in the wilderness that doesn't have trout in it. Take the time and pack in, either on foot or with the aid of horses or llamas, and you will not be disappointed." ■

Lower Animas

In Durango, there is about 7 miles of wade access via the Animas River Trail, which starts from the 32nd Street Bridge and extends downstream to the Rivera Crossing Bridge at Dallabetta City Park. To get to the 32nd Street Bridge (Memorial Park), take US 550 and turn left on 32nd Street, cross the bridge, and turn right on East 3rd Avenue. The parking lot is on the right at the cor-

ANIMAS RIVER

	JAN	FEB	MAR	APR	MAY	JUN	JUL	AUG	SEP	OCT	NOV	DEC

Midge (*Chironomidae*)

#18-22 Jujubee Midge, Rojo Midge, Barr's Pure Midge Larva, Brooks' Sprout Midge, Top Secret Midge, Griffith's Gnat

Blue-Winged Olive (*Baetis* spp.)

#16-22 Johnny Flash, Bad Boy Baetis, Mercury RS2, Engle's All Around Baetis, Parachute Adams, Vis-A-Dun, Sparkle Dun

Caddis
(*Brachycentrus* and *Hydropsyche* spp.)

#16-20 Phares' Caddis Candy, Landon's Larva, Lawson's Electric Caddis, Deep Sparkle Pupa, Barr's Graphic Caddis, Larry's High-Vis Caddis

Golden Stonefly (*Perlidae*)

#10-12 Barr's Tungstone, 20 Incher, Tyler's Fakey Nymph, Madam X, Rogue Parastone

Pale Morning Dun
(*Ephemerella* spp.)

#16-20 Barr Emerger, Pheasant Tail, Sparkle Dun, Parachute Adams

Terrestrials

#10-16 black Foam Beetle, Dave's Hopper, Schlotter's Foam Flying Ant, Chernobyl Ant, BC Hopper

Sculpin

#6-10 Meat Whistle, Lawson's Conehead Sculpin, Will's Stinging Sculpin, Mercer's Egg Sucking Rag Sculpin, Trick or Treat

---

ner of East 3rd Avenue and 29th Street. From the Lightner Creek confluence to Rivera Crossing Bridge is Gold Medal water, which is artificial flies and lures only, with a posession and size limit of two fish over 16 inches. Boat (raft and drift) launches are at 32nd Street, 9th Street, High Bridge, and Rivera Bridge.

In town, the river is similar to the Blue River as it flows through Dillon, including some wary fish that can require several changes in flies and techniques before you fool them. "For being a freestone," Will Blanchard, owner of Animas Valley Anglers, explains, "the fish at times act more like tailwater trout. The Animas frustrates experienced anglers and guides alike. Personally, I like that. Small mayflies, midges, tan and gray caddis, foam hoppers, beaded nymphs, and long streamers should be in every angler's fly box when fishing the Animas. Be prepared to cast a lot of flies to them."

Past Durango on US 550, the Animas flows through Ute Indian Reservation lands. Fishing can be very good, but you must obtain the reasonably priced permits through a vendor such as Duranglers on Main Avenue. If you want to explore this water, the shop can provide the regulations and designated access points.

According to the Southern Ute website: "The Animas River between the northern Reservation boundary and Weasleskin Bridge is managed for trophy trout fishing. This stretch of water has special regulations as follows: Artificial flies and lures only with barbless hooks. Absolutely no bait fishing allowed in this section. Two trout bag and possession limit, with each fish measuring 16 inches or greater in total length. All trout under 16 inches must be immediately returned to the water."

Hatches

The Animas has a healthy population of insects, but the main attraction is the caddis after runoff. "The number one hatch on the Animas is the caddis," says John Flick. "They start in early June when the river is big and muddy and continue most of the summer. Early in the season, they are size 12 to 14, and they

Angus Drummond searches the emerald green water of the Piedra River with a nymph. The Piedra is located off US 160 east of Durango and runs along CR 622 north of Chimney Rock. LANDON MAYER

Dark skies generally mean good fishing. In addition to great hatches, the Animas also fishes well with streamers, especially in high, off-color water or stormy low-light conditions that make the fish abandon caution and spread out to feed. WILL BLANCHARD

get smaller and less dense as the summer progresses. The trout love to feed on these bugs, many times in the film during an emergence, and swinging soft hackles and wets flies can be deadly."

Following the caddis, Pale Morning Duns and Blue-Winged Olives hatch from June through October, and during the winter, midges. Flick states, "There is also a huge population of sculpins in the Animas. Spring and early summer, when the river is high and colored, is the best time to fish streamers, either with a short sinking-tip line or extra lead on the leader." Use #6-10 olive Lawson's Conehead Sculpins, #8-14 Trick or Treats, #4-8 tan or olive Meat Whistles, and #8-12 Animas River Specials, a deer-hair-head streamer designed by John Flick.

Engle's All Around Baetis

Hook:	#18-22 Tiemco 101
Thread:	Black 10/0 Gudebrod
Tail:	Brown Antron
Rib:	Fine gold wire
Body:	Muskrat dubbing, and narrow pearlescent Mylar
Hackle:	Quail body feather (blue)

Barr's Uncased Caddis Larva (Green)

Hook:	#12-16 Tiemco 2302
Bead:	Black
Weight:	.015-inch-diameter lead wire
Thread:	Black 8/0 Uni-Thread
Tail:	Olive Z-lon
Rib:	3X monofilament
Shellback:	Olive Fly Specks Thin Skin
Body:	Caddis green Nature's Spirit Emergence dubbing
Thorax:	Black ostrich herl

Johnny Flash (Olive)

Hook:	#20-24 Tiemco 2488
Thread:	Olive 8/0
Tail:	Olive hackle fibers
Abdomen:	Thread
Wing:	Pearl Krystal Flash
Thorax:	Olive dubbing

Tyler's Fakey Nymph

Hook:	#10-18 Tiemco 2488
Thread:	Black 70-denier Ultra Thread
Bead:	Gold or color to match
Tail:	Ring-necked pheasant tail fibers
Rib:	Copper wire
Abdomen:	Pheasant tail fibers
Thorax:	Peacock Ice Dub
Flashback:	Pearl Mirage Tinsel
Legs:	Small round rubber legs
Hackle:	Brown hen

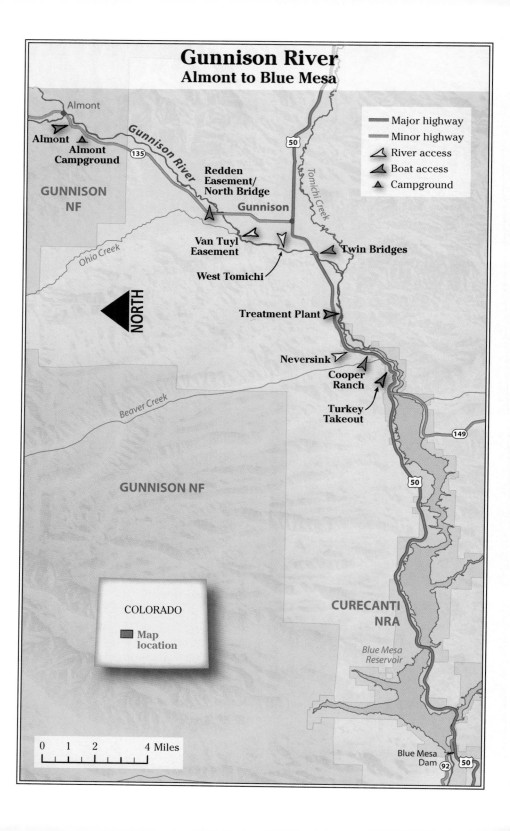

CHAPTER 17

Gunnison River

Forming in Gunnison County at the confluence of the Taylor and East rivers, the Gunnison River is the fifth-largest river in Colorado, running 180 miles long. Flowing through Blue Mesa, Morrow Point, and Crystal reservoirs, the river eventually cuts through one of the longest, narrowest, and deepest gorges in the world, the Black Canyon of the Gunnison. At the outlet of the canyon, it receives the North Fork of the Gunnison, and then downstream near Delta is joined by the Uncompahgre River.

Most days on the Gunny are good days, but fall is a magic time on this river—Gunnison-area guide and co-owner of Gunnison River Guides Jason Booth calls it the "epic season." Not only is the foliage stunning, but there is a run of kokanee salmon that make their way up the Gunnison from Blue Mesa Reservoir and readily take bright flies such as #14-18 red Copper Johns and #16-18 Flashtail Mini Eggs (4 mm).

Because they do not feed when they spawn, these landlocked salmon are striking out of aggression, and early in the run they put up a great fight. Following the kokanee are many lake-run brown trout in the prespawn stage and large rainbows. This is one of the best times to hook into a true deep-dwelling trophy from Blue Mesa Reservoir, while the fish are looking for the high-protein eggs produced by the salmon. As Booth says, "My favorite time to fish on the upper Gunnison is September and October. Every afternoon you get a BWO hatch. There is great sight-fishing for large rainbows and browns behind schools of spawning kokanee salmon. Fish feed hard at this time of the year." Pat Dorsey, who grew up fishing Gunnison Country, says, "I have experienced this myself. It is a lot like targeting rainbows in British Columbia and Alaska behind sockeye salmon. You'll sight-fish to 'bows sitting behind the areas where the kokanee have dug redds in the substrate. Nymphing can be explosive with egg patterns."

To get to the Gunnison from Denver, take I-70 West to CO 470 East and use US 285 South to enter the mountains. Follow US 285 South all the way to

The trails leading into the Black Canyon of the Gunnison River are not easy, but if you are up for the challenge, the reward is often unpressured water in a gorgeous setting.
ROSS PURNELL

Jason Booth holds one of many large trout found in the Gunnison River above Blue Mesa Reservoir. In high flows large trout will migrate upriver. JASON BOOTH

Poncha Springs, and then take US 50 West to Gunnison. For access from Colorado Springs, take I-25 to US 24 West to Johnson Village, then take US 285 South to Poncha Springs and US 50 West to Gunnison.

From Almont to US 50 special regulations are artificial flies and lures only with a possession and size limit of two browns 16 inches—all rainbows must be returned. Observe the closure signs near the reservoirs.

Almont to Blue Mesa Reservoir

The headwaters start south of Almont on CO 135, approximately 10 miles north of Gunnison at the confluence of the East and Taylor rivers. The first wade access is from Almont to Almont Campground, for approximately 1¹/2 miles, and then the Redden Access is 8 more miles downstream via pullouts. The flow of the river at the merger of the Taylor and East rivers is fast and wide, with numerous pockets, riffles, and deep runs and breaks throughout.

The water can change drastically in the early seasons of the year from runoff and release from the Taylor River. This is one of the main reasons fishing from a boat is most productive. You can float the upper river at 800 cfs or greater in a hard boat from Almont to Twin Bridges, or in an inflatable raft if flows are lower. An option to consider is the Class II section running 4 miles long, with a put-in at Almont and a takeout at North Bridge. "The upper river has limited access," says Dorsey. "It is best fished via personal watercraft, raft, or drift boat. For a hard boat, you need around 800 cfs, or you'll beat up your boat."

From the Redden easement, you can head south another mile to Palisades Park and take the trail to the Van Tuyl access. Taking Spencer Road west, take a left on Tin Cup Highway and follow it to access the park. The Palisades Park will be on your right. The trail offers approximately 1¹/2 miles of wade access on the east side of the river and a little less than that on the west side.

Farther downstream another half a mile, take a right onto CO 50 west to Twin Bridges access, which offers wade access on the north side of the river as well as a boat launch. Continue downstream by heading west on US 50. There is access at West Tomichi Riverway Park and Gunnison Water Park. From here, there is public water on both sides just past CR 32 and on down to the reservoir. While you can put in here and keep floating to McCabe's, there is a big drop named Psychedelic Drop below Twin Bridges that most people avoid in the area (unless you want to portage river-right). Four miles farther downstream is Neversink and Cooper Ranch Access. Alternatively, continue down CO 50, put in at McCabe's and take a 4-mile float to Turkey Take-Out, which is the last ramp before Blue Mesa Reservoir. "This is not your normal takeout," Pat Dorsey says. "You are literally taking your boat out in the reservoir. Lake levels vary depending on the time of year and flows. If the reservoir is full, you will row the boat through the lake; if the reservoir is low, the exposed river channel will allow you to navigate down to the Turkey Creek entrance. Again, there is no boat ramp per se, just back your trailer down to the reservoir/river. This can be muddy, especially after snowmelt or rainfall, so plan accordingly, otherwise you might get your truck stuck."

Dorsey says, "On my days off, I love to float the Gunnison. I float from Almont down to North Bridge and North Bridge to Twin Bridges, but I especially like the float from McCabe's Lane to Turkey Creek. It reminds me a lot of the Madison between Varney Bridge and Burnt Tree. It has nice riffles, runs, midchannel shelves, and the fishing is really good. Spring and fall, there are some nice lake-run trout."

According to Dorsey, this section of the river also hosts a great Trico hatch, or more accurately, fish that actually key in on the Tricos that emerge throughout the entire river. "While Tricos hatch on much of the river, it's rare to find fish keying on Tricos unless you are fishing the lower river. The best area to target this hatch is between McCabe's Lane and Turkey Creek, where the river widens and has well-defined midchannel shelves, gravel bars, and long, glassy runs. One of my favorite areas for this hatch is the braided section above Cooper Ranch."

The lower section of the upper stretch of the Gunnison River before entering Blue Mesa Reservoir has plenty of walk and wade access in areas like Cooper Ranch and Neversink in the Curecanti National Park, which has 2 miles of public water that Jason Booth says is "very readable and scenic with a good number of rainbows, browns, and in the fall, kokanee salmon and spawning browns out of Blue Mesa." This lower stretch is a great area to pursue spring-run rainbows and fall-run browns known to exceed 20 inches. Hit the deep runs and tailouts, in addition to the head of each run in the shallow, highly oxygenated water.

Also below Blue Mesa Dam are two reservoirs, Morrow Point Reservoir and Crystal Reservoir. You can access them by following the signs a short

Pat Dorsey fooled this fish with a #18 Mercury RS2. Many anglers are surprised when they first fish the river how large these trout can be on average. CDOW has attempted to stock whirling disease–resistant rainbows, as well as cutthroat trout, in hopes the natural populations will come back, because browns now outnumber them on this waterway. There is also a small population of cuttbows. LANDON MAYER

drive off US 50 near the town of Cimarron. If you keep heading west on US 50 past Cimarron, you will see a sign for the Black Canyon National Park. Turn north off US 50 onto CO 347 to enter the park. After you enter, take your first right onto East Portal Road and follow to parking, picnicking, camping, and fishing at the East Portal. You will drive down a paved 16-degree-grade road to access the river below Crystal Reservoir.

High Water and Hatches

Before mid-May, the water on the river is low and clear, but during runoff the river turns off-color and swells considerably and many anglers are intimidated by its size. At this time, fishing can be good. "I think the biggest overlooked component on this river is fishing it during runoff," says Pat Dorsey. "I have had some of my best fishing on this river when the river is flowing from 2,500 to 3,000 cfs. I have netted 30-plus fish on days when there is not another angler on the river and when the average angler might think

Fishing during the Blue-Winged Olive hatch in the fall can be terrific near the Chukar Trail, Gunnison Gorge. Always make sure you false-cast downstream of the fish in calm water to prevent any movement from above the trout. ANGUS DRUMMOND

Pat's Rubber Legs is a local favorite on the Gunnison River and one of the most effec-tive flies in the state in areas where stoneflies are found. LANDON MAYER

things are hopeless. The river can be on fire when the flows kick up and turn off-color. I have seen it where trout are spitting up massive amounts of worms from overfeeding in these conditions. Fish a bright red or pink San Juan Worm, Chamois Leech, or Mercury Caddis along the edges. The fish are typically stacked up there. If you find one fish, you'll generally find several more."

In late June, stoneflies begin to migrate to the river's edge. You can fish big, ugly nymphs in the softer water along the river's edge, around or below the overhanging willows. During high water, streamers can be very effective as well when the trout disperse around the river, allowing more trout to see a streamer retrieve. Following the stoneflies, there is a steady stream of Blue-Winged Olives, caddis, stoneflies, and Green Drakes best matched with a dual-fly rig such as #12-16 Furimsky's Foam Drake trailing a caddis pupa like a #14-16 Barr's Graphic Caddis or #14-16 Beadhead Caddis Pupa. To match the Blue-Winged Olives, Pale Morning Duns, and Red Quills, I also like a plain #12-18 Parachute Adams with a #16-20 PMD or BWO Barr's Emerger, #18-20 Sparkle Wing RS2, or #14-20 red, olive, or natural Pheasant Tail dropper.

Of all the rivers in the state, my favorite river to float is the Gunnison—from targeting larger trout that have swum upstream from Blue Mesa Reservoir to a multiple-day float through the stunning Black Canyon. A raft trip in the canyon and gorge section is a trip of a lifetime. ANGUS DRUMMOND

Black Canyon

Established in 1999, the Black Canyon of the Gunnison River is one of the country's newest national parks. From the rim, the views of this massive gorge—formed by the action of water and rock scouring down through hard Proterozoic crystalline rock—will leave you amazed. This 13-mile stretch of water can be fished by foot from trails leading down to the river or by traveling upstream with a guide in a jet boat from Gunnison River Pleasure Park. Pack trips to the river from local guide services like Black Canyon Anglers will let you bring all the gear you need to float and camp

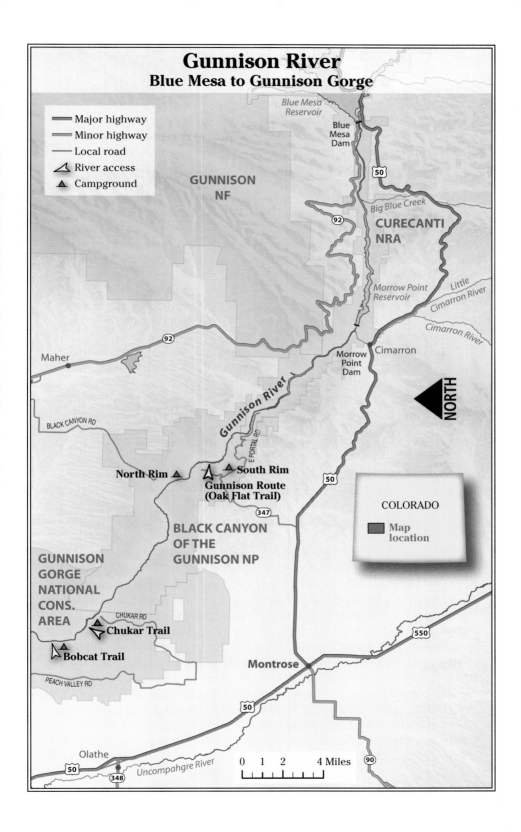

Gunnison River
Blue Mesa to Gunnison Gorge

— Major highway
— Minor highway
— Local road
⊿ River access
▲ Campground

Blue Mesa Reservoir

Blue Mesa Dam

GUNNISON NF

92

50

Big Blue Creek

CURECANTI NRA

Morrow Point Reservoir

Little Cimarron River

Cimarron River

92

Maher

Gunnison River

Morrow Point Dam

Cimarron

NORTH

BLACK CANYON RD

E PORTAL RD

North Rim ▲

⊿ ▲ South Rim
Gunnison Route
(Oak Flat Trail)

50

347

COLORADO

■ Map location

BLACK CANYON OF THE GUNNISON NP

GUNNISON GORGE NATIONAL CONS. AREA

CHUKAR RD

⊿▲ Chukar Trail

550

⊿▲ Bobcat Trail

Montrose

PEACH VALLEY RD

50

Olathe

50

348

Uncompahgre River

0 1 2   4 Miles

90

Flowing from the western slope of the San Juan Mountains near the rustic Colorado town of Ouray to Delta, the Uncompahgre meanders through some of the best scenery in the state before reaching the Gunnison. With a majority of the river above Ridgway Reservoir remaining private, the main attraction is the 2-mile stretch below the dam referred to as Pa-Co-Chu-Puk that continues down through Montrose. Known as one of the newest tailwaters in the state, the restoration project that started in 1992 has turned this tailwater into one of Colorado's great escapes.

With catch-and-release waters revealing deep runs and large pools, there is a strong population of 14- to 18-inch rainbows, browns, and cutthroat. The most sought-after location to fish, especially in the winter, is directly below Ridgway Reservoir. Continuing south on US 550, you can reach this tailwater fishery by entering Ridgeway State Park, approximately 15 miles south of Montrose. The area is well-marked; a park pass is required on all vehicles. Access to the river by foot is easy, with a path following the water in the 1 1/2-mile tailwater. In late May and June, when flows can increase to over 400 cfs, use caution when moving about the water.

The Uncompahgre River runs along US 550 with access in Montrose at the River Way Trail. Take US 550 south to East Oak Grove Road, turn right, and go three short blocks to Rio Grande Avenue. Additional in-town access is off US 550 and Chipeta Road near the Ute Indian Museum, as the trail runs behind the museum. ■

in the majestic landscape. With an abundance of wildlife, the canyon is also home to some impressive brown and rainbow trout that are willing to take big flies. It is hard to find a wilderness adventure like this anywhere in the United States.

To access the South Rim of the Black Canyon from Montrose, take US 50 East to CO 347 North. For the North Rim, take US 50 to Delta and take CO 92 East past Hotchkiss. Continuing on CO 92, take a right just past Crawford onto Black Canyon Road and follow it into the park. Ben Olson, guide and manager of Black Canyon Anglers, explains, "There really are no overlooked access areas, and the maps for the Gunnison Gorge (blm.gov/co/st/en/nca/ggnca.html) and Black Canyon National Parks (nps.gov/blca/planyourvisit/maps.htm) are very well done. They show you all access points and ask that you stay on these trails to preserve the area."

The easiest river access is at the South Rim's East Portal Trail from East Portal Road, which offers over 2 miles of river. Below Crystal Reservoir, the river can be fished by navigating along the banks. Camping is located in designated campgrounds on the north or south rim. A free inner-canyon backcountry permit can be obtained at the South Rim Visitor Center or the North

Rim Ranger Station. This permit is required to hike into the canyon. Tyler Befus, author of *A Kid's Guide to Fly Fishing*, says that one of his favorite places to fish in Colorado is the Gunnison River below Crystal Dam. "It is the only place that you can drive close to the Black Canyon," he says. "The river below grows some very large rainbows and browns. It is also one of the most beautiful places you will likely fish in Colorado."

Alternatively, the most popular access to the canyon is found on the Gunnison Route, also on the South Rim. Follow the Oak Flat Trail at the west side of the visitor center until you come to the river access sign (about 0.3 mile). Go right and follow the steep trail down. The total distance to the river is about a mile, and there is primitive camping at the river. While there are other trails, this one has the least amount of drop (only 1,800 feet). Still, anglers should make sure that they have adequate provisions and know enough about self-rescue to make safety a priority. Olson says, "You need to be in great shape to hike these trails, but you are rewarded for the effort you spend. You enter complete solitude, rarely seeing another person, but if you do, you can guarantee they are fishermen that share the same addiction and passion for the outdoors that you do."

From the North Rim, the SOB Trail next to the North Rim Campground on Black Canyon Road is a 2-mile, 1,800-foot drop with very loose rock and intense sun, but rewards fly fishers with 2 miles of river access during low flows. Park at the Ranger Station and walk west about 25 yards to the beginning of the trail. While there are other trails such Long Draw, Slide Draw, Tomichi and Warner Routes, they are often extreme or long and offer access to only a short stretch of water.

Gunnison Gorge

The Gunnison Gorge Wilderness is in the middle of the Gunnison Gorge National Conservation Area. According to BLM, "It encompasses approximately 17,784 acres of public lands, including 14 miles of the river, extending from the northwestern boundary of the Black Canyon of the Gunnison National Park north to a point approximately one mile downstream from the confluence of the Smith Fork and the main stem of the Gunnison River." Ben Olson recommends a trip into the gorge for lightly pressured trout. "If you enjoy hiking into low-pressure sections of Gold Medal water rivers I would send you into the Gunnison Gorge. The Gunnison Gorge is Class III water that has great walk-wade access. I would recommend going with a seasoned outfitter for your first float trip through the gorge."

To access the Gunnison Gorge National Conservation Area, continue on US 50 to Montrose where it heads north. Just outside of Olathe, head east on Falcon Road until you hit Peach Valley Recreation Site. The road will then turn north, and you can access the Gunnison Gorge from this road where there are four well-marked trails with roads bearing their names. Chukar

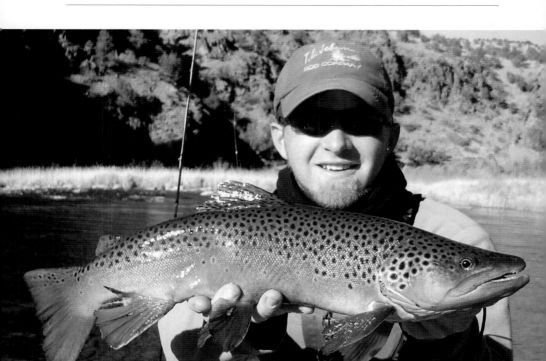

Ben Olson holds a large Gunnison River brown. BEN OLSON

Trail is the access point for boaters wishing to float the river, and you can fish up- or downstream from this access. Chukar Road is the first right upon entering the area, and after 7 miles, it leads to the trailhead. This trail, which drops approximately 550 feet in little over a mile, is the easiest and most heavily traveled route.

If you continue on Peach Valley Road you can also take a right on Bobcat or Duncan Roads to access those trails; however both are steep and loose with most of Bobcat being undeveloped. Instead, for an alternative to Chukar to avoid crowds, continue to Ute Road and take the Ute Trail. While it is a 4 1/2-mile, 1,200-foot drop, it also has over 4 miles of river access and makes an excellent overnight adventure.

From Chukar you can hire mules to pack down gear for one-, two-, or three-day float trips, in which you will cover 14 miles of one of the most pristine rivers in the state. Going with an outfitter is strongly recommended for your first trip, as there are a ton of logistical hoops to jump through and up to Class IV rapids at some levels. While Chukar is the easiest of the trails to use to reach the water, it still can test the strength of any angler in the hot sun. The last takeout is at Pleasure Park in the BLM Gunnison Forks Day Use Area, and the rest of the Gunnison to Austin has no wading access as it is all private land.

In the canyon, the trout use the sheer granite rock faces plunging into the river as ambush locations during the June Salmonfly hatch. When the stoneflies land or crawl on the rocks, the trout will leap out of the water and take them off the rocks or strike them down and then crush them in the water. When fishing to trout in the canyon—at all times, not just during stonefly hatches—concentrate on the slick water or cooling edges by the shadows of the rock walls.

But the Gunnison has other great hatches besides the hard-to-hit Salmonflies. "The most overlooked hatches on the Gunnison River are our four smaller species of stoneflies," Olson says. "Following the Salmonfly hatch is a Golden Stone hatch, then Yellow Sallies, little green stones, and brown stones, all of which can be as good if not better than our Salmonfly hatch with fewer people on the water. The time frame is end of June to mid-July."

Streamer fishing can be very good, and an overlooked technique: "One of my favorite techniques for this river is a double streamer rig. I tie two big

The most popular attraction in the canyon is the Salmonfly hatch in May and June. If you can time it right, which is tough, the hatch can provide awesome fishing with #4-8 Rogue Stones and Pat's Rubber Legs. ANGUS DRUMMOND

streamers about 18 inches apart with loop knots to add more movement and undulation to the flies. I use 0X tippet and strip these flies back to the boat as inconsistently as possible. Bait fish do not swim consistently—they are very sporadic. One of the most successful retrieves is two strips—pause—one strip—pause—three strips—pause, then recast. It is a lot of work but very effective. The Gunnison Gorge consists of 90 percent brown trout and 10 percent rainbows. Anyone who has done a lot of fishing for browns knows how opportunistic they are, and the fact that they are suckers for a streamer," Olson noted.

Olson's confidence flies for this river are a #6 Articulated Leech, a #16-20 Tungsten Beadhead Flashback Pheasant Tail on a curved hook, a #12-16 Miracle Nymph tied with a chartreuse underbody, #18-20 Barr's BWO and PMD Emergers, and a #6-10 Girdle Bug. "These patterns are flies I always carry, since they imitate the most readily available insects in the river."

One final tip: If you are hiking in, one thing that I have seen others do to avoid scaling rocks to get upstream to the next pool or to get to the other, less-pressured, side of the river is to use inexpensive inner tubes that are easy to pack in. Try this at your own peril, but they seemed to work for the people I saw using them, and I made a mental note to pack in one of them on my next trip.

Lake Fork

Often overlooked, the Lake Fork of the Gunnison can provide anglers with a great side trip while visiting the Black Canyon area. With the headwaters beginning in the San Juan Mountains and continuing into Lake San Cristobal, this river provides almost 14 miles of public access from the lake to Blue Mesa Reservoir. The Lake Fork of the Gunnison River provides excellent opportunities for anglers to catch brown and rainbow trout in the 12- to 16-inch range, with some fish over 20 inches. Public access has been improved significantly in the last 20 years on the Lake Fork, with several areas that were previously private property now open to the public for fishing.

As the Lake Fork freezes in the winter and reaches an unfishable 1,200 to 1,400 cfs during runoff, the best time to hit this river is from mid-July to October when the flows are better for wading. Kokanee angling is also popular during their fall migration in areas downstream of Red Bridge.

There is a wealth of insect life on the river, similar to the upper section of the Gunnison River from Almont to Blue Mesa Reservoir. It starts with midges and Blue-Winged Olives during a small window in April before runoff; later, the water drops and the true bloom of insects arrive: stoneflies, caddis, Pale Morning Duns, Green Drakes, and Red Quills supply the trout with a wealth of protein.

To access the Lake Fork, follow the directions for the Gunnison, but take CO 149 toward Lake City just west of the town of Gunnison. Public access

GUNNISON RIVER

	JAN	FEB	MAR	APR	MAY	JUN	JUL	AUG	SEP	OCT	NOV	DEC
Midge (*Chironomidae*)												
#18-24 Mercury Black Beauty, Disco Midge, Rainbow Warrior, Brooks' Sprout Midge, Befus' Adult Midge, Griffith's Gnat												
Blue-Winged Olive (*Baetis* spp.)												
#18-22 CDC Loop Wing Emerger, Flashback Pheasant Tail, Johnny Flash, Furimsky's BDE, Parachute Adams												
Caddis (*Brachycentrus* and *Hydropsyche* spp.)												
#16-20 Buckskin, Phares' Caddis Candy, Graphic Caddis, Mercer's Little Brown Bug, Mercer's Z-Wing Caddis, Puterbaugh's Foam Caddis, Peacock Caddis												
Salmonfly (*Pteronarcys californica*)												
#4-8 Girdle Bug, 20 Incher, Pat's Rubber Legs, Jackson's Ugly Bug, Rogue Foam Stone, Puterbaugh's Foam Salmonfly												
Golden Stonefly (*Perlidae*)												
#8-12 Mercer's Poxyback Biot Golden Stone Nymph, black Rubber Leg Hare's Ear, Tungstone, Pat's Rubber Legs, Stimulator, Chernobyl Ant												
Little Yellow Sally (*Isoperla* sp.)												
#14-18 yellow Copper John, Mercer's Poxyback Little Yellow Stone, Tungsten Prince Nymph, Befus' Slow Water Sally, yellow Puterbaugh's Foam Stone, Stimulator												
Pale Morning Dun (*Ephemerella* spp.)												
#16-18 Dorsey's Mercury PMD, Burke's Hunchback Two-Tone, Mercer's Trigger Nymph, Beadhead Flashback Barr Emerger, Lawson's Cripple, Sparkle Dun												
Green Drake (*Drunella grandis*)												
#12-16 Mercer's Poxyback Emerger, 20 Incher, Furimsky's Foam Drake, Lawson's Green Drake, Compara-dun												
Red Quill (*Rhithrogena* sp.)												
#14-18 Copper John, Pheasant Tail, A. K.'s Red Quill, Parachute Adams												
Terrestrials												
#8-16 Crystal Stimulator, Schlotter's Foam Flying Ant, BC Hopper, Amy's Ant												
Streamers												
#6-10 Slumpbuster, White Leech, ginger Meat Whistle, Conehead Autumn Splendor, black Circus Peanut												
Worms and Eggs												
Micro Worm, Flashtail Mini Egg, Nuke Egg, Otter's Egg, Wire Worm												

begins from the CO 149 bridge just below Lake San Cristobal, downstream to Vickers Ranch up to 10 feet above the high-water mark. Parking is located at either the CO 149 bridge or the BLM sign across from the Crystal Lodge. Below the ranch, access the west side through the parking area on Round Top Road. This area has access 30 feet above the high-water mark.

Continuing downstream on CO 149, Baker Canyon has two parking lots well-marked on the left-hand side of the road, with almost 2 miles of access to High Bridge Gulch and an additional 1 1/2 miles of east-side access just past this to Devils Creek. Another 2-mile stretch of public water starts just before Trout Creek, with parking just before and after the creek. This access is on

Pat Dorsey fishes just upstream from Blue Mesa Reservoir. Fall is a magic time on the water, with low pressure and willing fish. LANDON MAYER

both sides of the river, and there is a boat launch and camping at the Gate Campground.

Farther down, just as CO 149 leaves the river, take a left onto Lake Fork Road to enjoy 7 miles of public water from Gorsuch Ranch to the Gateview Campground. Parking is well-marked, with more camping at Red Bridge. Both Gateview and Red Bridge have boat ramps, with Gateview being the last takeout before Blue Mesa Reservoir.

Circus Peanut (Black)

Rear Hook:	#4-6, 3XL TMC 5263
Tail:	Black marabou
Rear body:	Black Cactus Chenille
Rear hackle:	Black strung saddle hackle
Legs:	Red barred Sili Legs
Connection:	17-pound American wire, looped through rear hook eye, lashed to front hook shank
Front hook:	#4-6 long streamer hook
Front body:	Black Cactus Chenille
Front hackle:	Black strung saddle hackle
Eyes:	Painted red dumbbell eyes

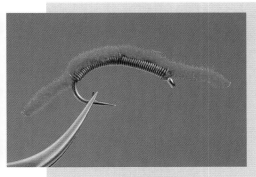

San Juan Worm (Red)

Hook: #12-16 Tiemco 3761
Thread: Red 6/0
Wire: Red (medium)
Body: Red Ultra Chenille

Rogue Parastone

Hook: #4-8 Tiemco 200
Thread: Black or orange 3/0 monocord
Abdomen: Orange closed cell foam
Underwing: Mottled gray/black Web Wing
Flash: Root beer Krystal Flash
Overwing: Black elk hair
Hackle: Black
Thorax: Orange Superfine
Legs: Black round rubber (medium)

Pat's Rubber Legs

Hook: #6-12 Daiichi 2220
Weight: Lead wire
Thread: Black 8/0
Legs: Super Floss, Spanflex,
         or Flexi Floss
Body: Chenille, solid or variegated

Meat Whistle (Ginger)

Hook: #3/0-1/0 Gamakatsu 90-degree
            jig hook
Cone: Gold
Thread: Tan 6/0 Uni-Thread
Rib: Blue Ultra Wire (Brassie)
Body: Blue Diamond Braid
Tail/wing: Ginger rabbit zonker strip
Legs: Barred blue Sili Legs, blue
            holographic Flashabou
Collar: Ginger marabou

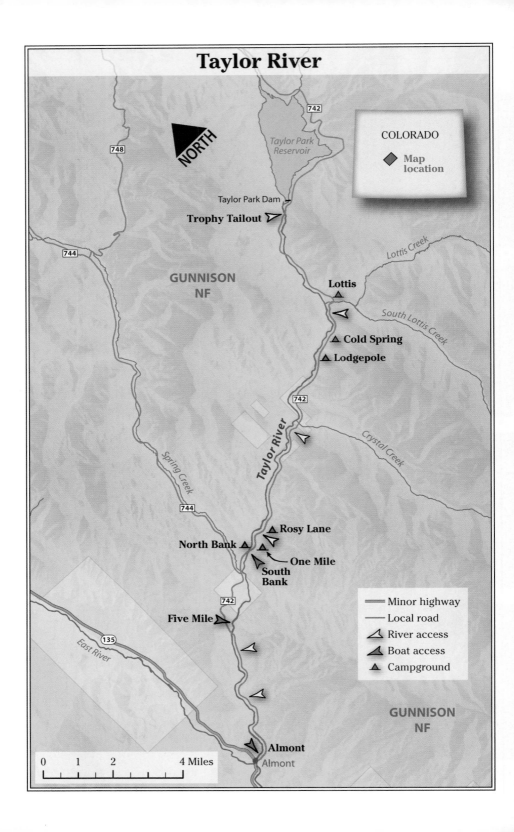

Taylor River

COLORADO

◆ Map location

748

742

Taylor Park Reservoir

Taylor Park Dam

Trophy Tailout

744

GUNNISON NF

Lottis Creek

Lottis

South Lottis Creek

△ Cold Spring

△ Lodgepole

742

Taylor River

Crystal Creek

Spring Creek

744

△ Rosy Lane

North Bank △ △

One Mile

South Bank

742

Five Mile

135

East River

GUNNISON NF

Minor highway
Local road
River access
Boat access
Campground

Almont
Almont

0   1   2   4 Miles

NORTH

CHAPTER 18

Taylor River

Taylor River and Taylor Park are named after Jim Taylor, one of the first men to discover gold in the area. Starting in the high country, the river descends past several fourteeners, eventually entering Taylor Reservoir. This pristine area has a gorgeous setting surrounded by the Collegiate Peaks. While the gold rush is long over, the new riches of huge trout and quality fishing thrive in the river today.

As one of two rivers (the East is the other) that meet the Gunnison River in Almont (20 miles downstream of Taylor Dam), this river is home to some of the largest resident river trout in the United States thanks to the Mysis shrimp. Giants over 20 pounds have been landed, with 23 pounds being the largest I have seen in person. "In March and April, Taylor is one of the only places where you walk past 25-inch fish, because there are a good number of 30-plus-inch fish in this stretch this time of the year," says Jason Booth, co-owner of Gunnison River Guides. "There is always the chance of a trout pushing 34 inches and probably 15-plus pounds."

Taylor Reservoir is one of three, including Ruedi and Dillon, that are supplied with Mysis shrimp to feed trout in these large bodies of water, and the Mysis get washed into the river below. With such an abundant food supply, there is a healthy supply of rainbow, cuttbow, brown, cutthroat, and brook trout in the upper stretch of the river. It is common to hook into fish ranging from 3 to 10 pounds on any trip, but it is not just the size that makes them trophies. These trout are brilliantly colored due to their diet of shrimp. Rainbows big and small look like they were striped with red lipstick; browns have shades of pink along their bellies; and cutthroats' fins and bellies turn Ferrari red.

But the trout do not rely solely on shrimp for food. They also feast on a wide range of hatches, including Green Drakes. The bug is one that will get the large trout in the upper stretch of the river to break the surface to take a dry, and let me tell you your heart will beat so hard you can feel it in your ears when an 8-pounder smacks a dry off the surface.

Taylor River fish are some of the most beautiful in the world. The black spots covering this male rainbow's body reminded me of the leopard 'bows in Alaska. Keeping the fish in the water when taking pictures is easier on the trout. JAY NICHOLS

When fishing below the dam, it is imperative that you look before you take a step. The rivers in this section can hold high flows of 400-plus cfs, but the river is not wide. With every step you take the trout can feel the vibrations in the water and detect you moving, causing them to spook. A partner on the high bank can help guide you. JAY NICHOLS

Front Range access comes from either US 285 South (from Denver) or US 24 West (from Colorado Springs) to Johnson Village. After the pass opens sometime in May, depending on the weather, you can drive directly to the headwaters by continuing toward Buena Vista on US 24 and then turning left onto Cottonwood Pass Road, approximately 4 miles north of Johnson Village. This gravel washboard road leads you through Cottonwood Pass, over the Continental Divide, to Taylor Park Reservoir. The rest of the year, continue on US 285 South to Poncha Springs and connect to US 50 West to Gunnison. In Gunnison, turn north onto CO 135 and veer right onto FR 742 at Almont toward Taylor Park Reservoir.

Headwaters

The Taylor River above the reservoir, including Texas Creek and Willow Creek, is not pursued by many, though it can be great dry-fly fishing for hungry brookies, rainbows, and browns ranging in sizes from 10 to 14 inches, with the occasional big fish willing to move out of Taylor Reservoir in high flows. To fish this stretch, take FR 742 above Taylor Reservoir and park at one of the pullouts and parking lots at the reservoir's inlet.

Early and late seasons (spring/fall) on this stretch can be tough. The prime time to concentrate here is after runoff in summer through early fall.

The fish can be wary, especially when you are fishing the beaver ponds, so tread with care and make every step count before you cast. Attractor dry flies, with or without droppers, are the way to go here.

Trophy Tailout

Most of the Taylor's trophy trout are in a 325-yard stretch below Taylor Dam. Here, at one of the most famous trophy trout fisheries in the world, you have an honest shot at a 30-inch resident trout. Unlike most other trophy trout waters, these fish do not migrate from a lake or the sea—they live within the same section of river their whole lives, and become giants from the Mysis, midges, mayflies, and caddis. The entire Taylor River is catch-and-release only with artificial flies and lures.

Where there are lots of large trout there are crowds. To beat the crowds, time your trip for the winter, or early or late in the day in the summer and fall, so that you can fish over trout that are less pressured. Frigid weather in the

A view of the Hog Trough. Just around the bend, there is no fishing. Trout will migrate back and forth between this open and closed water, depending on time of year and fishing pressure. JAY NICHOLS

Usually a trout's white mouth gives away its presence in the water, but this giant is on such a heavy shrimp diet its mouth is pink. ANGUS DRUMMOND

winter (it's often below zero) keeps anglers at bay and gives you the chance to fish the water below the dam in relative solitude.

While there are great hatches in the summer, the fish are wary from foot traffic and leader-shy and they move out of their normal holding waters. With this in mind, your best chance at numbers and size is looking in the unfamiliar water or the riffled runs, breaks, and pockets between drop-off points. Also, be cautious of spawning beds and maneuver around them. Some people are tempted to fish to spawning trout or think that is the only time to catch them, but that is false. Pre- or postspawn is the best time for size and quality of the fish, while they are still concentrating on feeding in the winter, early spring, and late fall.

There are four main sections of the public water in the mile downstream from Taylor Dam before the first stretch of private water: the water above the bridge on FR 742 that is closest to the dam, the Hog Trough (which is still in this upper section but closer to the bridge), the Avalanche Hole (which is downstream of the bridge), and finally a section of water just before the private water.

The major parking lot to access the water directly below the dam is located next to the first bridge crossing the Taylor, with additional pullouts 200 feet downstream, just above the footbridge that marks the beginning of private water. In the upper stretch, you can walk up the caretaker's access road but you cannot fish past the cable marked with signs that read "No

Flowing south from Emerald Lake and north of Crested Butte, the East River makes its way to Almont, where it joins with the Taylor to create the Gunnison. Nestled in an untouched ranching valley north of the Gunnison River, this wild trout river flows beneath the towering 12,000-foot peaks lining both sides of this pristine landscape.

Traveling north, the East River parallels CO 135, passing through the Almont Triangle State Wildlife Area. This is also known as the Roaring Judy Fish Hatchery. As designated wild trout water, this section of the East River is the first and only location to fish before reaching Crested Butte and has a healthy population of rainbows, browns, cutthroats, and brookies ranging from 8-18 inches, with the average being 8 to 14 inches. When you are imitating any of the hatches on the East, such as the Green Drakes or PMDs, trail a beadhead imitation like a #14-18 Prince Nymph close to the dry on the surface (12 inches).

In addition to the trout, kokanee salmon run up the East from the Gunnison River, allowing anglers a chance to pursue them in a small-water setting. While spawning kokanee do not eat, they will hit bright imitations like 4 mm orange, pink, or green egg patterns, #16-18 red San Juan Worms, and #14-18

red Copper Johns out of aggression. This can be very exciting during the beginning stages of their journey, before these land-locked sockeye salmon begin to deteriorate from within and turn bright red. Long, bolting runs with leaping displays out of the water can make every fight rewarding.

To access the East River, which is mostly private, take CO 135 north from Gunnison. The East River runs along CO 135, starting at the bridge in Almont. From this point to the Roaring Judy Fish Hatchery the river has been designated Wild Trout Water, with access above and below. Just past milepost 14, turn left (west) off the highway, cross the bridge, and park in the public parking area. River access is via trail. Parking is also available off of CO 135. Then follow the path through a dense stand of cottonwoods and willows to the river. ■

The uniquely colored Pale Morning Duns are an important hatch on the Taylor River. JAY NICHOLS

Fishing Allowed." This area of the river is important and worth checking out on every trip. Above this cable lies a stretch of water where the new state record is lying in solitude. A rise in water flow can, in some cases, push the giants into public water. Downstream a good 10-plus yards, a series of riffled runs begins and ends with rocks that provide great pockets, deep pools, and undercuts for large trout to hold. The riffled water also supplies great cover.

Farther downstream above the bridge, the Hog Trough is another deep 100-yard stretch that has plenty of rock structure providing cover for trout. While this 300-plus-yard stretch of the upper river is short in length, it makes up for size in the giant trout that dwell in its shallows and depths. Because this area is heavily fished, make sure you are casting to a feeding fish and not one hunkered down on the bottom. One trick is to remain low and wait until your target is feeding. Forget using your indicator here—the surface is too smooth.

The river then travels under a bridge and turns right, traveling into the Avalanche Hole, the most famous run in the whole river. Numerous avalanches have descended into the river from the mountain peaks, creating a huge, deep, slow-moving run, with depths reaching 10-plus feet, that hosts giant trout. One of my favorite ways to catch aggressively-feeding trout in this run is with streamers. While it is common to use a sink-tip line to achieve depth, keep a streamer moving in the same water column where the trout are holding. Having to switch spools or reels is an inefficient way to change disciplines. Instead, try using long leaders with heavily-weighted flies or one of my favorites: attaching a sinking leader to the fly line, which will allow you to change your rig quickly. Light-colored streamers like #6-12 tan Lawson's Conehead Sculpins can be seen by numerous fish in the depths of the dark run. It is also easier to see while it darts through the run, giving you the visual of the take.

Downstream from the Avalanche Hole, there is 100-plus yards of water that contains everything from deep, slow-moving runs to pocketwater moving through boulder fields and extended riffled runs. This section of the Taylor River is my favorite to locate trophy trout in because they are harder to see in the diverse water settings, making it challenging to find the trout. On the other hand, when you do find them they are often unpressured and willing to take the fly while settled in areas like in front of rocks.

The private section of the Taylor is long and, for the most part, untouched. In the first half of the private water there are very large trout that hold or take refuge like those below the dam. Before spawning or during high water, the fish move upstream into accessible public water, not just because fish move upstream when they spawn but because there is a lot of great habitat upstream in the public water.

For accuracy, sink rate, and stealth, leader design is an important but often overlooked aspect of your setup. Jason Booth, co-owner of Gunnison River Guides, says that his best technique for big fish in clear water is more tippet and less leader, so that when he presents the drift to the fish, the tippet cuts through the water, sinking the fly faster with less drag. "I like to build off a 7¹/₂-foot 4X leader, cut off 12 inches, add 3 feet of 4X fluorocarbon to my first fly, and 5X fluorocarbon to my second fly at 20 inches."

Lower Section to Almont

Since many come to the Taylor for the hogs right below the dam, the lower stretch is often uncrowded, which is great for those anglers who are in know about the great fishing down there. Lined with pine trees in a gorgeous, boulder-filled, pocketwater setting, the approximately 20 miles of river to

Jason Booth holds a monster buck rainbow. When the Taylor runs low and clear it is perfect for sight fishing, but stealth is paramount. "I show up very early in the morning and hike the whole place from bottom to top, noting to myself where all the larger fish are hanging, looking for the fish over 30 inches," Booth says. "These fish are very spooky and leader-shy, so I like snow camo for apparel, fluorocarbon leaders and tippet, and subtle strike indicators." JASON BOOTH

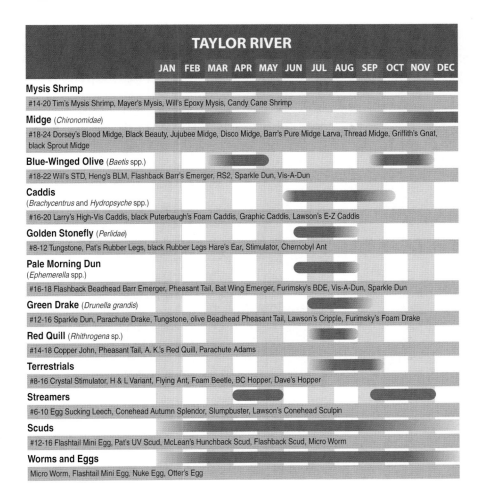

TAYLOR RIVER

	JAN	FEB	MAR	APR	MAY	JUN	JUL	AUG	SEP	OCT	NOV	DEC

Mysis Shrimp

#14-20 Tim's Mysis Shrimp, Mayer's Mysis, Will's Epoxy Mysis, Candy Cane Shrimp

Midge (*Chironomidae*)

#18-24 Dorsey's Blood Midge, Black Beauty, Jujubee Midge, Disco Midge, Barr's Pure Midge Larva, Thread Midge, Griffith's Gnat, black Sprout Midge

Blue-Winged Olive (*Baetis* spp.)

#18-22 Will's STD, Heng's BLM, Flashback Barr's Emerger, RS2, Sparkle Dun, Vis-A-Dun

Caddis
(*Brachycentrus* and *Hydropsyche* spp.)

#16-20 Larry's High-Vis Caddis, black Puterbaugh's Foam Caddis, Graphic Caddis, Lawson's E-Z Caddis

Golden Stonefly (*Perlidae*)

#8-12 Tungstone, Pat's Rubber Legs, black Rubber Legs Hare's Ear, Stimulator, Chernobyl Ant

Pale Morning Dun
(*Ephemerella* spp.)

#16-18 Flashback Beadhead Barr Emerger, Pheasant Tail, Bat Wing Emerger, Furimsky's BDE, Vis-A-Dun, Sparkle Dun

Green Drake (*Drunella grandis*)

#12-16 Sparkle Dun, Parachute Drake, Tungstone, olive Beadhead Pheasant Tail, Lawson's Cripple, Furimsky's Foam Drake

Red Quill (*Rhithrogena* sp.)

#14-18 Copper John, Pheasant Tail, A. K.'s Red Quill, Parachute Adams

Terrestrials

#8-16 Crystal Stimulator, H & L Variant, Flying Ant, Foam Beetle, BC Hopper, Dave's Hopper

Streamers

#6-10 Egg Sucking Leech, Conehead Autumn Splendor, Slumpbuster, Lawson's Conehead Sculpin

Scuds

#12-16 Flashtail Mini Egg, Pat's UV Scud, McLean's Hunchback Scud, Flashback Scud, Micro Worm

Worms and Eggs

Micro Worm, Flashtail Mini Egg, Nuke Egg, Otter's Egg

Almont (about half of which is private) offer anglers deep, slow-moving runs in a never-ending supply of fast-water breaks around the endless rock structure. You can spend hours covering only a few hundred yards with the number of small holding areas within the river. Because the water is warmer farther from the dam, hatches seem better down here as well.

While the trout on this lower stretch are not as large on average, the possibilities of water to fish and hatches make it a true piece of heaven, especially when the water below the dam is crowded. During the summer months—after runoff into fall—is a great time to find hatches of *Baetis*, PMDs, Red Quills, Yellow Sallies, and Green Drakes.

During the high water flows of summer, the lower stretch is also a great opportunity to throw attractor patterns like a #14-18 Royal Wulff, #16-18 GTH Variant, or #16-18 ant imitations. Trout in high-water conditions feel safe in

The large trout living below the dam attract the most anglers, leaving the lower river often untouched. JAY NICHOLS

various water, making them good targets to take a dry off the water's surface because they are not as wary of predators above. This makes the lower section a great addition to the make of the Taylor River.

The first public access after the tailwater section starts just below Lottis Creek Campground and runs approximately 3 miles down to Lodgepole Campground, with parking clearly marked at each area. Lottis Creek Campground also happens to be the only campground open year-round, something to keep in mind when planning your late-fall to early-spring trips. As is the case through most of the Taylor, parking is well-marked; the mostly paved parking lots and pullouts have regulations posted. The next parking is at Rosy Lane or One Mile Campgrounds, with a couple of miles of river access and an additional pullout between North Bank and Granite Campgrounds.

If you want to float the river, there is boating access at South Bank, but it is generally used by experienced boaters only and the river is not passable downstream without private landowner permission. It is better to use the Five Mile River Access, as the river here is only Class II and can be traveled to Almont. Always check with a local shop to discuss your route before navigating the river by boat.

Past Granite is a private fishing lodge, and access picks back up at Five Mile River Access with an additional paved pullout just past the bridge. The next access is at the Gunnison Mountain Park nature trail and the Gunnison Mountain Park pullout. From here, there are a couple more pullouts: one 1 1/2 miles upstream from Almont at the confluence of Spring Creek with the Taylor, and others just before the bridge in town and 200 yards upstream from the bridge.

Time of Day

It's generally true that the earlier you get to the water, the better your chances are of getting prime water or casting to unpressured trout. But there are also disadvantages to getting on the water too early on the Taylor. For example, if you show up at 6:00 a.m. in the top section where the giants dwell, the canyon walls prevent the sun from hitting the water's surface until 8:00 or 9:00 a.m. The time between can create steam rising from the water's surface and cooler water temperatures, making the trout lethargic and not as willing to move on a fly. Lastly, if you blind-cast over trout you cannot see, the fish will spook and retreat to different water or become wary. These are the challenges you will face when you are trying to sight-fish to the trout. To overcome this, concentrate on areas on the river where the water's surface runs smooth, like the Hog Trough. Look for trout in areas where you know from the previous day or past experiences that they are holding.

Once the sun does hit the water on the Taylor, I prefer to fish the section below the dam when the water temps increase and the trout become active in feeding. This is your chance to cast to a giant before it is spooked or walked over during the day. While this may only last an hour or two, it is worth the pursuit before the crowds show up. Once the concentration of anglers reaches its peak before noon, explore the rest of the Taylor River, either the lower stretch to Almont or the headwaters. Then as the sun disappears behind the canyon walls, the trout begin to move around again and fishing can be productive.

Mayer's Mysis

Hook:	#14-18 TMC 200R
Thread:	White Uni-Thread
Abdomen: (medium)	Pearlescent Hareline flat tinsel
Thorax:	White Hareline ostrich herl
Wing case:	Pearlescent Hareline flat tinsel (medium)
Eyes:	Black rubber legs (medium)
Antennae:	White Swisher's Wiggly Hackle

Brook's Sprout Midge (Black)

Hook: #18-26 Tiemco 2488
Thread: Black 8/0 Uni-Thread
Post: White foam
Abdomen: Tying thread
Hackle: Black
Tail: Black yarn

Furimsky's Foam Drake (Green Drake)

Hook: #10-14 Tiemco 100SP-BL or 2487
Thread: Olive dun 8/0
Body: Live Fly Foam (1/8")
Tail: Black calf tail hair
Hackle: Olive dyed grizzly saddle
Thorax: Peacock herl
Wing: Blue dun McFlylon

Blood Midge

Hook: #18-24 Tiemco 2487
Thread: Red 6/0
Head: Spirit River Hi-Lite silver glass bead (extra small)
Body: Red 6/0
Rib: Fine copper wire
Thorax: Peacock herl

Flashtail Mini Egg

Hook: #18-22 Tiemco 2487
Thread: Orange GSP 50
Tail: Flashabou
Body: Orange/apricot Glo Bug Yarn

Fly Shops and Outfitters

Fly shops and outfitters are some of the best resources for up-to-date fishing information throughout the state.

Animas

Anasazi Angler
12895 Highway 140
Hesperus, CO 81326
(970) 385-HOOK
anasaziangler@earthlink.net

Animas Valley Anglers
264 W. 22nd St.
Durango, CO 81301
(970) 259-0484
gottrout.com

Caddis Company
600 Main Ave. #208
Durango, CO 81301
(970) 382-9978
caddiscompany.com

Duranglers
923 Main Ave.
Durango, CO 81301
(970) 385-4081
duranglers.com

Arkansas River

Anglers Addiction
1401 N. Main St.
Pueblo, CO 81003
(719) 296-5886
coloradoflyfishingservices.com/
anglers-addiction.html

ArkAnglers
517 Highway 24 S.
Buena Vista, CO 81211
(719) 395-1796

943 W. Highway 50
Pueblo, CO 81008
(719) 543-3900

7500 W. Highway 50
Salida, CO 81201
(719) 539-4223

arkanglers.com

Arkansas River Tours
P.O. Box 337
Cotopaxi, CO 81223
(800) 321-4352 or (719) 942-4362
arkansasrivertours.com

Arkansas River (continued)

Arkansas Valley Adventure
40671 Highway 24 N.
Buena Vista, CO 81211
(719) 486-2827
coloradorafting.net

Blue River Anglers
281 Main St.
Frisco, CO 80443
(888) 453-9171
blueriveranglers.com

Breckenridge Outfitters
100 N. Main St.
Breckenridge, CO 80424
(970) 453-4135
breckenridgeoutfitters.com

Dvorak Expeditions
17921 Highway 285
Nathrop, CO 81236
(719) 539-6851
dvorakexpeditions.com

The Peak Fly Shop
301 E. Highway 24
Woodland Park, CO 80863
(719) 687-9122
thepeakflyshop.com

Royal Gorge Anglers/ SoCO Guide Service
49311 W. Highway 50
Cañon City, CO 81212
(888) 994-6743 or (719) 269-FISH
royalgorgeanglers.com

Big Thompson River
Bob's Fly Shop
406 S. Lincoln Ave.
Loveland, CO 80537
(970) 667-1107
bobsflytying.com

Colorado Skies Outfitters
11020 S. Pikes Peak Dr. #105
Parker, CO 80138
(720) 851-4665
coloradoskiesoutfitters.com

Elkhorn Fly Rod and Reel
3121 W. Eisenhower Blvd.
Loveland, CO 80537
(970) 227-4707
elkhornflyrodandreel.com

Estes Angler
338 W. Riverside Dr.
Estes Park, CO 80517
(970) 586-2110
estesangler.com

Estes Park Mountain Shop
2050 Big Thompson Ave.
Estes Park, CO 80517
(970) 586-6548
estesparkmountainshop.com

Front Range Anglers
2344 Pearl St.
Boulder, CO 80302
(303) 494-1375
frontrangeanglers.com

Kirks Flyshop
230 E. Elkhorn Ave.
Estes Park, CO 80517
(970) 577-0790
kirksflyshop.com

Laughing Grizzly Fly Shop
10675 Ute Hwy.
Longmont, CO 80504
(303) 772-9110
laughinggrizzlyflyshop.net

Sasquatch Fly Fishing Adventures
2515 Tunnel Rd.
Estes Park, CO 80511
(970) 586-3341 x1153
sasquatchflyfishing.com

Scot's Sporting Goods
870 Moraine Ave.
Estes Park, CO 80517
(970) 586-2877
scotssportinggoods@gmail.com

St. Peters Fly Shop
202 Remington St.
Fort Collins, CO 80524
(970) 498-8968
stpetes.com

Blue River

Anglers All
5211 S. Santa Fe Dr.
Littleton, CO 80120
(303) 794-1104
anglersall.com

Blue River Anglers
281 Main St.
Frisco, CO 80443
(970) 668-2583
blueriveranglers.com

The Blue Quill Angler
1532 Bergen Pkwy.
Evergreen, CO 80439
(303) 674-4700
bluequillangler.com

Breckenridge Outfitters
100 N. Main St.
Suite 206, Town Square
Breckenridge, CO 80424
(970) 453-4135
breckenridgeoutfitters.com

Colorado Skies Outfitters
11020 S. Pikes Peak Dr. #105
Parker, CO 80138
(720) 851-4665
coloradoskiesoutfitters.com

Cutthroat Anglers
400 Blue River Pkwy.
Silverthorne, CO 80498
(970) 262-2878
fishcolorado.com

Golden River Sport
806 Washington
Golden, CO 80401
(303) 215-9386
goldenriverports.net

Mountain Angler
311 S. Main St.
Breckenridge, CO 80424
(970) 453-4665
mountainangler.com

Cache La Poudre

St. Peter's Fly Shop
925 E. Harmony Rd. #200
Fort Collins, CO 80525
(970) 498-8978
stpetes.com

Colorado Skies Outfitters
11020 S. Pikes Peak Dr. #105
Parker, CO 80138
(720) 851-4665
coloradoskiesoutfitters.com

Kirks Flyshop
230 E. Elkhorn Ave.
Estes Park, CO 80517
(970) 577-0790
kirksflyshop.com

Jax Outdoor Gear
1200 N. College Ave.
Fort Collins, CO 80524
(970) 221-0544
jaxmercantile.com

St Peter's Fly Shop
202 Remington St.
Fort Collins, CO 80524
(970) 498-8968
stpetes.com

Colorado River

Alpine Angling
995 Cowen Dr. #102
Carbondale, CO 81623
(970) 963-9245
roaringforkanglers.com

Alpine River Outfitters
97 Main, Unit E102
Edwards, CO 81632
(970) 926-0900
alpineriveroutfitters.com

The Blue Quill Angler
1532 Bergen Pkwy.
Evergreen, CO, 80439
(303) 674-4700
(800) 435-5353
bluequillangler.com

Colorado River (continued)

Blue River Anglers
281 Main St.
Frisco, CO 80424
(970) 668-2583
blueriveranglers.com

Breckenridge Outfitters
100 Main
Breckenridge, CO 80424
(970) 453-4135
breckenridgeoutfitters.com

Colorado Skies Outfitters
11020 S. Pikes Peak #105
Parker, CO 80138
(720) 851-4665
coloradoskiesoutfitters.com

Cutthroat Anglers
400 Blue River Pkwy.
Silverthorne, CO 80498
(970) 262-2878
fishcolorado.com

Fly Fishing Outfitters
1060 W. Beaver Creek Blvd.
Avon, CO 81620
(970) 845-8090
flyfishingoutfitters.net

Frying Pan Anglers
132 Basalt Center Cir.
Basalt, CO 81621
(970) 927-3441
fryingpananglers.com

Gore Creek Flyfisherman
193 Gore Creek Dr.
Vail, CO 81657
(970) 476-3296
gorecreekflyfisherman.com

Mo Henry's Trout Shop
540 Zerex
Fraser, CO 80442
(970) 726-9754
mohenrys.com

Mountain Angler
311 S. Main
Breckenridge, CO 80424
(970) 453-4665
mountainangler.com

Taylor Creek Fly Shop
183 Basalt Center Cir.
Basalt, CO 81621
(970) 927-4374
taylorcreek.com

Conejos River
Conejos River Anglers
34591 Highway 17
Antonito, CO 81120
(719) 376-5660
conejosriveranglers.com

Conejos River Outfitters
320 West 7th Avenue
Antonito, CO 81120
(719) 376-6040
conejosriveroutfitters.com

Fox Creek Store
26573 Highway 17
Antonito, CO 81120
(719) 376-5881
foxcreekstore.com

Wolf Creek Anglers Fly Shop
266 E. Highway 160
Pagosa Springs, CO 81147
(970) 264-1415

001 Brown Dr.
P.O. Box 263
South Fork, CO 81154
(719) 873-1414
wolfcreekanglers.com

Denver Area Shops
Bass Pro Shop
7970 Northfield Blvd.
Denver, CO 80238
(720) 385-3600
basspro.com

Charlie's FlyBox
7513 Grandview Ave.
Arvada, CO 80002
(303) 403-8880
charliesflyboxinc.com

Denver Angler
6870 S. Yosemite St.
Centennial, CO 80112-1407
(303) 403-4512
denverangler.com

Discount Fishing Tackle
2645 S. Sante Fe Dr.
Denver, CO 80223
(303) 698-2550
discountfishinginc.com

Front Range Anglers
2344 Pearl St.
Boulder, CO 80302
(303) 494-1375
frontrangeanglers.com

Hook Fly Fishing
2030 E. County Line Rd.
Highlands Ranch, CO 80212
(720) 920-9780
hookflyfishing.com

Orvis Denver
2701 E. First Ave.
Denver, CO 80206
(303) 355-4554
orvis.com/denver

Trout's Fly Fishing
1303 E. 6th Ave.
Denver, CO 80218
(303) 733-1434
troutsflyfishing.com

Eagle River

Alpine River
97 Main St., Unit E102
Edwards, CO 81632
(970) 926-0900
alpineriveroutfitters.com

Breckenridge Outfitters
101 N. Main St.
Breckenridge, CO 80424
(970) 453-4135
breckenridgeoutfitters.com

Colorado Skies Outfitters
11020 S. Pikes Peak Dr. #105
Parker, CO 80138
(720) 851-4665
coloradoskiesoutfitters.com

Cutthroat Anglers
400 Blue River Pkwy.
Silverthorne, CO 80498
(970) 262-2878
fishcolorado.com

Fly Fishing Outfitters
1060 W. Beaver Creek Blvd.
Avon, CO 81620
(970) 845-8090
flyfishingoutfitters.net

Gore Creek Flyfisherman
193 Gore Creek Dr.
Vail, CO 81657
(970) 476-3296
gorecreekflyfisherman.com

Minturn Anglers
102 Main St.
Vail, CO 81657
(970) 827-9500
minturnanglers.com

Mountain Angler
311 S. Main St.
Breckenridge, CO 80424
(970) 453-4665
mountainangler.com

Roaring Fork Anglers
2205 Grand Ave.
Glenwood Springs, CO 81601
(970) 945-0180
roaringforkanglers.com

Fryingpan River

Alpine Angling
995 Cowen Dr. #102
Carbondale, CO 81623
(970) 963-9245
roaringforkanglers.com

Crystal Fly Shop
208 Main St.
Carbondale, CO 81623
(970) 963-5741
crystalflyshop.com

Frying Pan Anglers
132 Basalt Center Cir.
Basalt, CO 81621
(970) 927-3441
fryingpananglers.com

Roaring Fork Anglers
2205 Grand Ave.
Glenwood Springs, CO 81601
(970) 945-0180
roaringforkanglers.com

Taylor Creek Fly Shops
183 Basalt Center Cir.
Basalt, CO 81621
(970) 927-4374
taylorcreek.com

Gunnison River

Almont Anglers
10209 N. State Highway 135
Almont, CO 81210
(970) 641-7404
almontanglers.com

Black Canyon Anglers
P.O. Box 180
7904 Shea Rd.
Austin, CO 81410
blackcanyonanglers.com

Cimarron Creek
317 E. Main St.
Montrose, CO 81401
(970) 249-0408
cimarroncreek.com

Dan's Fly Shop
723 Gunnison Avenue
P.O. Box 220
Lake City, CO 81235
970-944-2281
dansflyshop.com

Dragonfly Anglers
307 Elk Ave.
Crested Butte, CO 81224
(970) 349-1228
dragonflyanglers.com

Gunnison River Expeditions
14494 F Rd.
Delta, CO 81416
(970) 874- 8184
gunnisonriverexpeditions.com

Gunnison River Fly Shop
300 N. Main Street
Gunnison, CO 81230
(970) 641-2930
gunnisonriverflyshop.com

Gunnison River Guides
Almont CO, 81210
(970) 596-3054
gunnisonriverguides.com

High Mountain Drifters
201 W. Tomichi
Gunnison, CO 81230
(970) 471-5829
highmtndrifters.com

Rigs Fly Shop & Guide Service
565 Sherman, Suite 2
Ridgway, CO 81432
(970) 626-4460
fishrigs.com

Sportsman Outdoors and Fly Shop
238 S. Gunnison
Lake City, CO 81235
(970) 944-2526
lakecitysportsman.com

Telluride Outside
121 W. Colorado Ave.
Telluride, CO 81435
(970) 728-3895
tellurideoutside.com

Three Rivers Resort & Outfitting
130 CR 742
Almont, CO 81210
888-761-FISH
willowflyanglers.com

Rio Grande
Animas Valley Anglers
264 W. 22nd St.
Durango, CO 81301
(970) 259-0484
gottrout.com

Conejos River Anglers
34591 Highway 17
Antonito, CO 81120
(719) 376-5660
conejosriveranglers.com

Duranglers
923 Main Ave.
Durango, CO 81301
(970) 385-4081
duranglers.com

Ramble House/Creede Guide and Outfitters
116 Main St.
Creede, CO 81130
(719) 658-2482
ramblehouse.net

Rio Grande Angler
13 S. Main St.
Creede, CO 81130
(719) 658-2955
riograndeangler.com

Wolf Creek Anglers Fly Shop
Pagosa Springs
266 East Highway 160
Pagosa Springs, CO 81147
(970) 264-1415

South Fork
001 Brown Dr.
P.O. Box 263
South Fork, CO 81154
(719) 873-1414

wolfcreekanglers.com

Roaring Fork
Alpine Angling
995 Cowen Dr. #102
Carbondale, CO 81623
(970) 963-9245
roaringforkanglers.com

Alpine River Outfitters
97 Main St., Unit E102
Edwards, CO 81632
(970) 926-0900
alpineriveroutfitters.com

Colorado Skies Outfitters
11020 S. Pikes Peak Dr. #105
Parker, CO 80138
(720) 851-4665
coloradoskiesoutfitters.com

Crystal Fly Shop
208 Main St.
Carbondale, CO 81623
(970) 963-5741
crystalflyshop.com

Cutthroat Anglers
400 Blue River Pkwy.
Silverthorne, CO 80498
(970) 262-2878
fishcolorado.com

Frying Pan Anglers
132 Basalt Center Cir.
Basalt, CO 81621
(970) 927-3441
fryingpananglers.com

Roaring Fork Anglers
2205 Grand Ave.
Glenwood Springs, CO 81601
(970) 945-0180
roaringforkanglers.com

Fly Fishing Adventures at the Little Nell
675 E. Durant Ave.
Aspen, CO 81611
(970) 920-4600
thelittlenell.com

Roaring Fork (continued)

Taylor Creek Fly Shops
183 Basalt Center Cir.
Basalt, CO 81621
(970) 927-4374
taylorcreek.com

Rocky Mountain National Park

Kirks Fly Shop
230 E. Elkhorn Ave.
Estes Park, CO 80517
(970) 577-0790
kirksflyshop.com

Elkhorn Fly Rod and Reel
3121 W. Eisenhower Blvd.
Loveland, CO 80537
(970) 227-4707
elkhornflyrodandreel.com

Estes Angler
338 W. Riverside Dr.
Estes Park, CO 80517
(970) 586-2110
estesangler.com

Estes Park Mountain Shop
2050 Big Thompson Ave.
Estes Park, CO 80517
(970) 586-6548
estesparkmountainshop.com

Front Range Anglers
2344 Pearl St.
Boulder, CO 80302
(303) 494-1375
frontrangeanglers.com

Laughing Grizzly Fly Shop
10675 Ute Hwy.
Longmont, CO 80504
(303) 772-9110
laughinggrizzlyflyshop.net

Rocky Mountain Anglers
1904 Arapahoe Ave.
Boulder, CO 80302
(303) 447-2400
rockymtanglers.com

Sasquatch Fly Fishing Adventures
2515 Tunnel Rd.
Estes Park, CO 80511
(970) 586-3341 x1153
sasquatchflyfishing.com

St. Peters Fly Shop
202 Remington St.
Fort Collins, CO 80524
(970) 498-8968
stpetes.com

South Platte River

Anglers All
5211 S. Santa Fe Dr.
Littleton, CO 80120
(303) 794-1104
anglersall.com

Angler's Covey
295 S. 21st St.
Colorado Springs, CO 80904
(719) 471-2984
anglerscovey.com

ArkAnglers
517 Highway 24 South
Buena Vista, CO 81211
(719) 395-1796

943 W. Highway 50
Pueblo, CO 81008
(719) 543-3900

7500 W. Highway 50
Salida, CO 81201
(719) 539-4223

arkanglers.com

The Blue Quill Angler
1532 Bergen Pkwy.
Evergreen, CO 80439
(303) 674-4700
bluequillangler.com

Blue River Anglers
281 Main St.
Frisco, CO 80443
(970) 668-2583
blueriveranglers.com

Breckenridge Outfitters
101 N. Main St.
Breckenridge, CO 80424
(970) 453-4135
breckenridgeoutfitters.com

Colorado Skies Outfitters
11020 S. Pikes Peak #105
Parker, CO 80138
(720) 851-4665
coloradoskiesoutfitters.com

Colorado Trout Hunters
4398 South Youngfield St.
Morrison, CO 80465
(303) 325-5515
coloradotrouthunters.com

Cutthroat Anglers
400 Blue River Pkwy.
Silverthorne, CO 80498
(970) 262-2878
fishcolorado.com

Flies and Lies
8570 S. Highway 67
Deckers, CO 80135
(303) 647-2237
fliesnlies.com

Golden River Sport
806 Washington
Golden, CO 80401
(303) 215-9386
goldenriverports.net

The Hatch Fly Shop
34375 US Highway 285
Pine Junction, CO 80470
(303) 816-0487
thehatchflyshop.com

Landon Mayer Fly Fishing
Woodland Park, CO 80863
(719) 210-0619
landonmayer.com

Mile High Angler
3250 S. Lafayette St.
Englewood, CO 80113
(303) 324-1854
milehighangler.com

Mountain Angler
311 S. Main St.
Breckenridge, CO 80424
(970) 453-4665
mountainangler.com

Orvis Cherry Creek
2701 E. 1st Ave.
Denver, CO 80206-5605
(303) 355-4554
orvis.com/denver

Orvis Park Meadows
8433 Park Meadows Center Drive
Lone Tree, CO 80124
(303) 768-9600

The Peak Fly Shop
5632 N. Academy Blvd.
Colorado Springs, CO 80918
(719) 260-1415

301 E. Highway 24
Woodland Park, CO 80863
(719) 687-9122
thepeakflyshop.com

Royal Gorge Anglers
1210 Royal Gorge Blvd.
Canon City, CO 81212
(888) 994-6743
royalgorgeanglers.com

South Platte Anglers
315 Elm St.
Hartsel, CO 80449
(719) 930-3260
southplatteanglers.com

South Platte Fly Shop
405 E. Highway 24
Woodland Park, CO 80863
(719) 686-8990
southplatteflyshop.com

Taylor River
Almont Anglers
10209 N. CO 135
Almont, CO 81210
(970) 641-7404
almontanglers.com

Taylor River (continued)

Cimarron Creek
317 E. Main St.
Montrose, CO 81401
(970) 249-0408
cimarroncreek.com

Dragonfly Anglers
307 Elk Ave.
Crested Butte, CO 81224
(970) 349-1228
dragonflyanglers.com

High Mountain Drifters
201 W. Tomichi Ave.
Gunnison, CO 81230
(970) 471-5829
highmtndrifters.com

Harmel's Taylor River Fly Shop
Harmel's Ranch Resort
6748 CR 742
Almont, CO 81210
(800) 235-3402
harmels.com

Gunnison River Fly Shop
300 N. Main St.
Gunnison, CO 81230
(970) 641-2930
gunnisonriverflyshop.com

Gunnison River Guides
132 Deer Path Ln.
Almont, CO 81210
(970) 596-3054
gunnisonriverguides.com

Willowfly Anglers
Three Rivers Resort
130 CR 742
Almont, CO 81210
(970) 641-1303
willowflyanglers.com

Williams Fork River

Blue River Anglers
281 Main St.
Frisco, CO 80443
(970) 668-2583
blueriveranglers.com

Blue Quill Angler
1532 Highway 74
Evergreen, CO 80439
(303) 674-4700
bluequillangler.com

Breckenridge Outfitters
100 N. Main St.
Breckenridge, CO 80424
(970) 453-4135
breckenridgeoutfitters.com

Cutthroat Anglers
400 Blue River Pkwy.
Silverthorne, CO 80498
(970) 262-2878
fishcolorado.com

Mile High Angler
3250 S. Lafayette St.
Englewood, CO 80113
(303) 324-1854
milehighangler.com

Mountain Angler
311 S. Main St.
Breckenridge, CO 80424
(970) 453-4665
mountainangler.com

Yampa River

Bucking Rainbow Outfitters
730 Lincoln Ave.
Steamboat Springs, CO 80477
(970) 879-8747
buckingrainbow.com

Steamboat Flyfisher
35 5th St., Unit 102
Steamboat Springs, CO 80487
(970) 879-6552

Yampa River Outfitters
2305 Mount Werner Cir., Gondola
Square
Steamboat Springs, CO 80487
(877) 783-2628
steamboatflyfisher.com

Straightline Sports
744 Lincoln Ave.
Steamboat Springs, CO 80477
(970) 879-7568
straightlinesports.com

Lodging and Camping

The overnight accommodations listed here are a sample of what is available in the area. There are many more places to stay overnight. The places listed below were selected because they are reasonably priced, comfortable, and tailored for the outdoorsman. For more information on camping, go to forestcamping.com.

Animas

Best Western Durango Inn and Suites
21382 Highway 160 W.
Durango, CO 81303
(970) 247-3251
bwdurangoinn@frontier.net

Econo Lodge
2002 Main Ave.
Durango, CO 81301
(970) 247-4242
econolodge.com

Purgatory Campground
26 miles north of Durango on US 550 on the east side of the road (8 miles north of Haviland Lake); 14 RV/tent campsites on 6 acres with drinking water and toilets. Just across from Durango Mountain Resort (Purgatory Resort). Gas, groceries, and a RV dump station are 2^{1}/$_{2}$ miles south on US 550.

The Rochester Hotel
726 E. Second Ave.
Durango, CO 81301
(970) 385-1920
rochesterhotel.com

The Rodeway Inn of Durango
2701 Main Ave.
Durango, CO 81301
(970) 259-2540
rodewayinn@frontier.net

Strater Hotel
699 Main Ave.
Durango, CO 81301
(970) 247-4431
strater.com

Arkansas River

Best Western Vista Inn
733 N. Highway 24
Buena Vista, CO 81211
(800) 809-3495

Arkansas River (continued)

Comfort Inn
315 E. Highway 50
Salida, CO 81201
(800) 228-5150

Comfort Inn
311 Royal Gorge Blvd.
Cañon City, CO 81212
(719) 276-6900

Days Inn
407 E. US Highway 50
Salida, CO 81201
(800) 329-7466

Five Points Campground
Mile marker 260 on US 50, between the towns of Cañon City and Cotopaxi.

Gateway Inn and Suites
1310 E. Highway 50
Salida, CO 81201
(719) 539-2895

Hampton Inn
102 McCormick Pkwy.
Cañon City, CO 81212
(719) 269-1112

Hecla Junction Campground
About a mile north of the CO 291 exit on CO 285, between mile markers 135 and 136. Turn east onto CR 194 and drive 2.4 miles to the end of the road.

Poncha Lodge
10520 W. Highway 50
Poncha Springs, CO 81242
(800) 315-3952

Railroad Bridge Campground
Take US 24 into Buena Vista. Turn east at the only stoplight in town, travel two blocks past the railroad tracks, and turn left on N. Colorado Avenue, which turns into Chaffee CR 371. Drive 6.2 miles to the campground.

Rincon Campground
8 miles east of Salida off of CO 50 at mile marker 231 between the towns of Swissvale and Howard.

Ruby Mountain Campground
South of Buena Vista on US 285, between mile markers 144 and 145. Turn east on Chaffee CR 301, and then turn right onto CR 300. Drive 2.4 miles to the campground.

Vallie Bridge Campground
From CO 50 at mile marker 239 between the towns of Howard and Coaldale, turn north on Fremont CR 45. This is a boat-in/walk-in only campground, with 102 sites total.

Woodland Motel
903 W. 1st St.
Salida, CO 81201
(800) 488-0456
woodlandmotel.com

Big Thompson River

The Appenzell
1100 Big Thompson Ave.
Estes Park, CO 80517
(970) 586-1122
appenzellinn.com

Riverview Camping and RV Park
7806 W. Highway 34
Loveland, CO 80537
(970) 667-9910
riverviewrv.com

Seven Pines Cabins and RV Park
2137 W. Highway 34
Drake, CO 80515
(970) 586-3809
7pinescabins.com

Two Eagles Resort
1372 Big Thompson Canyon
Loveland, CO 80537
(970) 663-5532
2eaglesresort.com

Blue River

Best Western Ptarmigan
652 Lake Dillon Dr.
Dillon, CO 80435
(970) 468-2341
bestwesterncolorado.com

Days Inn Silverthorne
580 Silverthorne Ln.
Silverthorne, CO 80498
(970) 468-8661

McDonald Flats Campground
From Silverthorne, take CO 9 north
14.8 miles, turn left onto Heeney Road
(CO 30), and go 2.1 miles. Turn right at
campground sign onto the gravel road
and go 0.2 mile to campground; 12 sites
with no RV hookups.

Peak One Campground
On I-70, take exit 203 for Frisco/Breck-
enridge (CO 9). At the end of the ramp,
turn south onto Summit Blvd. (CO 9
south) and go 2.2 miles; turn left at
sign, and go 0.2 mile; turn left at sign
and go 0.7 mile. Turn left into campground; 74 sites with no hookups.

Quality Inn
530 Silverthorne Ln.
Silverthorne, CO 80498
(970) 513-1222
qualityinn.com

Cache La Poudre

Ansel Watrous Campground
From Rustic, take CO 14 east 18.6
miles; 19 sites with no RV hookups.

Archer's Poudre River Resort
33021 Poudre Canyon Hwy.
Bellvue, CO 80512
(970) 881-2139
poudreriverresort.com

The Armstrong Inn
259 S. College Ave.
Fort Collins, CO 80524
(970) 484-3883
thearmstronghotel.com

Best Western University Inn
914 S. College Ave.
Fort Collins, CO 80524
(970) 484-2984
bwui.com

Jack's Gulch Campground
From Rustic, take CO 14 east 5.1 miles
to Pingree Park (CR 63 E) sign. Turn
right onto Pingree Road and go 6.3
miles to campground sign; 64 sites,
20 with RV electric hookups.

Mountain Park
From CO 14, the campground is 8 miles
east of Rustic; 52 sites, 31 with RV electric hookups.

forestcamping.com/dow/rockymtn/
roos.htm

Colorado River

Allington Inn and Suites
215 Central Ave.
Kremmling, CO 80459
(970) 724-9800
allingtoninn.com

Canyon Motel
221 Byers Ave.
Hot Sulphur Springs, CO 80451
(970) 725-3395

Cedar Lodge Motel
2102 Grand Ave.
Glenwood Springs, CO 81601
(970) 945-6579
cedarlodgemotel.net

The Hotel Denver
402 7th St.
Glenwood Springs, CO 81601
(970) 945-6565
thehoteldenver.com

Colorado River (continued)

Lone Buck Campground
3.5 miles west of Hot Sulphur Springs on US 40.

Pumphouse Campground
From Kremmling, take CO 9 south about 1 mile to Grand CR 1 (Trough Road). Go west on Trough Road for 10 miles, and turn right onto Pumphouse access road; 18 sites, no RV access.

Stillwater Campground
In Granby, at intersection of US 40 and US 34, take US 34 east 8.6 miles to campground; 124 sites, 20 with water and electric hookups.

Trail Riders Motel
215 W. Agate Ave.
Granby, CO 80446
(970) 887-3738

Conejos River

Aspen Glade
From Antonito, take US 285 south 0.3 mile to CO 17. Continue straight on CO 17 and go 15.4 miles to the campground; 32 sites with no RV hookups.

Mogote
From Antonito, take US 285 south 0.3 mile to CO 17. Continue straight on CO 17 and go 13.2 miles to campground; 40 sites with no RV hookups.

Mogote Meadow Cabins & RV
34127 State Highway 17
Antonito, CO 81120
(719) 376-5774
mogotemeadow.com

Narrow Gauge Railroad Inn
5200 State Highway 285
Antonito, CO 81120
(719) 376-5441
narrowgaugerailroadinn.info

Eagle River

AmericInn Lodge
85 Pond Rd.
Eagle, CO 81631
(800) 634-3444
americinn.com

Comfort Inn Vail
285 Market St.
Eagle, CO 81631
(970) 328-7878
comfortinn.com

Inn at Riverwalk
27 Main St.
Edwards, CO 81632
(970) 926-0606
innandsuitesatriverwalk.com

Yeoman Park
Take exit 147 off I-70 to Eagle. Go south 0.3 mile to a yield sign. Turn right onto US 6 and go 0.1 mile to Capital Street. Turn left and go 0.4 mile to a stop sign and sign for Yeoman Park. Go 10.2 miles on CR 307/Brush Creek Road (which eventually becomes FR 400) to a Y intersection (FR 415). Bear left onto FR 415 and go 5.9 miles to Yeoman Park; 22 sites with no hookups.

Fryingpan River

Aspenalt Lodge
157 Basalt Center Cir.
Basalt, CO 81621
(970) 927-3191
aspenalt.com

Comfort Inn and Suites Carbondale
920 Cowen Dr.
Carbondale, CO 81623
(970) 963-8880
comfortinn.com

Days Inn Carbondale
950 Cowen Dr.
Carbondale, CO 81623
(970) 963-9111
daysinn.com

The Green Drake
220 Midland Ave.
Basalt, CO 81621
(970) 927-4747
green-drake.com

Little Mattie
In Basalt, off CO 82, turn at the Ruedi Reservoir sign and follow the road 2.1 miles to a stop sign. Turn left onto Midland Avenue (which becomes Frying Pan Road) and go 14.8 miles to the campground and boat ramp sign. Turn right, then immediately left, and go 0.8 mile to campground; 19 sites, no hookups, waste station.

Little Maude
Follow same directions as for Little Mattie, but proceed only .2 mile to campground; 21 sites with flush toilets and no hookups.

Gunnison River
Black Canyon Motel
1605 E. Main St.
Montrose, CO 81401-3808
(970) 249-3495
blackcanyonmotel.com

Black Canyon of the Gunnison
nps.gov/blca/index.htm

Curecanti National Recreation Area
nps.gov/cure/index.htm

Gunnison Gorge (BLM)
blm.gov/co/st/en/nca/ggnca/gorge.html

Water Wheel Inn
37478 US 50
Gunnison, CO 81230
(970) 641-1650
waterwheelinnatgunnison.com

Western Motel
403 East Tomichi Ave.
Gunnison, CO 81230-2030
(970) 641-1722
westernmotel-co.com

Western Motel
1200 E. Main St.
Montrose, CO 81401-5821
(970) 249-3481
westernmotel.com

Rio Grande
Allington Inn & Suites
182 E. Frontage Rd.
South Fork, CO 81154
(800) 285-6590
allingtoninn.com

Marshall Park
From Creede, take CO 149 south (toward Lake City) 5.6 miles, turn left onto Middle Creek Road, and go 0.4 mile to campground; 15 sites with no hookups.

River Hill Campground
From Creede, take CO 149 south (toward Lake City) 19.3 miles to the Rio Grande Reservoir sign (Forest Route 520). Turn left onto FR 520 and go 0.5 mile to the Y intersection. Bear left, staying on FR 520, and go 9.3 miles to the campground; 19 sites with no hookups.

Snowshoe Motel
202 E. 8th St.
Creede, CO 81130
(719) 658-2315
snowshoelodge.net

The Spruce Lodge
29431 W. Highway 160
South Fork, CO 81154
(719) 873-5605
sprucelodges.com

Roaring Fork

Cedar Lodge Motel
2102 Grand Ave.
Glenwood Springs, CO 81601
(970) 945-6579
cedarlodgemotel.net

Comfort Inn & Suites Carbondale
920 Cowen Dr.
Carbondale, CO 81623
(970) 963-8880
comfortinn.com

Days Inn Carbondale
950 Cowen Dr.
Carbondale, CO 81623
(970) 963-9111
daysinn.com

Difficult Campground
From Aspen, take CO 82 east 2.7
miles to campground; 47 sites with
no hookups.

The Hotel Denver
402 7th St.
Glenwood Springs, CO 81601
(970) 945-6565
thehoteldenver.com

Rocky Mountain National Park
For more information, see nps.gov/
romo/planyourvisit/camping.htm.

Aspenglen Campground
On US 34 just west of the Fall River
Entrance Station; 54 sites.

Best Western Silver Saddle
1260 Big Thompson Ave.
Estes Park, CO 80517
(970) 586-4476
estesresort.com

Columbine Inn
1540 Big Thompson Rd.
Estes Park, CO 80517
(970) 586-4533
estescolumbineinn.com

Glacier Basin Campground
On Bear Lake Road, approximately
6 miles south of the Beaver Meadows
Entrance Station; 150 sites.

Longs Peak Campground
Approximately 9 miles south of Estes
Park on Route 7; 26 sites.

Moraine Park Campground
Above the meadows of Moraine Park
on Bear Lake Road, approximately
2 1/2 miles south of the Beaver Meadows Entrance Station; 245 sites.

Paradise RV Park
1836 CO 66
Estes Park, CO 80517
(970) 586-5513
paradiservcolorado.com

Silver Moon Inn
175 Spruce Dr.
Estes Park, CO 80517
(970) 586-6006
silvermooninn.com

Spruce Lake RV Park
1050 Mary's Lake Rd.
Estes Park, CO 80517
(970) 586-2889
sprucelakerv.com

Timber Creek Campground
Along the Colorado River in the
Kawuneeche Valley on US 34, approximately 10 miles north of Grand Lake;
98 sites.

South Platte River

Chapparal Park General Store (RV Park)
19015 CR 59
Hartsel, CO 80449
(719) 836-0308
chaparralparkgeneralstore.com

Country Inn
723 W. Highway 24
Woodland Park, CO 80863
(719) 687-6277
woodlandcountrylodge.com

Eleven Mile State Park
There are nine different campsites in the park, each with different amenities. Rocky Ridge campground offers the only electrical sites and is nestled among trees and rocky outcrops. Loops A, B, and D offer electrical hookups; loops C and E have trees. North Shore and Witchers Cove campgrounds offer open lakeshore sites and convenient access to boat ramps.

parks.state.co.us/Parks/ElevenMile/Camping/Pages/ElevenMileCamping.aspx

Taylor River
Comfort Inn Gunnison
911 N. Main St.
Gunnison, CO 81230
(970) 642-1000
comfortinn.com

Lakeview Campground
In Almont, at the intersection of CO 135 and CR 742, take CR 742 for 22 miles; 65 sites, 22 with electric hookups.

Lodgepole Campground
In Almont, at the intersection of CO 135 and CR 742, take CR 742 for 14.2 miles to campground; 16 sites with no hookups.

Lottis Creek
In Almont, at the intersection of CO 135 and CR 742, take CR 742 for 16.7 miles to the campground; 27 sites, two with electric hookups.

Onemile
In Almont, at the intersection of CO 135 and CR 742, take CR 742 for 8.3 miles to the campground; 25 sites, 22 with electric hookups.

Rosy Lane
At the intersection of CO 135 and CR 742 in Almont, take CR 742 for 8.7 miles to the campground; 19 sites, one with electric hookups.

Seasons Inn
412 E. Tomichi Ave.
Gunnison, CO 81230
(970) 641-0700

Three Rivers Resort and Outfitting
130 CR 742
Almont, CO 81210
(888) 761-FISH (3474)
willowflyanglers.com

Western Motel
403 E. Tomichi Ave.
Gunnison, CO 81230
(970) 641-1722
westernmotel-co.com

Williams Fork
Allington Inn and Suites
215 W. Central Ave.
Kremmling, CO 80459
(970) 724-9800
allingtoninn.com

Canyon Motel
221 W. Byers Ave.
Hot Sulphur Springs, CO 80451
(970) 725-3395

Yampa River
Duffy Mountain
Take US 40 west approximately 19 miles from Craig to CR 17. Take CR 17 south for approximately 10 miles, following the signs for public access, and go left at the cattle guard on BLM Road 1593.

Elk Run Inn
627 W. Victory Way
Craig, CO 81625
(970) 826-4444
elkruninn.com

Yampa River (continued)

Iron Horse Inn
333 South Lincoln Ave.
Steamboat Springs, CO 80487
(970) 879-6505
ironhorseinnsteamboat.com

Juniper Canyon
Take US 40 west out of Craig 20 miles
to Moffat CR 53, which is on the south
(left) side of the highway. Take CR 53
for 3.6 miles to CR 74. Take a sharp
right turn and drive approximately
3/4 mile to the site.

Rabbit Ears Motel
201 Lincoln Ave.
Steamboat Springs, CO 80487
(970) 879-1150
rabbitearsmotel.com

South Beach Campground
3 miles south of Craig on the west
side of US 13.

Super 8
200 S. Highway 13
Craig, CO 81625
(970) 824-3471
super8.com